# ENEMY OF THE STATE

# ENEMY

# OF THE STATE

## THE TRIAL AND EXECUTION OF SADDAM HUSSEIN

**MICHAEL A. NEWTON**
**and MICHAEL P. SCHARF**

ST. MARTIN'S PRESS NEW YORK

www.stmartins.com

Grateful acknowledgment is made to the Holocaust Museum for permission to reprint a photo from the Adolf Eichmann trial in Jerusalem and one from the International Military Tribunal in Nuremberg. The views or opinions expressed in this book, and the context in which the images are used, do not necessarily reflect the views or policy of, nor imply approval or endorsement by, the United States Holocaust Memorial Museum.

Library of Congress Cataloging-in-Publication Data

Newton, Michael A.
Enemy of the state : the trial and execution of Saddam Hussein / Michael A. Newton & Michael P. Scharf.—1st ed.
p. cm.
ISBN-13: 978-0-312-38556-9
ISBN-10: 0-312-38556-0
1. Hussein, Saddam, 1937–2006—Trials, litigation, etc. 2. Trials (Crimes against humanity)—Iraq—Baghdad. 3. Trials (Murder)—Iraq—Baghdad. I. Title.
Includes bibliographical references.

KMJ41.H87 N49 2008
345.567'470235—dc22 2008021087

First Edition: September 2008

10 9 8 7 6 5 4 3 2 1

Dedicated to Riyadh and John
and all those who have sacrificed at
the altar of freedom and human dignity

# CONTENTS

# ACKNOWLEDGMENTS

The nature of this material and the ongoing conditions inside Iraq prevent a lengthy enumeration of the many people whose perspectives, wisdom, courage, and candor made this book possible. Foremost among those are the judges, prosecutors, and staff of the Iraqi High Tribunal and the members of the Regime Crimes Liaison Office who gave us the unparalleled opportunity to assist in one of history's most extraordinary trials and provided incredible insights during the writing of this book.

We especially express our deep gratitude to Judge Aref Abdul Razaq al-Shahen, the president and chief appeals judge of the tribunal, who provided us many of the photos that appear with the tribunal's permission in this book. Appreciation also goes to Judith Cohen of the U.S. Holocaust Memorial Museum for the photos of the Nuremberg and Eichmann trials, and to the American patriot (who has asked to remain unnamed) who provided the photo of Saddam taken immediately after his capture.

In addition, several people deserve special recognition for the assistance they have furnished us. Jean Sasson was a special friend and source of guidance, as were Mark Ellis, Marieke Wierde, Miranda Sissons, Bruce MacKay, Eric Blinderman, and Ra'id Juhi. We are also indebted to our agent, Peter Rubie, who had faith in this project, and to our editors at St. Martin's Press,

Phil Revzin and Jenness Crawford, along with their great team, who improved our text in innumerable ways.

We are also deeply appreciative of the institutional support provided by Vanderbilt University Law School and Case Western Reserve University School of Law. We offer special thanks to the following Vanderbilt and Case Western Reserve students who provided us research assistance: Christine Lillie, Casey Kuhlman, Linda Toth, Preeti Kundra, Julie Chandler, Jetta Sandin, and Meggin Sowers.

Finally and most importantly, we would like to thank our wives, Jeanne Newton and Trina Scharf, and our families, who permit us to live, work, and write in ways that often complicate their own lives.

# ENEMY OF THE STATE

# PROLOGUE

## HIGH CRIMES, HIGH DRAMA

**The room was hushed** as Saddam Hussein, the once powerful tyrant known around the world as the Butcher of Baghdad, was escorted before Trial Chamber 1 of the Iraqi High Tribunal at 12:21 P.M. on October 19, 2005. His composed and well-coifed appearance stood in sharp contrast to the disheveled and shaken old man with the long, gray-streaked beard and wild hair who had been pulled out of a hole in the ground by American soldiers two years earlier. As he passed the chief prosecutor, Ja'afar al-Moussawi, Saddam muttered an ethnic Iraqi insult in his direction.

This first trial for the newly established Iraqi High Tribunal was the long-anticipated response to the pent-up expectations of the Iraqi people. The trial would center around the events in a small Iraqi village rather than focusing on the massive campaigns of criminality that Saddam Hussein supervised throughout his reign. Rather than simply taking their vengeance on the deposed leader and his criminal cronies, the Iraqi politicians had risked the future of their country on a bold gambit—they believed that creating the tribunal and holding televised and transparent proceedings would help the country move forward into a new and better era. The trial itself was a historic first against the backdrop of high drama and an ongoing insurgency outside the courtroom. It was a domestic trial, incorporating international law and aspects of international procedures.

The Iraqis chose to prosecute a discrete and comparatively minor series of events that took place in an Iraqi village named Dujail in the wake of what Saddam regarded as an attempt on his life. Surprisingly to many outside observers, the Iraqis chose to prosecute Saddam as one of the defendants in the first trial rather than deferring until the jurists had more experience and the inevitable kinks of an entirely new judicial institution had been ironed out. From the outside, the decision to begin with such a comparatively minor case, and to include Saddam in the first trial, was seen by some as proof that the Dujail trial was a politically motivated fiasco from the beginning. In reality, the judges responsible for selecting Dujail and moving the case to trial had no connections to the politically dominant Dawa Party. If the Maliki government had been responsible for moving a politically motivated trial to the head of the docket, either the massive crime committed against Kurds during the Anfal campaigns or the brutal suppression of the Shiites in 1991 would have been more logical choices. As it happened, Dujail was simply the first case ready for trial. It proved to be a fateful choice. The chief judge, whose face was flashed around the world, was Iraqi, as were the other judges on the bench. The prosecutor and all of the lead defense counsel were members of the Iraqi bar. With the exception of one famous defense lawyer, there were no Westerners in the courtroom, although many Westerners, including the authors of this book, had worked in the background for more than a year, preparing the trial.

Millions around the world tuned in to the televised proceedings of what was called the trial of the century and the mother of all trials. One Iraqi woman who served as a translator and saw every minute of the nine-month-long trial said the most dramatic moment for her was the first time she saw the defeated tyrant seated as a criminal defendant in the dock while she went to do her job. For high drama, this case had it all: a strident former dictator inclined to glower menacingly at the television cameras that were just over the shoulders of the presiding judge; the backdrop of a coalition occupation fighting against insurgents claiming to represent the will of the Iraqi people; raucous and disruptive defense lawyers whose chief strategy was to challenge the legitimacy of the proceedings and focus the trial on the legality of the U.S. invasion of Iraq; mysterious assassinations of key trial participants; smoking-gun documents with Saddam's signature; and videotapes of the worst atrocities imaginable. Each witness who came to court to tell the story of his or her own terrible experience would represent thousands of compatriots who suffered in their own ways under the regime.

Saddam retained an animal magnetism that competed for domination with the judicial power from the first moments of the trial down to its dramatic conclusion. When the judge told him to stand and identify himself for the purposes of trial, as required by Iraqi procedure, the gray-bearded defendant, whose thick black hair had been combed carefully to cultivate the image of control and authority, stood up. Every viewer in the region watched intently to see whether he would bow to the power of the judge. Iraqis were riveted to their televisions. Signaling the themes that would run through the entire trial, when the judge referred to him as the former president of Iraq, Saddam retorted: "I didn't say 'former president,' I said 'president,' and I have rights according to the constitution, among them immunity from prosecution."

Saddam spoke in a powerful and aggressive manner. His voice rang across the courtroom and rose as his passion became evident: "Those who fought in God's cause will be victorious. . . . I am at the mercy of God, the most powerful." When the judge persisted, Saddam demanded, "Who are you? What does this court want?" Saddam Hussein al-Tikriti, deposed president of Iraq, added: "I don't answer this so-called court, with all due respect, and I reserve my constitutional rights as the president of the country of Iraq. I don't acknowledge either the entity that authorizes you or the aggression, because everything based on a falsehood is a falsehood."

On that October morning in the year 2005, Saddam embodied the age-old struggle between law and power, between process and privilege. His words unconsciously echoed those uttered by Charles I, king of England, as his trial at the hands of his own citizens began on January 20, 1648.

> I would know by what power I am called hither . . . by what Authority, I mean, lawful; there are many unlawful Authorities in the world, Thieves and Robbers by the highways; but I would know by what Authority I was brought thence, and carried from place to place, and when I know what lawful Authority, I shall answer. Remember that I

> am your King, your lawful King, and what sins you bring upon your own heads, and the Judgment of God against this land, Think well on it, I say, think well on it before you go further from one sin to a greater; therefore, let me know by what lawful Authority I am seated here, and I shall not be unwilling to answer, in the meantime I shall not betray my Trust. . . . Let me see a lawful Authority warranted by the Word of God, the Scriptures, or warranted by the constitutions of the Kingdom and I will answer.[1]

As the trial played itself out on worldwide television, one of its major themes was the persistent struggle of the judges to maintain control and conduct the proceedings with a demeanor and gravity appropriate to their importance. For every witness or complainant (as those who testify seeking monetary damages are termed in Iraqi law) who looked into the faces of the accused and testified about personal suffering, there were thousands more whose stories could have been heard. The Iraqi people watched, commented on, and critiqued every nuance of the trial process. One middle-aged Iraqi engineer from Basra told one of the authors over lunch one day that he believed it was a mistake to televise the trial because, he felt, it signified a distinctly different set of procedures than a "normal Iraqi trial," but, he added, once having begun to televise the proceedings, "it would be an even bigger mistake to stop the broadcasts."

The legal process formed the canvas against which an explosive mix of personalities, politics, power, and ego combined to produce the most important trial in the history of the region. Many of the decisions intended to increase the perception of fairness and demonstrate the rebirth of an Iraqi judiciary dedicated to restoring the rule of law ironically seemed only to increase the cynicism of the population and feed popular misconceptions of the trial as a form of American power. The newly established free press in the country had a field day. There were times when the insurgency raging outside the courtroom seemed directly linked to and fed by the events inside the courtroom. The tension between law and power, between truth and tyranny, was almost palpable to observers inside the courtroom. During the course of the trial, eight people associated with the process were murdered, including three members of the defense counsel and the brother of one of the prosecutors. Rather than succumbing to the manipulation of the murderers, the judges resisted outside pressures to move the trial to a safer location and forged ahead.

ON THE MORNING of November 5, 2006, the defendants came into court one by one to hear the verdict pronounced by the presiding judge. When Saddam's turn came, he entered with an arrogant strut. He refused to stand until the guards made him do so. When Saddam interrupted the reading of the verdict, Judge Ra'ouf Rasheed Abdel Rahman turned down the volume of Saddam's microphone and spoke over him. The court pronounced a verdict of "death by hanging" on Saddam for the crime of willfully murdering his citizens from the town of Dujail. "God curse the enemies in occupation," Saddam railed. He demanded that the Arab people "stand up" and proclaimed "death to the enemies of the nation." Appeals filed on December 3, 2006, were denied, and Saddam was hanged until he was dead on December 30, 2006.

The grainy and illicit images of the execution captured on a smuggled cell phone were flashed around the world, and the perceptions completely overwhelmed the official photographic record. The images of Saddam's death lent an eery air of dignity to the end of one of the cruelest tyrants of the twentieth century. The executioner's rope tightened around his neck and interrupted him halfway through the most sacred Islamic prayer, the Shahadah: "There is no god but Allah . . ." Nevertheless, he died not as the proud president of a sovereign nation, but as the enemy of a new state wobbling toward freedom from tyranny. He died as a convicted criminal whose crimes were documented in the trial and its 283-page judgment.

## THE JUDGMENT OF HISTORY

More than three years before his execution, as Saddam was bundled into an American Humvee for transport to the secure detention facility within the Camp Raider compound, a participant in his capture recalls thinking of the phrase attributed to Julius Caesar: "Veni, vidi, vici." The American forces felt that they came to Iraq with a clear mission—to liberate a country and evict a dictator. They saw a country that was struggling to get back on its own feet and was slowly grasping the realization that democracy isn't reserved just for other cultures. And they conquered the perceptions of those who felt Saddam Hussein would never be caught alive and overcame the perception of many that Iraq could not function without a dictator at the helm. Soldier M (some names have been omitted at the request of interviewees) was present when the dictator became only a high-value detainee, and he remembers that "many of us felt that the capture of Saddam Hussein that night would enable the country to begin to think on its own and begin to finally rid itself of a shadow of fear that cast itself over the population for the better part of three decades. The first free elections that some Iraqi citizens, including women, would take part in for the first time in their lives, a body of officials representative of the Iraqi people . . . these were some of the fruits of our labor, and we were proud to have contributed to them."

In fact, Saddam's capture was not the end in itself, but merely the beginning of the end. If Iraqis had simply executed Saddam without any pretense or fanfare, it would have essentially negated all of the aspirations to democratization and reform, because it would have symbolized an Iraq entrapped by revenge and factionalism. The formation of a tribunal, its staffing and training, the complex preparations for trial, and the public and transparent demonstration of the process of justice were all essential steps toward a revitalized Iraq dedicated to the rule of law. The Dujail trial represented the televised spectacle of Iraqis struggling to redefine the soul of their nation, even as it faced grave challenges to its existence as an organized society built on mutual respect and a commonality of interests.

AS IRAQI FORCES reeled before the victorious coalition in the Gulf War of 1991, the state newspaper controlled by the Baath Party falsely proclaimed the success of Iraqi arms: "Victory is not how many tanks or planes we or the enemy used; it's all steel that can get ruined. Victory is the face that you acquire in the history books." The Dujail trial processes and the subsequent sentences imposed on the discredited leaders of Iraq are pivotal events in the modern history of the Middle East. While the precise legacy of the Dujail trial remains unknown, its implications stretch worldwide. At a minimum, it symbolizes the struggle to implement law as a constraining and constructive force in lieu of violence, power, or passion. The trial processes remain muddled in misconception, mistranslation, and miscommunication, but Saddam was prophetic in declaring death to the enemy of the nation.

The judgment of history will certainly acknowledge that using the process of law to punish the "enemy of the state" marked a watershed in the saga of the Iraqi people. It was bold and idealistic in its aspirations. Its actuality was marked by missteps and miscalculations. The Dujail trial was caricatured in many minds as being an orchestrated show trial; the debates over holding a trial in the midst of an insurgency and over the fairness of showing the demeaning images of Saddam after his capture lingered in legal circles.

One thing that holds true is that the Iraqi judges succeeded in using domestic law to implement the substantive norms drawn from international law to hold Baath Party officials accountable for crimes committed against their own citizens, and in that pursuit felt very strongly that they were in the service of their nation and the larger rule of law.

The signers of the American Declaration of Independence ended that historic document with the explicit assurance that they pledged their lives, fortunes, and sacred honor to the pursuit of its principles. The courageous Iraqis, all of them involved in this process, made no less noble a gesture. Virtually every lawyer associated with the work of the tribunal suffered enormous personal and financial hardships, and their families often shared those hardships just as they shared the danger. There was very little about the Dujail trial that was predictable, yet its very audacity is inspiring. Though the Iraqi High Tribunal continues to hold trials, the saga of that first trial is one of courage and commitment to the rule of law. Yet it clearly failed in the short run to turn the tide of lawlessness within Iraq. The Dujail trial captured both the best and the worst aspirations of humankind. It was a legal process that took place against an intensely political backdrop as the Iraqis labored to restore the soul of a society. The legal process nonetheless served as a stage for the drama of human struggle; the history is colored by the law and its application and formation, but the events in the courtroom represented a very real tale of personalities and power.

This book documents the actual events of the Dujail trial rather than casually accepting the perspectives from distant and disparate points of observation. The Dujail trial was both revolutionary in its aspirations and at times rudimentary in its application. At its end, the Iraqis used the power of the law to destroy the raw power of the Baathist regime. They branded Saddam as the enemy of the state and forever ended the fear that gripped their society under his tyranny. This is their story.

# 1

## LIBERATION

**As the world watched** the enormous statue of Saddam Hussein al-Tikriti being pulled down in Iraq's Firdus Square on April 9, 2003, the logical impression was that the repressive Baathist regime had ended and that Iraq now stood at the doorway of a new era. Though it looked quite substantial, the statue was merely a hollow shell bolted to upright steel shafts running up the legs. Like Iraq itself, the great monument fell far more easily than expected.

The Iraqi army had melted away under the destructive wrath of Operation Cobra II,[1] which unfolded with surprising speed and momentum.[2] In the face of the military onslaught, the ruling Baath Party leaders either were killed or fled like startled rabbits and went into hiding. As Baghdad was liberated from the Baathist regime, thousands of Iraqis danced in the streets.

For more than three decades, the Iraqi people had lived in the shadow of the dictator referred to by his given name, Saddam. (After the Iraqi custom, Saddam's second name, Hussein, was his father's first name, and his third name, al-Tikriti, indicated his place of birth.) Saddam's image and will hung over the citizenry like a cloud of rancid cigar smoke. The Iraqi people could seemingly never escape his gaze as he looked down from the thousands of murals and portraits across the country. One Marsh Arab on the outskirts of Nassiriyah described the repressive malaise: "When Saddam was in office, we used to be afraid of the walls."[3]

As they toppled Saddam's regime, the coalition soldiers felt they had given a great gift of freedom to the Iraqi people. Though many Iraqis were in fact grateful, they remained uneasy about the future. They urged their new American friends to come back when "the real Baghdad" is reborn—a place of vibrant markets, parties, feasts, and family gatherings.

One of the authors of this book (Michael Newton) was in Baghdad in December 2003, just eight months after the invasion. First-person references in this chapter are to him.

ONE OF THE first Iraqis I encountered was a striking, dark-haired young college student who was working for the American administrators as an interpreter. When I asked her what she planned to do with her life after Saddam, she simply shrugged. All that she had known in her lifetime was an Iraq where privilege and tribe and power trumped hard work and individual innovation at every turn. The children of Baath Party officials enjoyed bonus points on their college exams and hence obtained admission to the schools of their choice. She explained to me that she had never imagined that her future could be determined by her dreams. It was only after some prodding and a sustained effort to gain her trust that the young student began to admit to the life goals and dreams that she had long repressed or dismissed as unattainable. She talked of boys and clothes and travel. She wavered between wanting a career in the fashion industry and one as a caterer, and it was in the very expression of her personal ambitions that the shimmering possibilities of a new Iraq became tangible and real.

In those first months after the fall of Saddam, a better life seemed so attainable for ordinary people. I listened as ordinary citizens began to tell me of their hopes after escaping the shackles of Baath Party rule; such words would have endangered their lives just months before. People told me of family members who had disappeared or fled under Saddam's iron fist, while showing me worn pictures of their loved ones. One older woman secretively sought me out to ask whether the persecution of Christians could be prosecuted as a crime against humanity and to discuss freedom of religion and belief.

This early period of the occupation later came to be called the "golden months" because anything seemed possible. When confronted with the 2006 Iraq Study Group observation that "pessimism is pervasive," one administrator nostalgically harkened back to the early spring of 2003, a time in which "optimism was omnipresent." The victorious coalition had a brief period of unopposed opportunity to establish the building blocks of a new and better society. At the same time, the uncertainty that people felt about their future and the deep societal scars that remained even after the Baathist power structures imploded made it plain that the transition to a peaceful and democratic Iraq, positioned to enjoy the fruits of freedom, would be arduous and bumpy at best.

To close observers, it soon became clear that pre-invasion assumptions about the ease with which Iraq could suddenly become an island of prosperity and peace by transitioning into institutionalized norms of democratic governance had melted like ice in the withering summer heat. The Bush administration had pointedly decided early on that the U.S. military should not be in the business of "nation building." American planners had spent the most time on what turned out to be the least difficult task—defeating the Iraqi army. Very little planning had been devoted to the most daunting challenge—building a new democratic Iraq in the face of a mounting insurgency. The paradox of prewar planning was that there were far too few U.S. forces to secure and protect the hundreds of suspected weapons of mass destruction (WMD) sites, much less to prevent WMDs from being smuggled out of Iraq or being transferred to the terrorist groups; the preemption of such transfers had been one of the very purposes for the war.[4]

In the run-up to the war, the Americans largely failed to anticipate an extended presence or the need to engage in institution building from the ground up. The images of widespread looting in Baghdad lingered; American forces had been too thinly stretched to protect the treasures of the National Museum. Nor could they seal the borders with Iran or Jordan. Coalition forces worked with little strategic guidance or concerted focus.

Superficial progress was nevertheless rapid. Freedom of the press was quickly restored; soon, 75 radio stations, 180 newspapers, and 10 television stations were established. Cell phone subscriptions exploded as Iraqis realized they could talk with each other without fear of being jailed. Satellite television was introduced to Iraq. During Saddam's era, anyone caught with a satellite dish was imprisoned and forced to pay a fine of 100 dinars. Iraqi lawyers later apologized that the regime had prevented them from remaining aware of current legal developments, and they thirsted to catch up to the most modern conceptions. Plans were made to reopen the Baghdad Stock Exchange, and soon realized in June 2004. Western civilians flowed in to staff the Coalition Provisional Authority, headquartered in Saddam's ostentatious Republican Palace on the banks of the Euphrates. At the same time, Saddam's shadow loomed in the consciousness of the people as his whereabouts remained a deep mystery. No one had seen him since the fast-moving armor of the U.S. Third Infantry Division had thundered toward Baghdad. Despite the trappings of progress, ordinary Iraqis remained bound in a sense of growing unease and disbelief.

As early as May 18, 2003, one of the most respected judges on the U.S. federal bench wrote during a visit to Iraq that "calm is slowly returning but families are still afraid. . . . Most of all they are afraid of an unknown future, afraid that Saddam will return or that the country will dissolve into anarchy because the Americans won't stay the course."[5] The insurgency became more organized and effective in conducting random acts of violence. Foreign fighters poured into the country with the express aim of killing and maiming Iraqi citizens to defeat the coalition forces by showing the limits of their strength. As summer bled into fall, more than three hundred American service members had been killed.[6] The guarded optimism that flowered during the spring of 2003 faded into a residue of uncertainty reminiscent of the fear that many Iraqis had experienced under the tyranny of the Baathist regime. Saddam remained at large as the tectonic plates of Iraqi society began to grind against the realities of running a nation and reestablishing order that could contain sectarian and tribal rivalries.

Internecine arguments increased as the Interim Governing Council (IGC) that had been quickly appointed by the occupation authorities began to meet. Rival political organizations quickly formed and jockeyed against each other in preparation for the inevitable rounds of elections that would distribute power. In many areas, the fissures that ran along tribal loyalty, family bonds, and religious perspective became the poles that attracted political support. Against this backdrop, the people of Iraq sustained a deep and visceral need to expose the crimes of the regime and witness an accounting for their suffering.

## THE MANHUNT

American forces began to plan and execute a series of raids to capture or kill the leading Baath Party leaders who had escaped during the lightning-fast invasion of Iraq. Saddam was depicted as the ace of spades in the pack of cards handed out to deploying American soldiers. The ace ran wild as a succession of operations designed to capture him failed. Saddam had built his career on his persona as the symbol of a unified and proud Iraq standing up to the Americans and the United Nations. The resourcefulness of the Iraqi leader was legendary, and his ruthless drive to retain and regain power was almost mythical to the Iraqi people. Most knew that the allies had sought to kill him with specially planned military strikes during the war—yet, he survived and was still at large. Iraqis wondered if the charisma and drive of the leader whose entire image had been built on defiance of the United States could somehow be enough to propel him to recapture his throne and resume his domination of Iraqi society. The undercurrent of tension built as the insurgency blossomed into a full-scale and sustained level of violence that was itself destabilizing and frighteningly real for ordinary citizens.

A military task force was assembled with a nimble command structure and a unique blend of special operations and conventional forces. The military objective was to kill or capture Baathist leaders with deadly efficiency. Saddam's sons Qusay and Uday—each with a $15 million bounty on his head—were killed on July 22, 2003, in a four-hour battle with U.S. troops in a hideout in the northern city of Mosul. Quietly, but with ever-increasing effectiveness, task force analysts began to map out the organizational dynamics of the social, family, tribal, and party connections that were essential to keeping Saddam in hiding. In what was dubbed "social network analysis" in the official counterinsurgency doctrine of the U.S. Army, military planners scraped together fragments of information and plotted the connections to construct a graphical chart of the insurgent infrastructure.[7]

The goal of social network analysis was to chip away at the enablers who supported Saddam and his coterie. The detailed compilation of a coherent underground support structure was painstakingly assembled as analysts charted the connections and characters that were sheltering

Saddam. Meanwhile, Saddam's aura seemed to grow as the weeks turned into months. Commentators across the Arab world mocked the United States as a toothless tiger, and the unease of the people seemed to deepen as fear of the regime's possible return persisted. The reality was that Saddam was on the run and afraid, but fear of him lingered in the Iraqi consciousness. According to one anecdote during this period, an Iraqi policeman looked into the backseat of a taxi as it tried to enter a police compound near Tikrit—and saw Saddam himself hiding beneath a blanket. The man's bladder emptied on the spot in a spontaneous reaction of fear and surprise.

Meanwhile, analysts inside the operations center tried to pierce this fog of fear and tribal loyalty as they pieced together a detailed diagram showing the structure of Saddam's secretive security network. The chart of connectivity was mounted on a three-foot-square board and eventually included hundreds of biographical details and interpersonal linkages. Social network analysis goes far beyond mere descriptive data about the members of an insurgent organization; it seeks to show a picture of the social and personal interactions that sustain and feed an insurgency. This technique gradually increased understanding about how the insurgency was functioning and the ways in which Saddam was being sheltered. Commanders began to understand the trends and tactics employed by the growing insurgency as analysts made constant adjustments to the network template and constantly reassessed which critical data points were missing.

As the intelligence tips flowed in, mission after mission after mission came up empty. Soldiers began to embark on missions with what one member of the task force would later term a "bitter optimism" born of so many dry holes and empty efforts. Literally dozens of missions were launched based on reported information about Saddam's whereabouts just hours prior. The seemingly unsuccessful missions contributed bit by bit to the planners' understanding, which in the routine cycle of missions led to more operations. The network analysis expanded to generate new missions and shifting priorities. A team of six hundred soldiers from the Fourth Infantry Division commanded by Major General Raymond Odierno flowed in to augment the special operations forces, bringing new energy and enthusiasm to the repetitive missions. The task force continued to scour the area around Saddam's hometown of Tikrit. The network of people preserving Saddam's freedom was strongest in that area based on their personal loyalties and family bonds. The tightly integrated social structure also helped to prevent informants from bringing details to the attention of intelligence analysts because of their own fears.

The space in which Saddam could maneuver tightened in late November 2003 as U.S. commanders captured people they had been hunting throughout the summer. "This was the inner circle," Lieutenant Colonel Steven Russell, commander of the Fourth Infantry Division's 1-22 Infantry Regiment, told *Time* magazine, and "we were taking pieces out of it." The upsurge in intelligence spawned an intensified series of raids that in turn produced new intelligence about the insurgency and Hussein's possible location. Each mission gained additional information, which in turn shaped the next raid. The social network analysis chart became even more crammed with tidbits of useful information.

On December 10, 2003, the IGC announced its success in drafting a statute for a special tribunal designed to prosecute the crimes committed by the Baathist regime against Iraqi society. For the military, the announcement had little effect; the mission remained the same. General Odierno later described the critical intelligence breakthrough that flowed from the detailed social network analysis. According to him, during the ten days or so preceeding Saddam's capture, American forces obtained key information from five to ten Iraqis who were key members of his enabling network, and "finally we got the ultimate information from one of these individuals."[8] Less than twenty-four hours after capturing a key member of the network of Sunni enablers that had supported Saddam's efforts to remain at large, American interrogators obtained snippets of information that would change the course of the region. The source, whose identity remains a tightly guarded secret, was known to have had contact with Saddam and at first revealed only general details about locations where he might be hiding, followed by the revelation that he would likely be hiding underground.[9]

At around 5:00 P.M. the source finally revealed that Saddam had hidden himself in a farmhouse on the edge of an otherwise nondescript Iraqi village named ad Dawr. That location fit the profile that had been painstakingly cobbled together over the months; U.S. units had previously conducted searches less than three miles away.[10] American commanders knew that they had missed Saddam by only hours on several other missions and hastily assembled the forces to respond to yet another promising bit of information.

## THE CAPTURE OF SADDAM

Operation Red Dawn began at around seven o'clock on the evening of Saturday, December 13, 2003.[11] After they cordoned off about two square kilometers surrounding the small farm near ad Dawr, about ten miles outside Tikrit, soldiers fanned farther out among the buildings, thinking that they could be following the worn script of previous failures. The Humvees drove along the road a short distance and then took a turn off the initial search area. One group redirected its efforts toward a set of ramshackle buildings that looked like a farm compound. There was an animal stench in the air, which mingled with the scent of some nearby fruit trees; the aromas created an odd perfume that was foreign and almost exotic to the Americans. There was no gunfire or enemy contact, but a growing sense of potential quickened their steps. The soldiers later described the place as "a dump." A shack stood to the left; beside it was an awning, sheltering more debris that was piled in corners and an equal amount of trash strewn throughout the area. Soldiers poked around the shadows and the piles of junk looking for anything that seemed out of place. They looked for the smallest indications, but did not sense that they were so close to Saddam's hiding place.

The night was cold and crisp, and the sounds of soldiers not so discreetly searching for anything on the property carried clearly: desert trousers brushing past the vegetation, the sound of boots fading as more troops fanned out across the acreage, low murmurs of voices in the distance. The occasional beam of a red-lensed Maglite flashlight doing wide sweeps across the ground contrasted with the clear night sky and gave the soldiers a surreal impression that this was yet another wrong location at the wrong time. They went about doing their jobs with the detached professionalism born of training. They strolled through the trees, almost as though they were willing the ground to reveal something, anything, to get this one over with. So much expectation had been built up that this mission would be *the one*. Soldier M, who was there that night and has never spoken publicly about the mission, remembers the feeling during the search of the area: "It was easy to free-associate your thinking, and—if you let it—your mind would play tricks on you as well. If Saddam was supposed to be in one of two different areas, who's to say that he couldn't be hidden amongst the trees and scrub vegetation near the farm area, or worse—already gone? I felt relieved when I saw some of the same quick head turns that I was making, where a soldier thought he heard something. . . . It always seems that, in those circumstances when you want a fast resolution, your mind plays tricks on you. You hear things, sense things that aren't there, but made the time pass faster. Innocuous boots walking on uneven ground suddenly gave pause, where you think it's somebody making their way through the darkness away from us." The tension grew as the knot of soldiers heard a hollow "thunk" sound, and then a comrade called out to get their attention. "Hey!" he said. Adrenaline surged as the situation quickly became all too real.

A few more soldiers moved to the immediate area and watched as some kind of brick or block was pulled up and moved to the side of this newly discovered hole. Flashlights were passed up and stuck down into the opening. One of the soldiers said something along the lines of "I think there's something down there." Almost at the same moment, another soldier found a tube sticking out of the ground less than ten feet away. The nervous tension almost hung in the air. The soldiers became extremely aware of every detail as their senses sharpened and time seemed to stand still.

The Arabic translator was standing right next to the hole. Soldiers asked him to order the person, if there really was one, to come out with hands up and surrender. The very real possibility of enemy contact quickened pulses. Leaning down over the hole, one of the Americans confirmed that "there's definitely something moving down there." The translator yelled out that some grenades would be dropped down into the hole if the person didn't get out. One of the soldiers looking down into the hole shouted, "Movement! We have someone coming up." More orders were yelled down, to drop any weapons and emerge hands first. A few of the soldiers right beside the hole grabbed at the body and yanked upward and outward; they deposited what looked like a homeless man onto the ground. Spines tingled as they realized the history that was being made. The wild hair and shaggy beard surprised some soldiers who imagined that Saddam would have kept his "presidential" appearance so as to marshal support while on the run and coerce the people to shield him as he eluded capture. When he was thrust face down on the ground, the interpreter yelled at him, "Who are you? What is your name?" The deposed dictator responded—after translation—"My name is Saddam Hussein, and I wish to surrender." Those closest by heard a spontaneous order from the American special operator to the translator that forever summarized the moment: "Tell him that President Bush sends his regards." What else needed to be said?

Around 8:30 P.M., the future of Iraq and the region was forever changed. The scruffy-looking man had once bragged about going down in a blaze of glory and defiance; he had terrified millions and buried thousands of his own citizens in mass graves scattered throughout the nation, yet all he could muster after hearing the translation was a dull, vacant stare. The troops pulled away the Styrofoam cover to reveal a hole about six by eight feet deep, barely wide enough for Saddam to wriggle into and lie down. Termed a "spider hole" by exultant military leaders, it provided just enough space to lie down; it was camouflaged with bricks and dirt, with an air vent that was sufficient to permit its occupant to remain underground for long periods. Saddam was unkempt and dirty. Inside the hole, American forces discovered $750,000 in one-hundred-dollar bills, as well as a pistol that was never fired.[12]

The former dictator was captured quickly and with no loss of life. "No way he could fight back," crowed General Odierno at a press conference held in Tikrit. "He was caught like a rat." By 11:00 P.M. Camp Raider Base was buzzing with excitement and triumph, and morale had soared. Saddam was searched, shaved, immediately identified by other detainees, and imprisoned while DNA tests were obtained for absolutely positive identification. One Iraqi woman said, "It's like he's a goat," as she watched images of the shaggy and obviously rattled tyrant being searched that were broadcast on worldwide television the next day.

The takedown was rich with irony, and even in those formative moments carried the seeds of controversy that would later infect the trial of Saddam. He was captured just across the river from one of his many ornate palaces. Iraqis delighted to see him emerge from hiding underground like an animal. The contrast showed just how powerless he was at the hands of the coalition forces. Although the insurgency could have been fed by images of a defiant and dignified Saddam being treated with cruelty by imperialist occupiers, the former dictator's blank stare was captured in a photograph that inspired no nationalist fervor across Iraq or in the broader Arab world as it was broadcast around the world. Saddam would later try to rebuild his shattered image by appealing to the insurgents more than a dozen times as his televised trial progressed. Secretary of Defense Donald Rumsfeld, who had been publicly frustrated by the earlier failures to capture Saddam, exulted: "Here was a man who was photographed hundreds of times shooting off rifles and showing how tough he was, and in fact, he wasn't very tough, he was cowering in a hole in the ground, and had a pistol and didn't use it and certainly did not put up any fight at all." He added, tauntingly, that in "the last analysis, he seemed not terribly brave."[13]

## TO TRIAL

The momentum for a trial began almost immediately after the takedown. President George W. Bush publicly predicted that "now the former dictator of Iraq will face the justice he denied to millions."[14] Restating the goals of the ongoing American presence, he went on to promise that Iraqis would "not have to fear the rule of Saddam Hussein ever again. All Iraqis who take the side of freedom have taken the winning side. The goals of our coalition are the same as your goals—sovereignty for your country, dignity for your great culture, and for every Iraqi citizen, the opportunity for a better life." Saddam's capture at the hands of U.S. military forces paved the way for his later charges that the process of bringing him to trial was merely an extension of Western power. Rather than maintaining the image of the omnipresent leader whose will was dominant in Iraqi society, he looked like a scruffy, defeated sixty-six-year-old man whose days would best be spent doing crossword puzzles and sipping chai tea at the market. No one will ever know with certainty, but it is likely that the strategy of disrupting the trial and denying its legitimacy was born in the minute that Saddam was humiliated before the cameras of the world.

Meanwhile, I was in the Convention Center conducting a training session for a group of judges and prosecutors who had been tentatively screened by the Iraqis to preside over war crimes trials. The roomful of Iraqis buzzed with enthusiasm and mystery as they began to meet. Each attendee had been through a selection process, and most dreamed of being named to a position in such a court. Many of the key participants in the Dujail trial received their first exposure to the principles of international criminal law during those long days of discussion. Though this was months before the Iraqi High Tribunal (IHT) would name anyone to formal positions, or even establish its structure, prosecutor Ja'afar al-Moussawi was a memorable participant.

The Iraqis gathered in a large rectangular auditorium with a table at its front on a raised platform from which the Western experts spoke. Translators sat behind a sheet of glass in booths to the left of the audience. This simultaneous translation allowed for good interchanges between the Iraqi lawyers and teaching staff. Some coalition political officials stopped by to signal their support for the discussions but did not remain in the room long enough to mingle with the Iraqis and listen to the issues they sought to raise. Most of the Iraqis wore suits, though a few wore traditional garb. One sheikh wore flowing white robes lined with intricate designs; he would be murdered during the months of unrest as the insurgency blossomed. Many of the younger men were quiet as they grappled with the new notions of international law presented to them. They tended to take careful notes and ask questions only during the breaks or during lunch in private conversations.

Early in the week, those who had suffered hardships at the hands of the regime tended to dominate the discussions as they told of their pain and tried to educate the visiting Westerners as to the particulars of their experience. Later, the dynamic changed markedly as the Iraqis became intrigued by the intricacies of applying international law to their own system. They wondered aloud about the challenges of integrating developments in international law into the comfortable contours of their own domestic procedures. Lunch discussions were lively, and I was pulled from table to table to answer questions. Almost all of the lawyers were eager for me to understand their perspectives on what had happened to Iraq under Baathist rule. They asked whether a court could truly be independent and impartial, as required by human rights standards, if its funding came through political channels. They debated which approach was preferable: the international practice of grouping all of the charges against a defendant into one megatrial or the Iraqi procedural code approach, by which a defendant is tried in a series of minitrials, each focusing on a particular incident. They wanted to know whether international law allowed for the combination of charges: that is, could the same acts be punished both as war crimes and as crimes against humanity? Could an act charged as an Iraqi crime also be characterized as a crime against humanity or even as genocide? They asked many questions about the differences between the responsibility of commanders and the individual responsibility attributed to the followers or those who had far less input into the joint criminal purpose. All of these issues would surface as key points of contention during the Dujail trial.

Those Iraqis were the first in the nation to read and discuss the legal content of the statute for the Iraqi High Tribunal that had been adopted by the IGC just a few days before. From the very beginning of our discussions, the Iraqi professionals referred to the end of Baathist rule as "the entombed regime." The reference was more tinged with hope and weariness than with confident prediction. Midmorning of December 14, 2003, the calm orderliness of our academic discussions in the Convention Center was rocked by the electrifying rumors that Saddam had been taken. Rumors flew around Baghdad that he had been captured by Kurds and handed over to Americans, and the press corps was alive with speculation. The Iraqi judges and lawyers studying the newly promulgated statute remained oblivious to the news until a cell phone rang and one of their number jumped to his feet from the back of the room to shout the good news.

The class immediately dissolved in a frenzy of joy and palpable relief as Iraqis literally jumped and hugged and cried on each other's shoulders. It was a scene of joyful pandemonium. Celebratory AK-47 fire began to crackle in the streets and lasted much of the night. The classes dissolved as the judges and prosecutors spontaneously left to return home before dark, when the celebrations might make travel more dangerous. Ironically, some Americans were injured accidentally as rounds that had been fired to celebrate the success of the U.S. Army rained down from the sky. Caught up in the electricity of the moment, one of the Iraqis in the room exclaimed, "Today is day one!" His spontaneous vision captured the sense of many Iraqis that the capture and prosecution of Saddam and the leading members of his regime was a watershed event for those dedicated to leading Iraq toward stability and sovereignty founded on respect for human rights and the rule of law.

Along with many of the judges, we went into the main press room and witnessed Ambassador Paul Bremer triumphantly proclaim the message that would change the course of Iraq: "We got him!"[15] Iraqis crowded to the front of the packed room. The sense of history hung in the air with unmistakable import. As soon as Ambassador Bremer uttered those three words, the journalists crowded at the front of the room erupted with joy. The release of tension and confirmation of the rumors that had been flying across Baghdad fueled intense emotions mingled with a rising sense of optimism for the future. Later, when General Sanchez showed video of the bearded, bewildered-looking fugitive undergoing a medical exam after his capture, Iraqis in the audience stood, pointed, and shouted, "Death to Saddam! Down with Saddam!" The tape showed him opening his mouth like an obedient child as American doctors conducted a medical exam to verify his condition as he entered custody.

The man whose entire persona was built on defiance to the West was humiliated as his confused and disheveled visage was transmitted around the world. The importance of this visual confirmation can hardly be overstated. The myth of the untouchable tyrant mocking the West in full control of his destiny was shattered. Rather than a well-groomed Saddam in a pressed shirt standing up to the invader, the world saw a humbled man with no pretense of power or control. Even today, the capture of Saddam remains as one of the key coalition triumphs. In the end, though, the trial itself would serve as the forum where Saddam found his voice and stood defiantly to rally the insurgency. The behind-the-scenes preparation for the trial of Saddam and other Baath Party officials began in earnest as soon as that press conference ended. As the enormity of the task became evident and the challenges mounted, the triumphant memories of that day sustained the Iraqis in their work on behalf of their country.

# 2

## THE GENESIS OF JUSTICE

**The institution that became known** to the world as the Iraqi High Tribunal was conceived long before the coalition invasion of Iraq in March 2003. Given the unyielding and often inexplicably cruel power of the regime, justice based on law and truth was only a dim aspiration for a generation of Iraqis. Thousands of Iraqis died with the cry for justice on their lips. The people suffered enormous personal and societal trauma under Baathist tyranny, and the origins of the Iraqi High Tribunal lie far beyond the polite discourse or formal protocols of international politics. Its roots are deeply grounded in the shared suffering of the Iraqi people rather than legalistic wrangling of world capitals.

In Saddam's Iraq, fear of the regime was the unifying factor and common experience that cut across the normal divisions of race, region, tribe, and religion. There is an old Iraqi proverb that was repeated to the authors as the Iraqis prepared to seek the justice that their nation needed: the cruelty of a relative hurts more than the cut of a sharp sword. The need for justice was visceral and keenly felt by those civilians who were unfortunate enough to experience the reality of Baathist power. As one jurist said to the authors, "Saddam was the real occupier of Iraq." He went on to explain that a society of order and rich culture and legal tradition had been hijacked for decades. Saddam's narcissism and irrationality were wrapped in a cloak of charisma and unconstrained power that had seeped into every corner of the culture. Even after the regime ended in 2003, ordinary Iraqis knew that a return to Baathist rule would mean swift executions for any person accused of having helped the coalition.

All Iraqis suffered in ways that few who did not live through Baathist tyranny could imagine. The regime dealt with any hint of real or imagined political opposition with an iron purpose and an icy coldness. Random cruelty was typical of Saddam's rule, even as he postured as the "father of the Iraqi people" and the "great protector of Iraq." The tale of one midlevel Baathist official was widely circulated and accepted by average Iraqis despite its possibly apocryphal nature. The official was summoned without explanation to appear before Saddam's throne in the Republican Palace in Baghdad. Given the experience of previous officials under similar circumstances, the man knew he could expect one of two possibilities: either he would be rewarded by Saddam or he would be sentenced to die. According to the story, when he was at last called into the room, he suffered a heart attack and fell dead at Saddam's feet.

Saddam's delusional megalomania and misplaced sense of destiny led Iraq into two disastrous invasions of neighboring nations. The Iraqi people and society suffered the full effects of these debacles. At one point during the Iran-Iraq War, young Iraqis were sent without weapons en masse ahead of advancing military units to serve as human mine clearers. Saddam decreed that deserters would have their ears cut off. After Saddam invaded and occupied the small nation of Kuwait to the south, a coalition of Western and Arab states administered a humiliating defeat to what had been the fourth largest army in the world. Eight of Saddam's crack Republican Guard divisions were annihilated into fragments that together could not have been cobbled into an effective force for further external aggression. His defeat during the one hundred hours of ground fighting in 1991 forced Saddam to withdraw back to Iraqi soil and made his voice impotent in the broader sweep of Arab politics.

During 1982, the same year in which Saddam orchestrated the campaign of crimes against a village named Dujail—crimes that would later lead to his trial and execution—the health minister dared to suggest that Saddam's resignation might speed negotiations for a cease-fire in the long-running and disastrous Iran-Iraq War that Saddam had begun. Saddam ordered the official, named Riyadh Ibrahim Hussein, to adjourn to another room to discuss the proposal. When the two retired, a shot rang out, and Saddam returned to the meeting. Riyadh's widow received his dismembered body some time later. In hindsight, she was one of the lucky widows among the thousands whose husbands were murdered by the regime. Many women could never remarry because the fate of their husbands could not be proven, as their bodies moldered beyond recognition in secret mass graves across the country.

For ordinary Iraqis fear was an inescapable aspect of life under Baathist rule. The correlative dominance of Saddam's will transcended the fissures of tribe, region, culture, language, or economic status that permeated every other aspect of Iraqi society. Under Saddam, Iraqis enjoyed nothing that resembled freedom of speech or freedom of the press. If civilians were caught with an illegal satellite dish in their thirst for uncensored information, they were fined and imprisoned. Even the weather forecasts were vehicles for the dissemination of propaganda. Saddam's presence permeated every facet of society for over thirty years. Schools, mosques, palaces, whole towns, airports, hospitals all bore his name. His image dominated the daily life of every Iraqi citizen. Schoolchildren chanted, "Saddam, oh Saddam, you carry the nation's dawn in your eyes."

At the same time, Iraqis were murdered, raped, imprisoned, mutilated, and traumatized as a routine feature of life under Saddam, even as he maintained the carefully cultivated image of a devout Muslim and the paternal keeper of Iraqis. Thousands of Iraqi mothers saw their children dragged off to mass graves. Thousands of Iraqis were taken in the dead of night, often with no explanation or trial, never to be seen again. Thousands more were tortured or raped by regime forces. Some members of Saddam's security apparatus carried business cards bearing the job title of "security rapist."[1]

Whole Iraqi families were imprisoned together for years, often for being of the wrong ethnic origin or the wrong tribal lineage. Kurds, whose distinct language, culture, and ethnic identity separated them from the ruling elite, felt the wrath of a bureaucracy bent on eliminating any hint of political opposition. While the regime propaganda shaped the news to suit the precise desires of the state, unlucky thousands were killed or imprisoned based on the cruel calculus from Baghdad that their identity or political views posed a threat to the regime. Life or death often hung on the whim or inexplicable mercy of a local political official or military officer or a momentarily inattentive guard. The Kurdish people were traumatized by wholesale military attacks directed against their villages. Some escaped the terror of military attacks and lived to survive imprisonment with their families. Many never saw their loved ones again, and had only the memory of homes and businesses to sustain them in their suffering. There were more than fifty documented uses of chemical weapons against Iraqi villages. During the eight coordinated campaigns that came to be known as the Anfal, thousands of villages were literally bulldozed to the ground as their inhabitants fled, or were imprisoned or transported to distant locations where they filled the mass graves prepared to receive their bodies.[2] Kurds thirsted to see the regime humbled.

Human rights organizations outside Iraq labeled the Anfal campaigns as genocide and actively advocated that the military and civilian officials responsible face prosecution for the grievous cruelties and crimes committed against the Kurds. Shiites also suffered at the hands of a hostile government and thirsted for vengeance. They longed for the day when their majority status could be leveraged to atone for the crimes suffered under Baathist tyranny. Many Sunnis also suffered at the hands of the regime, but they remained trapped in their conflicting tribal loyalties and welded to the privileges they enjoyed as Saddam's Sunni-dominated regime bestowed its largesse on those who suited its purposes.

In the immediate wake of the crushing defeat suffered by the regime at the hands of the victorious coalition in 1991, the Shiite majority rose in rebellion. The fires of Shiite discontent burst forth from across a wide swath of southern Iraq. Shiite men organized themselves to attack the regime militarily, and they succeeded in some places in taking control of government buildings. There is a widely circulated home video shot in the streets of Najaf as young Iraqi civilians fought street to street against the remnants of Saddam's armed forces. The video goes ominously silent as tanks roll down the street; the imminent doom of the rebels is obvious. The regime was merciless in crushing the 1991 uprising.[3] U.S. forces in the region did not invade Iraq to support the Shiite uprising.

One of those patriots who took up arms to fight for liberty and the basic rights of the Shiite majority against the oppression of the regime was named

Ali Shakir al-Khuzaii. At the time of the 1991 uprising, Ali Shakir was thirty-three years old and living with his wife and daughter in Thi-Qaar Governorate, Souq al-Shuyoukh Province. His experience typifies that of thousands of Iraqis. As the Iraqi army methodically crushed the rebellion, Shiite men were slaughtered and their homes destroyed. Using tactics similar to those that had been perfected against the Kurdish population, the Iraqi army separated men and boys from their families, and dispatched them for execution in prepared mass graves far from their villages. After the government regained control of his village, Ali's neighbors were ordered to vacate their homes. They were never seen alive again. Ali decided not to give himself up, but fled for safety. He was separated from his family for years, and his wife took on the responsibility for raising their daughter. Ali later graduated from the Baghdad law school and eventually escaped to join his family in the United States, where he became an American citizen.

Even today, he is fierce in his defiance against Baathist rule. "Saddam destroyed my country," he says with a powerful and deep anger. His voice is steady, with an unmistakable steely determination. Like so many of his countrymen, he longed to see a peaceful and free Iraq in which citizens could live without fear of oppression at the hands of the government. Ali vowed to stand up to the regime using the tool of law just as he had stood alongside his brethren and fought the Iraqi army. Like so many other Iraqis, Ali Shakir prayed for the day that justice could be done and the rule of law restored to a once proud civilization. When the opportunity presented itself, he was one of the first exiles to return to Baghdad in December 2003 to assist in the conduct of trials against the regime. His warm smile and seemingly tireless dedication would make him virtually indispensable in the service of judges, lawyers, witnesses, victims, and, ultimately, the truth. The judicial process for him was a logical extension of his deeply held conviction that opposing Baathist tyranny was his duty and his destiny.

## THE TALE OF DUJAIL

Against the wide swath of crimes committed by the regime and its leaders during Saddam's reign of terror, the incident that would prove to be his legal downfall is minor indeed. It could be dismissed as merely business as usual for the dictator and his minions. When the Iraqi investigators first mentioned it to the Americans who were assisting them in documenting the crimes of the regime, the Westerners had not even heard of those crimes or of that particular village.

The town was named after the Nahr al-Dujail, the picturesque tributary of the Tigris River that runs through the center of the village, bringing it life and prosperity. In a country largely made up of vast deserts of gritty sand, Dujail was known as a lush place of palm groves, citrus trees, and grapevines. The Dujail trial judgment describes the place as a "safe town . . . rich in fruit gardens irrigated from the Tigris River through canals and water pumps."[4] Shiites and Sunnis lived together in peace, and the people of Dujail enjoyed a good standard of living. It was only fifty miles north of Baghdad and connected by a modern paved road. This meant that Dujailis were in the middle of the privileged area of Iraq that later to came be known as the Sunni triangle.

For the people of Dujail, Thursday, July 8, 1982, was the day they became bonded by blood and suffering with all of the other Iraqis who felt the wrath of the regime. Today, Dujailis refer to the day as *al-karitha*—the disaster. One witness during the trial would call it "doomsday." The events will always reverberate through Iraqi history because Saddam's decisions that day and in the days to follow sowed the seeds of his eventual prosecution and conviction at the hands of his own citizens. The following description of events has been pieced together from the evidence presented during the Dujail trial, including witness statements, documents, and even the admissions of Saddam and the other defendants. The evidentiary record is detailed in chapter 6, which contains a day-by-day account of the trial.

Although it was the midst of the fasting month of Ramadan, the forty-five-year-old Iraqi leader decided to visit the small town located in the verdant Tigris Valley, just an hour's drive north of his main palace in Baghdad. Saddam had often passed by the appealing village, which lay just off of Highway 1, halfway between Baghdad and Saddam's hometown of Tikrit. In July 1982, the war that Saddam had begun with Iran was eighteen months old. Despite a specific provision of the Iraqi criminal code that made it a crime to use armed forces against an Arab neighbor, the Iraqi dictator had sent an invasion force of a hundred thousand troops into neighboring Iran because its people were Persian, and hence an enemy.

In reality, Saddam's reasons for attacking his eastern neighbor had little to do with ethnic tensions and everything to do with gaining control of oil outlets and increasing his influence in the Arab world. Although his commanders used thousands of often unarmed conscripts as human waves in attacking Iranian positions, the war was not going well for Iraq. As the war dragged on, the regime began a sustained campaign of persecution and punishment against Iraqi citizens, using the pretext that they were in collaboration with the "Persian enemy."

One of Saddam's targets was al-Dawa al-Islamiyah ("Islamic Call"), which had been founded in the early 1960s as an underground organization. By the 1980s, the organization had grown into the Dawa Party, a Shiite-dominated political group that was popular with the growing segment of the population that did not support the ongoing military campaigns against Iran. The Dawa Party's campaign for social change, along with its Shiite roots, earned Saddam's wrath. He signed a decree rendering membership in the Dawa Party a capital offense

Saddam's megalomania was so intense that he could tolerate no hint of dissent. Shortly after seizing power in 1979, he convened a meeting of high-level government officials in a large auditorium in Baghdad. A video shows Saddam sitting on the stage with a bored expression on his face as names are read out one by one. The officials who were gathered in the room are seen standing with a look of surprise and growing horror as they hear their names called. Saddam's guards escort them out of the room, and moments later shots ring out as they are summarily executed. Whether their "crime" was disloyalty, or poor management, or whether they were simply selected at random for a demonstration of Saddam's power, no one will ever know. This was just the way Saddam ran his country.

In his first three years in office, Saddam had become increasingly intolerant of domestic dissent. Dujail was a center of Dawa political persuasion, and many Dujailis opposed the unpopular war with Iran, rendering the town the perfect backdrop for the sequel to his 1979 demonstration. Making a deadly example of the Dawa stronghold would also serve to draw domestic focus away from the flagging military efforts against Iran.

In March of 1982, a meeting was held by a local Baath Party official at the Dujail youth center. The official, Ahmad Ibrahim Hassun al-Samarra'I, brought together the tribal leaders and said to the gathering: "O people of al-Dujail, you have deserters. You have al-Dawa Party." The town had been marked. Four months later, at midmorning on July 8, 1982, Saddam would arrive just as the sun was peeking over the date palms.

As the five cars of Saddam's presidential convoy rolled into town from Highway 1, the word of his visit spread rapidly. The first hint most residents had of Saddam's visit was when Baath Party officials ordered children out of school to stand at the roadside and welcome his motorcade. Though Saddam was not a popular figure in Dujail, many of the town's two thousand residents closed up their shops and gathered to get a glimpse of the man who ruled their country and their lives with an iron fist. Saddam routinely traveled in unmarked cars and used doubles to prevent assassination attempts, and typically, his forces gathered the people upon his arrival with no prior notice.

Sporting his trademark dark green beret and a khaki uniform festooned with the insignia of an Iraqi army general, Saddam rode in the backseat of the third car, a white Mercedes with bulletproof windows. Crowds ran alongside the posh automobile as it motored down the town's central thoroughfare. He motioned for the driver to stop a few hundred yards from the Baath Party headquarters so that he could step outside to wave to the cheering crowd. With an official cameraman in tow, Saddam strode down the main street lined with colorfully dressed men, women, and children, a fixed smile on his face below his Joseph Stalin mustache. Behind him, just out of camera range, anxious soldiers aggressively shoved people back with rifle butts.

In a touching moment caught on video, a young girl with dark, sullen eyes stepped forward to offer the imposing leader a cool drink. He patted her on the head, but despite the July heat, he declined the drink and moved on. Fearing poison, Saddam would never accept such courtesies from the people in this town. There had been several attempts on Saddam's life in the last year, and he had no intention of letting his guard down, even for a moment.

Holding a large microphone up to his lips, Saddam briefly addressed the cheering crowd from the second-floor roof of the Baathist headquarters, thanking them for sending their sons to war. He then climbed back into the Mercedes to proceed to the next stop on the north side of town where a new government-funded clinic had just opened. The dusty road snakes to the left and then to the right as it follows the contours of a large date palm grove behind a six-foot-high cement wall. Suddenly the car skidded to a halt and Saddam heard the unmistakable sound of rifle shots coming from the thick foliage behind the wall on the left side of the road. One, two, three, four . . . He counted a dozen in all. Saddam was unhurt and neither his car nor his guards suffered any injury.

He sent his security detail to dispatch the small band of attackers. Several more shots were fired, this time by his own men. The would-be assassins escaped, while Saddam's men killed two children who were in the wrong place at the wrong time. After the attack, Saddam played for the video camera as if nothing serious had happened. He briefly addressed another crowd, this time from the roof of the clinic. As word of the attack quickly spread, hundreds of Dujailis gathered to beg Saddam not to punish them.

"These small groups imagine they break the relationship between Saddam and the people," Saddam shouted over the loudspeaker to the mass of people, as they frantically screamed their allegiance, knowing the likely fate of those thought to be involved in any plot. Equating the attack on his car with attacks from Iran in the war, Saddam bellowed, "Neither these few shots nor the artillery bombardments will deflect us from the course we are taking. The days have gone when Iraq belonged to foreigners." Then he said the words that the crowd ached most to hear. "We distinguish between the people of Dujail and a small number of traitors in Dujail," he declared.

Yet Saddam and the officials who answered to him made no such distinction. This was the excuse he was looking for when he chose to visit Dujail that day. The town would pay. The people would pay. And, via the reporting of the state-controlled media, the rest of Iraq would learn the price of such treachery.

Saddam immediately sent for his half-brother Barzan al-Tikriti, head of the secret police known as the Mukhabarat, who arrived in the late afternoon to mete out a devastating retribution. But Saddam didn't wait for his half-brother's arrival to personally commence the interrogations, for he fancied himself a hands-on ruler, just like his heroes Stalin, Mussolini, and Napoleon. "Where were you going?" he asked a young man who had been seized near the site of the attack. Pleading for his life, the youth replied, "I'm fasting and was on my way home." Another man, being held between two soldiers, tried to prove his loyalty by calling out, "Please, sir, I'm in the Popular Army"—the Baath Party militia. Saddam ordered his men to escort them away, and the two were never seen in Dujail again. These moments were caught on videotape and played in the courtroom during Saddam's trial.

After about an hour, Saddam left Dujail just as the thirty-one-year-old Barzan swept in, accompanied by a score of tanks and helicopter gunships. Iraqi army units sealed the entrances and exits to the town; civilians who could not flee were taken into custody. Helicopters strafed civilians working the farms. Artillery shelled the neighborhoods. Soldiers moved in and dragged young men of military age from their homes. In the next few days, Iraqi forces began to arrest whole families. The men were separated from the women; children below the age of twelve remained with the women. The guards waved weapons over the families and called them traitors and Khomeiniites, followers of the leader of Iran.

Meanwhile, at his temporary headquarters on the outskirts of town, the thuggish Barzan spent several days personally interrogating over five hundred townspeople. Those willing to provide incriminating information about their neighbors (such as Abdallah Kasim Ruwayyid al-Mashari, his son Mizhir, and Ali Diyah Ali) were immediately released and rewarded with land confiscated from the families of those arrested. Those who were implicated in the attack—more than three hundred in all—received a one-way ticket to the dreaded Hakimiya detention facility in Baghdad, run by the detested Mukhabarat. In some cases, whole families, including young children, were sent to Hakimiya. "As a humane government, we don't like to break up families," Saddam would later comment.

At Hakimiya, many of the Dujailis perished during interrogation. More than one hundred people confessed; they would say anything, admit to anything, under the Mukhabarat's torture techniques. They were then transferred to the notorious Abu Ghraib prison to await trial before the Revolutionary Command Council Court. Other Dujailis were transported to a compound known as Liya, in the Samawah Desert, where they were held for years.

The townspeople were not the only target of Saddam's vengeance. Three months after the attack on Saddam's convoy, he sent former vice president Taha Yassin Ramadan, head of the Popular Army, back to Dujail to complete the town's annihilation. Under Taha's direction, the fields and orchards surrounding Dujail were razed and all of the fruit trees carted off and destroyed. More than 5,000 acres of fertile farmland were destroyed. In the words of the trial judges, the destruction took away the citizens' "lives and their children's lives in addition to taking their honor and freedom and dignity." Thousands of miles above, a satellite snapped before-and-after photos of the town, capturing the carnage.

The lifestyle and affluence of the families of Dujail died as the palm groves, orchards, and vineyards were ripped from the ground. In open court, Taha indignantly defended his actions in conceiving and implementing the destruction of the fruit farms: "Due to what has happened, it is natural and it is the government's right as long as there is a public interest at stake or a need for taking over of farms, buildings, or estates in exchange of an appropriate compensation." The "government's right" which he referred to was to punish all of the inhabitants of Dujail for the attack on Saddam's convoy. Destroying the sustenance and prosperity of an entire village is the epitome of acts "intentionally causing great suffering, or serious injury to the body or to the mental or physical health." These acts would provide the basis for convictions in open court for the "crime against humanity of inhumane acts."

Saddam issued medals of honor to the interrogators for their excellent work. He would later sign the death warrants for 148 citizens from Dujail based on a request from the chief judge of the Revolutionary Court, Awad Hamad al-Bandar. In convicting Awad for the crime against humanity of murder, the Iraqi High Tribunal would later conclude: "It had been proven beyond any reasonable doubt that the Revolutionary Court did not conduct any session for trying the victims of al-Dujail, but despite that it issued a death sentence against all of them by hanging to death on June 14, 1984." Judge Awad al-Bandar used the fig leaf of legal power to implement the political vengeance directed by Saddam.

## A WINDOW INTO THE SOUL

The Dujail trial, in which eight defendants faced justice, was a complex courtroom ballet, with profound sociological implications for the future of

Iraq. The very essence of government is to protect the people who claim its citizenship. The Dujail trial provides a window into our souls because it forces us to confront our own experience and to think through the depth of our own commitment to law and to justice. Should the government be entitled to destroy the rights of some citizens in order to preserve the essential rights of its entire population? Can the leaders of a free people be truly accountable to those within the scope of governmental authority, or will political factors always produce injustice and inconsistent application of the law?

The courtroom tension between the dictator whose word had been law and the judge who swore to be the servant of the law was the most obvious narrative. At a deeper level, the very conception of law as a constraining social force was on trial. The Dujail trial was not just about Iraq. Its themes implicate all free peoples who seek to live without fear that their future depends only on the largesse of government or the mercy of a madman. On the day that the Dujail trial started, Mustafa Hassan Ali al-Doujaily, who had been imprisoned for four years by the Baathist regime along with the surviving members of his family, told the Associated Press: "My family and I and almost all Iraqis hope Saddam will be executed. He is a killer. He likes blood."

On reflection, he added, "We want peace, and I want my children to live in peace forever." Fathers around the world would share such an aspiration. In open court, with the world watching, the Iraqis struggled to define the outer limits that governments should lawfully have available to defend their existence from real or perceived threats. Governments across the globe must confront grave threats to their citizens and way of life, but the proper use of government power is one of the preeminent questions of our time. In a sense, that small town, in an area little known beyond Iraq, on what began as a day like so many others, was the fulcrum marking the beginning of the end of Baathist tyranny over all Iraqis. Dujail also provided a benchmark for the progress of our own civilization.

# 3

# HAMMURABI WAS AN IRAQI: THE CREATION OF THE IRAQI TRIBUNAL

## HISTORY OF IRAQI JUSTICE

"Hammurabi was an Iraqi." Though not literally true, since Iraq did not then exist as a modern nation-state, it is historically accurate that long before the modern state of Iraq, Hammurabi reigned over Babylon from 1792 to 1750 B.C. and used his powerful army to establish a unified Mesopotamia. Almost any discussion with Iraqi lawyers and judges inevitably harkens back to the importance of Hammurabi as the cornerstone of Iraqi legal consciousness. The origins of legal rules for regulating social interactions can fairly be said to have developed initially in premodern Mesopotamia. Hence, the Iraqi legal culture is keenly conscious of its place in both regional and world history. Iraq itself is the modern repository for what remains of the civilizations and cities that shaped early human history. Students of world history know that the Akkadian and Sumerian empires changed the arc of history. The modern word "Iraq" actually derives from an old Akkadian word. The Babylonian Empire was centered within modern Iraq, and Saddam built an imposing (and what some have described as garish) palace high above the remains of Babylon as a tangible symbol that his power exceeded the ancient empire and that he represented the modern incarnation of its kings.

The Baathist regime cultivated the perception of linkage between itself and the Mesopotamian kings in a 1980 advertising section of *The New York Times:*

> Iraq was more than once the springboard for a new civilization in the Middle East and the question is now pertinently asked, with a leader like this man, the wealth of oil resources and a forceful people like the Iraqis, will she repeat her former glories and the name of Saddam Hussein link up with that of Hammurabi, Ashurbanipal, al-Mansur, and Harun al-Rashib?[1]

The world's first library was assembled during the reign of Ashurbanipal, and the Iraqi self-conception was one of learning and civilized culture across the centuries. Under Saddam, the will of the regime became the sole criterion for the affairs of Iraqi society. His word was law, both literally and figuratively. Saddam was merciless to his enemies, yet generous and graceful with his friends. He carried the style of a Tikriti with him to Baghdad—in accordance with Iraqi custom, his very name identified his regional affiliation, Saddam Hussein al-Tikriti. Tikrit was an area known for its violent nature, where everyone carried a weapon and bowed to no one until compelled by superior force. One of Saddam's coterie explained at the time, "There is no mystery about the way we run Iraq. We run it exactly as we used to run Tikrit."[2]

In contrast, Hammurabi's reign symbolizes the formation of law as the unifying force for society. Turning to the administration of his newly established empire, he issued a comprehensive and humane (for the time) legal code that was long believed to be the first and most important codification of law.[3] He expressly established the purpose of the code as a god-given mandate "to cause righteousness to prevail in the land, to destroy the wicked and the evil, to prevent the strong from plundering the weak, to go forth like the sun over the black-headed race, to enlighten the land and to further the welfare of the people." Despite recent discoveries proving that Hammurabi's twenty-eight-paragraph compilation built on earlier origins,[4] the code established what we in modern parlance would recognize as the "rule of law" in Mesopotamia. Iraq has a system of law that is unfamiliar to many Western lawyers, but it is far from the lawless backwater that it is frequently stereotyped to be. From the Iraqi perspective, the precept that law provides the basis of equality and justice among civilized peoples, and that it operates on a higher moral basis, above the vagaries of political power, derives from the Iraqi exemplar. By establishing the truth that the regime abandoned its fundamental role as the protector of the people in favor of persecution and the constant expansion of its own power, the trials of Saddam Hussein and his Baathist lieutenants at the hands of Iraqi jurists will forever mark the definitive contrast to the reign of Hammurabi.

Iraqi lawyers are proud of their legal traditions. Many still remember that when the League of Nations delegates came to Iraq in 1930, they were so impressed by the professionalism and integrity of the Iraqi bar that the quality of the judiciary was "a major factor" in their support of Iraq's accession to the League.[5] Other Iraqis observe with pride that the majority of jurists in the far-flung Ottoman Empire were Iraqi; some may even recall that Iraqis themselves were familiar with the subordination of society to the precepts of a written constitution. Lawyers from Baghdad demanded that the British should be bound by a written constitution even during the colonial period. In fact, similar to the Bill of Rights in the Constitution of the United States, all of the Iraqi constitutions since 1921 have contained positive assurances of the rights of the citizens.

Of particular note to the prosecution of Saddam Hussein and the other leading Baathists, Article 20 of the 1970 constitution enshrined the right of an accused to be presumed innocent until "proved guilty in a criminal trial." In evocative terms that resonate in the consciousness of the Iraqi bench, Article 20 proclaimed that "the right of the defence is sacred in all stages of investigation and trial in accordance with the provisions of law." These are more than words—they define the ideal that animates the Iraqi sense of justice, because in their system the role of the judge is to guide the search for truth rather than to referee between two opposing sides in a dispute. The defendants may speak to witnesses, but normally do so through the judge. There are no juries in such a code-based system because professional jurists are entrusted with the responsibility for sifting through all of the available facts and pieces of evidence to determine guilt or innocence based on the specific requirements of the law. Judges in civil law systems such as that in Iraq are charged with interpreting and applying the law while the prosecutor's function is simply to assemble facts and bring them before the judge. The prosecutor is not seen as the adversary of the defendant.

During the Dujail trial, the presiding judge recited the protections due to the defendants repeatedly from the bench in response to the demands of boisterous defendants or disrespectful defense attorneys. The presiding judge sought to remind the defendants, as well as the watching world, that he was committed to balancing the rights of the defendants against the larger need for the court to pursue justice and accountability for crimes committed against innocent people. The ethos of the Iraqi tribunal originated as one in which members of the Iraqi bar sought to establish a lasting example of the power of law as the vehicle for recognizing and protecting the individual human rights of the citizenry. One Iraqi man who claimed to have been imprisoned and tortured by the regime spoke for many of his peers: "I want the trial to be just because he was not just for all his life, for a single moment, over Iraq. But I wish there is, God willing, a transparent and just tribunal over him as it would be over any person or any other dictator."

The Iraqi ambassador to the United States, Samir Shakir Mahmood Sumaida'ie, points out that the Iraqi delegate was responsible for holding out during the negotiations among nations to ensure that the 1948 Universal Declaration of Human Rights provided for gender equality.[6] The Universal Declaration of Human Rights was adopted by the UN General Assembly on December 10, 1948, and over time became the cornerstone of the entire human rights superstructure that emerged after World War II. Symbolically, but by sheer coincidence, it was exactly fifty-five years later, on December 10, 2003, that the leaders of the Interim Governing Council in Iraq stood in a newly refurbished room before the world media to announce the formation of the Iraqi High Tribunal, which would ultimately be charged with meting out justice to Saddam and the other leading Baathists who destroyed the rule of law for nearly three decades. The first line of the Universal Declaration provides that recognition of the inherent dignity and of the equal and inalienable rights of all members of the human family is the foundation of freedom, justice, and peace in the world.[7] Under Saddam, the rule of law was broken beneath the iron rule of the tyrant's power and the fear that pervaded society.

The Code of Hammurabi is preserved on a stele of black basalt that is more than seven feet tall.[8] The stele was unearthed by French archeologists in 1901 and can be seen in the Louvre in Paris. Even when taken out of historical and cultural context, and seen by tourists with no insight whatever into the Iraqi legal community, it is impressive as a great monument to ancient civilization. Its columns of cuneiform writing remain the figurative center of the modern Iraqi legal system. Iraq is a civil law state whose jurists are strictly bound by the detailed provisions of the law. The very first paragraph of the Iraqi Penal Code of 1969 (known as Law No. 111) states: "There is only punishment of an act or omission based on a law which stipulates that it is a criminal offense at the time it is committed. No penalty or precautionary measure that is not prescribed by law may be imposed."[9] One respected lawyer explained that judges in Iraq are "not lawmakers—they are truth finders," and concluded that "anything not mentioned in the law does not exist."[10] This connotes that Iraqis understand the intricacies of legal procedure and accept that the law has its own inherent power. There is no recourse to vague and shifting tribal laws or informal codes—the law itself is determinative of any legal issue.

For example, Hammurabi's code contained no laws with religious overtones, and the Iraqi codes today are complete codifications that do not permit direct influence of sharia, or Islamic religious law, in the settlement of disputes or the regulation of society. The logo of the Iraqi High Tribunal shows the black basalt stele of Hammurabi centered over the outline of Iraq. The logo itself symbolizes the judges' goal that the rule of law be central to the operation of the tribunal as it paves the way for a restoration of the rule of law across Iraq. For the Iraqi lawyers, the stele of Hammurabi represented a time when law itself was dominant, and more than one Iraqi told us that "Saddam was the real occupier of Iraq because his regime displaced and destroyed the rule of law." Educated Iraqis understood that Saddam's Baathist tyranny really represented the regression of a modern secular society with a highly developed legal culture into a state of fear and barbarism that in many ways resembled the Middle Ages. Indeed, if a Westerner unfamiliar with Iraqi legal culture were to be so arrogant as to assert that the goal of the coalition occupation was to *build* the rule of law in Iraq, the locals would frequently remind him politely that Iraqis had been accustomed to order, and that the invasion merely paved the way for the *restoration* of the rule of law.

## THE TRANSITIONAL JUSTICE WORKING GROUP

Against this backdrop of legal culture that awaited their arrival, the coalition forces entering Iraq encountered a population with a visceral demand for justice. The final report of the Transitional Justice Project, completed during prewar meetings in Siracusa, Italy, under the auspices of the International Human Rights Law Institute, stated that "the overwhelming majority of Iraqi jurists" supported a national law to establish a "special national criminal court comprising Iraqi judges according to law no. 23/1971. It may be made up of a president and two members who can seek council from international experts or have international judges acting as experts."[11] Research conducted during the summer of 2003 by the International Center for Transitional Justice and the Human Rights Center at the University of California at Berkeley similarly found that Iraqis expressed a "clear and emphatic preference" that a court to prosecute the leading member of the Baathist regime be established in Iraq and operate under Iraqi control.[12] A Gallup Poll taken in August and September of 2003 found that 6.6 percent of Baghdad residents admitted to having had a member of their household executed by the regime. Gallup released its results on December 9, 2003, and extrapolated that roughly sixty-one thousand citizens had been executed by the regime in Baghdad alone. This represented 1 percent of the population—double the number of bodies found in Bosnia, where the body count had motivated the UN Security Council to create the International Criminal Tribunal for the Former Yugoslavia.[13] The people demanded justice. Observers reported that the Iraqi support for bringing Saddam and other leading Baath Party members to justice inside Iraq "appeared almost universal."[14]

Even in the midst of daily disorder and looting in the streets, Iraqis were relieved to be free of the fear that had gripped their daily lives under the regime. Iraqis truly felt liberated, but also apprehensive about the future. In the face of complaints from his peers that the Americans had cut down the old and beautiful rows of trees that lined the road between Baghdad and the airport, one Iraqi responded that even though the trees had been something of a national symbol, "the Americans can cut down every tree in Iraq if that is what it takes to bring us security and justice." He emphasized his sentiment with a raised index finger: "God bless America." The nation faced an uncertain future, but the people wanted the essentials of personal security, education, and the opportunity to forge a better future for themselves and their families. They wanted steady electricity and the chance to resume their education.[15] The war disrupted the rickety supply chain that Iraqis used to get their gasoline. By December 2003, gasoline that would normally cost 50 dinars was being sold for more than 400 dinars, and people had to wait in long lines. Iraqis complained and wondered why the greatest military power on Earth was powerless to provide such basic amenities. In typical regional fashion, rumors flew that the shortages were intentional. Against this backdrop, it was very clear to both the legal experts and the Iraqi population that prosecuting Iraqi officials would be a necessary step toward national restoration and a democratic Iraq that enjoyed stability and territorial integrity built on the rule of law.

A great deal has been written about the paucity of prewar planning, but the area of transitional justice is perhaps the best illustration of that fact. When he was named head of the Office of Reconstruction and Humanitarian Assistance upon its formation in January 2003, General Jay Garner was tasked with the enormous and complex task of coordinating coalition relief efforts in Iraq,[16] but he was specifically told to disregard the previous State Department–sponsored Future of Iraq Project.[17] This exclusion had the effect of discounting the perspective of the Iraqi exiles who had integrated their perspectives into the formal State Department report since 2002. The Working Group on Transitional Justice, which was merely one component of the larger State Department project, released its report on May 15, 2003.[18]

Shortly thereafter, an Iraqi American lawyer named Sermid al-Sarraf, who had assisted with the rule of law aspects of the project, "was carrying a copy of its 250-page report, trying to interest occupation officials. No one seemed to have seen it."[19] After his return from Baghdad, Sermid would testify on June 25, 2003, to a subcommittee of the Senate Judiciary Committee that "Iraqis are feeling like strangers in their own country. Either through neglect, lack of understanding, or for the sake of expediency, current efforts seem to be avoiding direct Iraqi involvement and their opinions in important decisions."[20] By the fall of 2003, one leading expert quite accurately observed in testimony to Congress that the "patterns of cooperation inside the Government broke down" during the early phase of the occupation and that in confronting tasks for which it had "no background or competence" the Department of Defense failed to invite the support of others inside the U.S. government with the required expertise.[21] Exporting the bureaucratic struggles from inside the Washington Beltway onto the Baghdad battlefield affected virtually every aspect of the postconflict transition, especially because the reality on the ground was that the insurgency gained strength every day and had not been anticipated by American contingency planning. The paralysis and delay caused by interagency fighting in Washington tragically created huge obstacles and inefficiencies for those on the ground in Iraq trying to fight the real enemies of the United States and the people of Iraq.

When the Coalition Provisional Authority was established in May 2003, an ambitious and brilliant lawyer named Sandy Hodgkinson was named to head its Office of Human Rights and Transitional Justice (OHRTJ). That office had a huge job and a minuscule staff, but it had the advantage of experts from the United States, as well as the United Kingdom, Canada, Australia, New Zealand, Spain, and the Czech Republic. Sandy is a slightly built energetic blur who did a masterful job of balancing competing constituencies and moving toward a holistic system of justice that would contribute to a future of peace and prosperity. She is an avid long-distance runner who is almost constantly in motion. Her intense personal commitment to human rights and the preservation of human dignity operates like a gravitational field to pull her colleagues toward a higher vision of the future. Sandy moved very quickly to establish a reporting office, staffed by Iraqis, which almost immediately began to collect enormously compelling testimony of the human rights abuses suffered at the hands of the regime. Some of those statements would later become evidence in the trials, but the very fact that they were being collected and that ordinary Iraqis who came to the office had a voice in documenting their suffering was a stark contrast to the treatment of Iraqi citizens at the hands of what they began to call "the entombed regime."

Even as she mobilized support for human rights investigations in Iraq, Sandy took on the Herculean task of moving the Washington bureaucracy toward a unified position that could be supported financially and politically with the resources of the U.S. government. She met repeatedly with officials at the highest levels to brief them on the importance of a prosecutorial strategy. Sandy envisioned what she termed a "holistic approach" that would ultimately include prosecutions as well as compensation to victims, processes for societal reconciliation and rebuilding of trust within communities, and a localized form of a Truth and Reconciliation process similar to those used in other postconflict zones.

Sandy's initial vision later led the U.S. Ambassador-at-Large for War Crimes Issues, Pierre-Richard Prosper, to postulate a so-called three-tier system for dealing with the massive numbers of crimes committed against the Iraqi people. At its pinnacle would be the special tribunal created to deal with a small number of perpetrators at the very highest level. Many more would be prosecuted in ordinary domestic Iraqi courts, provided that the resources and training were made available to ensure that they were prepared to apply the sophisticated modern international legal principles. And finally, the majority of offenders, particularly those at the lower levels of authority, would be handled using what Ambassador Prosper termed a "Truth-Revealing Process." The early conversations with Iraqis revealed that they envisioned a massive mechanism of perhaps fifteen trial chambers that would prosecute something on the order of five thousand defendants. Realizing that this would be unrealistic, Sandy firmly believed in the importance of beginning progress toward a viable court as quickly as possible. The larger goals of justice and social reconstruction would be thwarted if months went by with no tangible progress. Besides, vigilante justice might be the option of choice in Iraq if the people saw no indication that the crimes of the past would be prosecuted.

Washington politicians initially favored a hybrid tribunal that would be based on the dual authority of the United Nations and the government of Iraq, and would fully integrate international lawyers alongside Iraqis in the trial chambers, prosecutorial offices, and appeals panels. Though this hybrid model had been successfully implemented in Sierra Leone, where the trials were conducted in the immediate aftermath of a civil war, the final policy decision in Washington favored a decentralized approach that empowered Iraqis to create and maintain a tribunal under their own legal authority. From the time of that fateful decision, the United States and its lawyers on the ground were relegated to the role of assisting, advising, and supporting the Iraqis.

Meanwhile, on the ground, OHRTJ moved quickly to establish a Transitional Justice Working Group. Sandy's husband, Dave Hodgkinson, is a talented attorney in his own right who recognized that the integration of Iraqi perspectives and their personal commitment would be the vital ingredient in any successful justice efforts. Dave and Sandy had both served in the U.S. military and been key members of a team organized to train Iraqi lawyers and discuss the future of a free Iraq at a meeting held at the Defense Institute of International Legal Studies (DIILS)[22] in Newport, Rhode Island, in November 2000.[23] The DIILS training represented a major effort to bring together Iraqis who had fled the regime and foster candid debate over the constitutional and legal structures that might be created in a post-Saddam Iraq. That meeting was the first time that a constitution had been drafted by groups of Iraqis, and some of the participants in that November 2000 meeting were among those who returned to Iraq to help rebuild from the devastation of the Saddam era. Dave replicated the DIILS structure in Baghdad by organizing a series of seminars that brought together participants from across Iraq, international experts, and representatives of international organizations as well as nongovernmental organizations. The overall project to dismantle the bureaucracy of repression would prove daunting, but there was no lack of energy and enthusiasm on the part of the local population.

Dave explained that "justice is almost a sacred word" for Iraqis; "it has a deep ring and is very close to the Arab heart—almost akin to honor."[24] A seminar convened by the Transitional Justice Working Group under Dave's leadership attracted Iraqi lawyers from across the cultural and legal spectrum. The Iraqi participants in that seminar room self-selected which groups to attend. The room dedicated to investigations was very popular as participants sought to learn about the proper handling of documents and the best practices for handling evidence and coordinating the dimensions of a complicated investigation. Another meeting room was abuzz with discussions about the legal reform needed to move Iraqi society ahead. For Iraqi jurists, the text of the law itself has an authoritative power that makes amendments both time-consuming and important. These debates often became technical as highly motivated and educated lawyers debated which of the provisions of the extensive Iraqi civil and penal codes needed to be amended and in what sequence and to what purpose. The Iraqi participants in these early discussions focused almost exclusively on the need to create a tribunal because they feared overloading the fragile domestic judicial system, which itself was struggling in light of the insurgency.

In sharp contrast, the room dedicated to what was labeled "Truth and Reconciliation" had only one attendee. Iraqis did not want to focus on forgiveness or the task of merely documenting the crimes of the regime, and the nearly empty room demonstrated their priorities. The idea behind a Truth and Reconciliation Commission, as used in other parts of the world, is that compiling factual evidence of the record of the regime serves a useful healing purpose that can justify forgoing prosecution in some circumstances.[25] Western experts believe that community reconciliation and documentation can help to create a renewed cultural consensus that educates future generations and memorializes the exact nature of the abuses at the hands of lawless and undemocratic authorities.[26]

Iraqi law does contain an analog to the procedures developed in other parts of the world by permitting the court or magistrate to sentence a convicted person "to such penalty as is customary under tribal custom." The practice of suspending the sentence imposed by the court and deferring to tribal custom is predicated on the judge clearly establishing the guilt of the accused, and must be based on the finding "that it is in the interests of public order and consonant with justice that the case be so settled."[27] The translation of "Truth and Reconciliation" sounded like "forgive and forget" to Iraqi ears. In fact, one eminent scholar recommends the use of the term "historic commission" because it is rooted in regional experience and translates more directly into understandable Arabic. When Sandy Hodgkinson spoke to assembled Iraqis about Truth and Reconciliation, they were polite but visibly unengaged, even after the necessary linguistic explanations. The lone Iraqi who chose to attend that seminar group worked with American officials to design a reconciliation process involving local groups across Iraq, but the project died from lack of funding and the competing priority that Iraqis put on prosecutions.

The seminar room dedicated to prosecutions, by contrast, was packed to overflowing. Iraqis were standing in every available space. They wanted to talk about justice and accountability. They wanted more than public and international recognition of their suffering at the hands of the regime. They wanted punishment based on law. Iraqi leaders listened and responded.

## NEGOTIATING THE TRIBUNAL STATUTE

The impulse to punish Saddam and other leading Baathists was a thread running throughout U.S. policy toward Iraq from the end of the 1991 Gulf War.[28] The U.S. Congress appropriated $4 million to a UN War Crimes Commission[29] trust fund that could have been available at some unspecified time in the future if a UN tribunal had been established based on the model that would later be developed for the Balkans and in response to the genocide in Rwanda.[30] Through the years, there were repeated calls in Congress for the formation of an International Criminal Court for Iraq or another international tribunal for prosecuting Saddam.[31] When coalition forces moved into Baghdad and Saddam's regime melted, the American and British forces became legally responsible for Iraqi civilians and institutions under the international law of occupation as they swept aside the existing governmental structures.[32]

In mid-April 2003, the American and British forces formally notified the UN Security Council of the legal state of occupation.[33] As early as April 9, 2003, Pierre-Richard Prosper told *Newsday*, "We will work with Iraqi people to create an Iraqi-led process that will bring justice for the years of abuses that have occurred." In a resolution, adopted at light speed by any normal UN measure, the Security Council unanimously required the coalition members to "comply fully with their obligations under international law including in particular the Geneva Conventions of 1949 and the Hague Regulations of 1907."[34] In this important resolution, the Security Council specifically highlighted the need for an accountability mechanism "for crimes and atrocities committed by the previous Iraqi regime." British authorities decided to dispatch a retired army attorney, Colonel Charles Garroway, to assist the transitional justice effort. Garroway is one of the most capable and experienced international lawyers in the world on the details of atrocity law, having represented Her Majesty in the negotiations for the elements of crimes for the International Criminal Court. His intellectual firepower is paired with a keen wit and a gregarious nature that made him a tremendous resource for Sandy Hodgkinson as she fought to get OHRTJ off the ground.

Using its inherent powers under occupation law and the power granted by the Security Council, the Coalition Provisional Authority proclaimed its purposes using declarative terms that echoed the pronouncements of the Allied forces that occupied German soil at the end of World War II:[35] "The CPA is vested with all executive, legislative, and judicial authority necessary to achieve its objectives, to be exercised under relevant UN Security Council resolutions, including Resolution 1483 (2003), and the laws and usages of war."[36] Under international law, when the coalition displaced the Iraqi government, it assumed the broad legal obligation to "take *all* the measures in [the occupant's] power to restore, and ensure, as far as possible, public order and safety" (emphasis added).[37] In the authoritative French, the occupier must preserve *l'ordre et la vie publics* (public order and life).[38] Even in the early days of the occupation, it was clear to close observers that prosecution of leading Baath Party officials could act as a pressure relief valve to help meet the needs of impatient groups of victims in Iraq who had long harbored dreams for personal revenge and score settling. Even if the CPA could have avoided its legal obligations to assist the Iraqi people, no responsible official sought to sustain conditions that would lead to the widespread vigilante justice that was on display in the wake of the 1991 Shia uprisings as Baath Party officials were hacked to death by mobs of furious citizens.[39] These imperatives resulted in a clear requirement in Security Council Resolution 1483 that the CPA exercise its temporary power over Iraq in a manner "consistent with the Charter of the United Nations and other relevant international law, to promote the welfare of the Iraqi people through the effective administration of the territory."

The CPA touted its subsequent creation of a twenty-five-member Interim Governing Council on July 13, 2003, as a "major step" toward the longer-term goal of a "unified and stable, democratic Iraq that provides effective and representative government for the Iraqi people; is underpinned by new and protected freedoms and a growing market economy; is able to defend itself but no longer poses a threat to its neighbors or international security."[40] From the CPA perspective, the IGC was a needed step in transitioning authority over day-to-day functions to respected Iraqis who knew their nation and its needs. The IGC was composed of distinguished Iraqis that in the aggregate formed the most representative set of national leaders in Iraq's history. The council was composed of thirteen Shiite Muslims, five Sunni Muslims, five Kurds, one Christian, and one Turkoman. Its members had spent their adult lives enmeshed in Iraqi politics or opposing the regime in one form or another, and many of them would later be elected by the Iraqi people to prominent political positions.[41] The UN Security Council welcomed its formation and committed to a UN mission to Iraq to support the goals of political stability and the preservation of human rights.[42] The IGC was, however, caught in a perfect storm of political factors that dramatically undermined its effectiveness in steering Iraqi politics and created a perception of illegitimacy on the part of those outside its narrow sphere of influence.

The bitter international division over the legality of invading Iraq continued to spawn poisonous international debate over each step taken by those charged with administering the chaotic situation on the ground. Charles Garroway wrote, with typical British understatement, that "the Gulf War of 2003 was controversial in its origins and in its outcome."[43] The International Crisis Group typified the skepticism from outside Iraq.

> While it can accurately be described as the most broadly representative body in Iraq's modern history, selected as it was by the CPA in consultation with pre-chosen political parties and personalities, the Interim Governing Council simply lacks credibility in the eyes of many Iraqis and much of the outside world. On paper, it enjoys broad powers; in reality, few doubt the deciding vote will be cast by the U.S. A gathering of political leaders with weak popular followings, very little in common between them, no bureaucratic apparatus and a clumsy nine-person rotating presidency at its helm, it is doubtful that it can become an effective decision-making body.[44]

Inside Iraq, the people suffered daily from the privations of economic and social disruption and from the spreading insurgency. The increasingly clear effects of American mistakes and miscalculations, such as the disbanding of the Iraqi military, compounded the political difficulties.[45] The horrific truck bomb that destroyed the UN compound on August 19, 2003, caused an immediate withdrawal of international expertise, which in turn helped sustain the perception that everything done by the IGC was under American political control. The reality on the ground was far more complex, as American officials understood little of the intricacies of Iraqi political maneuverings and even less about the informal avenues of influence that are the real keys to getting concrete results in Iraq. On a more intangible level, the bombing at the UN headquarters killed the Secretary-General's Iraq representative, who was widely believed to have been the target of the blast. Sergio Vieira de Mello was a fifty-five-year-old Brazilian diplomat, silver-haired, square-jawed, and as smooth as he was experienced. His death was devastating. He had helped to oversee the investigation of human rights abuses in Kosovo, Cambodia, East Timor, and Cyprus, and was serving as High Commissioner for Human Rights before walking into danger in Baghdad. His absence deprived the Iraqis of an international voice and credibility that might have been critical in advocating on their behalf and explaining the need for international support to the investigation and prosecution of Saddam and his regime.

Sergio de Mello might have been the only diplomat on Earth with the experience and international credibility to forge an alliance between the Iraqi tribunal and the wider community interested in the prosecution of what those in the business term "the crimes of most serious concern to the international community as a whole." Ambassador Prosper had informed diplomatic circles of the American view that a purely international tribunal along the lines of those established in Rwanda and the Balkans would be counterproductive. Prosper was clear that the United States would provide technical, logistical, legal, and financial assistance to an Iraqi-led tribunal, but that "the international community should help too."

In the early summer of 2003, Sergio de Mello had already begun to meet with the administrator of the CPA, Paul Bremer, on the issue of a tribunal. His untimely death, coupled with the precipitous UN withdrawal from Iraq, meant that the process of negotiating a framework for prosecutions was truly opaque to the outside world of diplomats and legal debaters. Commentators would later complain that the UN had no role in establishing the Iraqi tribunal, even though all UN employees were withdrawn from Iraq at the precise period the negotiations began. In the wake of the UN withdrawal from Iraq and escalating sectarian division, even the apportionment of political power by the CPA was panned by the International Crisis Group because it reflected "how the Council's creators, not the Iraqi people, view Iraqi society and politics, but it will not be without consequence. Ethnic and religious conflict, for the most part absent from Iraq's modern history, is likely to be exacerbated as its people increasingly organize along these divisive lines." Confounding the external expectations, the very first decision of the Iraqi council illustrated that the issues of justice and accountability cut across sectarian and tribal lines. After all, Hammurabi was an Iraqi.

On its very first day of authority, the IGC created a Legal Affairs Subcommittee to respond to human rights abuses and reestablish judicial processes for administering justice. One member of the IGC later explained the importance of this, the council's first decision: "The justice we bring is not the justice of vengeance. It is an important part of healing. In the end, it is right that we do it our own way." The Iraqi aspirations were similar to those expressed in other tribunals faced with massive crimes. The International Criminal Tribunal for Rwanda had written that its fundamental purpose in prosecuting the *genocidaires* was to "contribute to the process of national reconciliation and to the restoration and maintenance of peace."[46] From its outset, the effort to prosecute Saddam Hussein would be spearheaded by Iraqis and was conceived to be in the service of the Iraqi people. In practice, this meant that the United States and its allies could cajole, coax, and coach, but the deliberations and decisions that would determine success or failure would be in Iraqi hands.

## LEGAL COLONIALISM OR LOCAL CONVENIENCE?

Judge Dara Nur al-Din was described by Judge Gilbert S. Merritt, himself one of the most respected federal judges in the United States, as a cross between Nelson Mandela and Sir Thomas More.[47] When Judge Merritt went to Iraq in May 2003 at the request of the Department of Justice, he was tasked with assessing the Iraqi judicial system and its capacity for rebuilding. He, too, heard the refrain "Hammurabi was an Iraqi." When he explained to local lawyers that he wanted to speak with the most respected judge in Iraq, he was repeatedly told that he should find Judge Dara. Judge Dara was fifty-six at the time of the invasion. He is a barrel-chested man with muscular arms and shoulders and gray hair and mustache. Iraqi lawyers describe him as "a dignified scholar" or "a man of great integrity." Even through a translator Judge Merritt found Judge Dara's warm and easy manner to be coupled with a quick sense of humor.[48] An anonymous Iraqi lawyer told Judge Merritt that Dara "combines bravery, straight talk, and great intellect."

Judge Dara's personal history is compelling, but also emblematic of the many professionals who fought to preserve the real Iraq from Saddam's deprivations. The judge was sentenced by one of Saddam's Special Courts to two years of confinement at Abu Ghraib prison because he dared to defy the regime. After the Baghdad planning commission took some land on the outskirts of the city without paying any compensation to the landowners, the case came before Judge Dara in the Court of First Instance. Judge Dara found that the confiscation violated a provision of the 1970 Iraqi constitution. As he explained it to his American counterpart, "When I refused to back down, I was imprisoned and brought before a special revolutionary court for trial. When I again said my decision was correct under the law, I was sentenced to two years in prison. I am not the only judge who has gone to jail. My friend Judge Alia al-Jaqubi on my court went to jail with me. We shared a cell together at Abu Ghraib, a prison of seventeen thousand built for three thousand." Judge Dara was living proof that the judiciary was one Iraqi institution that even Saddam's power could never completely destroy. Hammurabi was an Iraqi, indeed.

Western human rights lawyers argued that, after decades of Baath Party domination, an international tribunal was necessary because the Iraqi judiciary had been destroyed by the insidious effects of Baathist political influence. Judge Dara and others like him embodied the simple truth that the value of authentic justice had been sustained by courageous judges all along. Judge Dara explained that Saddam dismissed nine members of the Supreme Court because they followed their conscience and refused to order the death penalty for a man who had accidentally shot one of Saddam's guards; such punishment was not authorized for that type of crime under Iraqi law. Though he is retired now, Judge Dara takes pride in his place in an Iraqi judiciary that he described as having been the best in the Arab world. He comes from a line of distinguished Iraqi lawyers. He was never a spineless pawn under Saddam's control, but served the law in pursuit of the larger purpose of justice and in the interests of the Iraqi people. For Judge Dara and many other Iraqis, these precepts are not merely esoteric theories; they are the professional and personal code by which they live. Judge Dara was no puppet of Saddam, and he would be deeply offended at the implication that he was merely serving the interests of the Americans as he supervised the efforts to debate a statute to create a court to prosecute the Baathist leaders that committed such crimes against the people.

Judge Dara was the head of the Legal Affairs Subcommittee that began to meet in the fall of 2003 to hammer out a process and structure for prosecuting Saddam. The subcommittee met frequently and for lengthy periods of time as it grappled with the complex procedural and political hurdles to establish a viable tribunal. Participants in those debates characterize Judge Dara as overseeing the effort with a charismatic and deliberative purpose that earned the deep respect of his subcommittee. Despite his short stature, his booming voice cut through the confusion and debate to shed insight and wisdom on the intricate legal issues confronting the group. As they worked, members of the CPA Transitional Justice Working Group attended and assisted, but the process was most definitely Iraqi. It was collaborative and comprehensive, though it occasionally bordered on combative as the dozen or so men debated. There were a handful of legal experts from outside Iraq (including author Michael Newton) who were asked to review successive drafts and offer constructive comments. In each case, the subcommittee decided the issue by common consensus after much debate and chai tea.

Critics have noted that the statute of the tribunal was written in English and only later translated into Arabic and have assumed that proved that the entire effort was merely a subterfuge for the exercise of American power. Judge Dara had a great deal of legal experience, but like domestic judges around the world, he had little expertise in distilling and applying the principles of international law to the complex facts that would be at issue in cases against the leading Baathists. None of the leading cases in the field of international criminal law were available in Arabic, and Saddam had refused to permit Iraqi lawyers to maintain current expertise in the body of law needed to prosecute officials for genocide, war crimes, and crimes against humanity, for obvious reasons. The IGC appointed an Iraqi expatriate named Salem Chalabi who had been living in London and working as a highly paid corporate lawyer to serve as the draftsman and coordinator of the document.

Salem, who goes by the name Sam when in Western circles, is a short, balding lawyer who was in some sense a ready-made lightning rod because his uncle was the controversial founder of the Iraqi National Congress (INC). Rumors of shady dealings and financial improprieties surrounded Achmed Chalabi like cigar smoke. The INC had received millions of U.S. dollars through the years, much of which was ostensibly provided to gather evidence of war crimes for use at an auspicious moment. Achmed secured his seat on the Interim Governing Council, and later headed up the politically charged De-Baathification Commission.

Salem Chalabi, forty-one years old, had long been the most vocal and knowledgeable Iraqi proponent for a tribunal to prosecute Saddam and other leading officials. Salem's preparations for service began as early as 1993, during his pursuit of a law degree at Northwestern Law School in Chicago, when antiregime dissidents asked him to write a report for the Iraqi National Congress that laid out the case for an Iraqi tribunal under Security Council auspices.[49] Salem was the INC representative at the DIILS seminar in November 2000, and advocated for a tribunal to anyone who would listen. For those prone to view the drafting exercise as an extension of American politics—victor's justice wrapped in Iraqi robes—Salem was an American proxy whose appointment by the IGC derived only from American power. Conversely, American human rights lawyers criticized his later appointment as the administrator of the Iraqi tribunal on the grounds that it was announced by the INC rather than Iraqi political officials.

Judge Dara did not see himself as working for American interests, or European interests, or even the interests of humanity: he was an Iraqi serving Iraq. Salem Chalabi explained that American politics had no role in his appointment, but that he was selected by the Iraqi governing council "because they knew I was the one pushing this the hardest."[50] His uncle's influence was certainly no hindrance.

When Charles Garroway arrived in Baghdad in August 2003, he received the draft of a statute establishing a tribunal that had been prepared by Salem Chalabi. The August 2003 draft was prepared as a composite document that built on Iraqi law and was what Garroway describes as an "amalgam" of the Nuremberg, Rwanda, Yugoslavia, and Sierra Leone statutes, as well as some phrases borrowed from an earlier proposal that had been prepared by the world-famous and widely admired Egyptian academic Cherif Bassiouni. None of the other tribunal documents were written in Arabic, and Salem's draft had been based on the English-language versions of the works that at the time were seen as the most authoritative in the world. Chalabi kept his drafts in English to permit easier editing and incorporation of language from the provisions of other tribunals around the world (which are all in English). When he received the draft, Garroway was told that the statute was to be promulgated in three days.[51] He spent an intense twenty-four hours preparing a detailed memorandum that documented the gaps, inconsistencies, and legal flaws of the draft he had received. Salem persuaded the Interim Governing Council that more time would be needed to iron out the key areas, and they agreed to the delay because of the desire to produce an Iraqi text that would be compatible with the provisions of the other tribunals in the world.

## THREE KEY LEGAL CORNERSTONES

The earliest drafts of a statute began to circulate in August 2003, though there had been some proposals floated outside Iraq even before the invasion in April. The Legal Affairs Subcommittee grappled with many issues, but the scaffolding of what would become the tribunal structure emerged on the foundation laid by three early decisions. As a starting point, the Legal Affairs Subcommittee emphatically rejected suggestions that the legal authority of the tribunal should derive from the power of the UN Security Council. One of the interesting historical paradoxes behind the trial of Saddam Hussein is that his crimes had served as a major impetus behind the formation of the international tribunal in the Balkans. Under Chapter 7 of the UN Charter, all power from all of the states in the world is conveyed to the UN Security Council to "maintain or restore international peace and security."[52]

After discussions revealed that an international tribunal to try Saddam was supported by France, Belgium, and Luxembourg, the acting president of the Council of Ministers of European Communities wrote a letter to the secretary-general of the United Nations on April 16, 1991, that sought legal clarification that such a tribunal would be within the power of the Security Council.[53] The International Criminal Tribunal for the Former Yugoslavia (ICTY) was later established on the basis of a groundbreaking 1993 resolution marking the first exercise of Chapter 7 authority to create a judicial process.[54] One of the benefits of such an approach is that the tribunal enjoys derivative power to require sovereign states to cooperate with its investigations and prosecutions based on the fact that all the members of the United Nations have a treaty obligation to "accept and carry out the decisions of the Security Council."[55]

On a conceptual level, for Iraq, an international court with international judges applying international law would have been immune to the concerns of domestic politics or the pressure of the populace. Such an impartial bench could have overturned the immunity of Iraqi officials with barely a ripple of commentary from the legal afficionados outside Iraq. The Legal Affairs Subcommittee decided instead that an international tribunal superimposed by the Security Council would create a crisis of legitimacy within Iraq that would destroy the tribunal. A participant in the process confided that the drafters "didn't want political trials." Given the bitter feelings toward the Security Council as a creature of world politics, the Iraqis felt that a court relying on its power would be popularly rejected. Setting aside the withdrawal of the UN staff after the murder of Sergio de Mello, the UN sanctions imposed on Iraq had created disdain for its legitimacy among the population. At the same time, Iraqis knew that civilians were being dragged from their cars and beaten to death. There was very little support for trusting the cumbersome UN bureaucracy with a task as vitally important to the future of Iraq as trying the regime while innocent Iraqis continued to die for months in the face of glacial UN progress toward justice. The idea of a pan-Arab tribunal integrating judges from across the region was quickly rejected for similar reasons. Even if a tribunal founded on legal authority from outside Iraq had been able to function inside the war zone, the benefits of imposing punishments in a manner acceptable to the international community would likely have been negated by its form of neocolonism wrapped in judicial robes.

The decision to create an Iraqi institution founded on Iraqi domestic law was a comfortable one for judges steeped in the tradition of Hammurabi. It nonetheless created second- and third-order effects that reverberated to the very last days of the trial and the appeal. The Coalition Provisional Authority order that delegated authority to the Iraqi leaders to promulgate the statute nevertheless required that the tribunal meet "international standards of justice."[56] Dave Hodgkinson was an active participant in the debates and believes that "to them it was an Iraqi institution" that would require only the addition of "little things here and there" to gain international legitimacy. The Legal Affairs Subcommittee engaged in lengthy debates, trying to find a workable synthesis of underlying Iraqi procedure with relevant international legal principles. For the first time in

Iraqi law, the concepts of crimes against humanity, war crimes, and genocide would be imported from the international precedents.

Judge Dara was the dominant and authoritative presence in the room; his booming voice cut through the overlapping circles of discussion. The room was always crowded, and progress at times was slow as the Iraqis darted about like fireflies pursuing a series of legal issues rather than engaging in an orderly and dry esoteric discussion. For them, this was *the* challenge facing post-Baathist Iraq, and they advocated their various positions with energy and passion.

The earliest drafts also contained two controversial paragraphs that were later deleted. The two provisions that did not make it into the text later adopted by the IGC would have criminalized crimes of aggression (based on the Nuremberg precedent) and crimes against the environment. Legal experts agreed that these two provisions were insufficiently defined in international law, and that prosecution for those offenses would be fundamentally unfair because of the human rights principle that no one should be convicted for crimes defined and penalized after their commission.[57] This protection is familiar to Americans as the constitutional principle that they cannot be punished on the basis of ex post facto laws. The International Covenant on Civil and Political Rights, which Iraq ratified in 1971, states that same principle, as follows: "No one shall be held guilty of any criminal offence on account of any act or omission which did not constitute a criminal offence, under national or international law, at the time when it was committed."[58]

The final text closely mirrored the prohibitions on genocide, crimes against humanity, and war crimes that are found in the Rome Statute of the International Criminal Court. The ICC statute has been accepted by 110 nations around the world, including all of the members of the European Union. Salem Chalabi would later explain that the drafters designed the text to gain international legitimacy in order to "ensure it is not seen as a symbol of victory because it follows international procedures."

The drafting committee required that the trial chamber be guided by the "general principles of criminal law" derived from the Iraqi Criminal Procedure Code,[59] but specifically included authority for the judges to "resort to the relevant decisions of international courts or tribunals as persuasive authority for their decisions."[60] The international tribunals have developed a complex and rigorous body of case law interpreting the precise legal questions arising in prosecutions for genocide, war crimes, and crimes against humanity. American authorities arranged for a contractor to translate many of the leading international decisions into Arabic for the first time so that they could be studied and applied by the judges. As one judge told Michael Newton during a meeting in January 2005, "I should know more about the international case than what the lawyers tell me it says." The Iraqis sought to produce decisions that would be consistent with practice around the world. In time, the judgment in the Dujail case would rely in part on the precedents of the international tribunals in explaining the legal reasoning of the judges, and would include many references to international cases.

In order to meet international expectations of authentic justice, the trial chamber must "ensure that a trial is fair and expeditious and that proceedings are conducted in accordance with this Statute and the rules of procedure and evidence, with full respect for the rights of the accused and due regard for the protection of victims and witnesses."[61] The Iraqi drafters mirrored other tribunal statutes as well as the guarantees of the International Covenant on Civil and Political Rights by providing that[62]

1. All persons shall be equal before the tribunal.
2. Everyone shall be presumed innocent until proven guilty before the tribunal in accordance with the law.
3. In the determination of any charge, the accused shall be entitled to a public hearing, having regard to the provisions of the statute and the rules of procedure made hereunder.
4. In the determination of any charge against the accused pursuant to the present statute, the accused shall be entitled to a fair hearing conducted impartially and to the following minimum guarantees:
   a. To be informed promptly and in detail of the nature, cause, and content of the charge against him.
   b. To have adequate time and facilities for the preparation of his defense and to communicate freely with counsel of his own choosing in confidence. The accused is entitled to have non-Iraqi legal representation, so long as the principal lawyer of such accused is Iraqi.
   c. To be tried without undue delay.

d. To be tried in his presence, and to defend himself in person or through legal assistance of his own choosing; to be informed, if he does not have legal assistance, of this right; and to have legal assistance assigned to him, in any case where the interests of justice so require, and without payment by him in any such case if he does not have sufficient means to pay for it.
e. To examine, or have examined, the witnesses against him and to obtain the attendance and examination of witnesses on his behalf under the same conditions as witnesses against him. The accused shall also be entitled to raise defences and to present other evidence admissible under this statute and Iraqi law.
f. Not to be compelled to testify against himself or to confess guilt, and to remain silent, without such silence being a consideration in the determination of guilt or innocence.[63]

In order to help achieve these rights, while gaining international credibility, the Legal Affairs Subcommittee agreed to one symbolic and crucial last-minute edit. All of the drafts, as well as the final text, required that the president of the tribunal appoint qualified international advisers to augment the investigative, trial, and appeals judges. The Iraqis knew that they were unfamiliar with the contours of the international crimes and sought the expertise of non-Iraqi lawyers to assist them. Coming from the Hammurabi tradition, they had resisted the advice of non-Iraqi experts to include international judges on the bench. The subcommittee felt that Iraqi judges would be best positioned to apply the criminal laws drawn from international law in a manner that best fit with Iraqi legal practice. They felt that Iraqi judges would be most recognizable and acceptable to the Iraqi people. On the last night of debates, and in the final round of edits, the Iraqis yielded to the persistent advice of outside experts and added a provision that permitted the appointment of non-Iraqi judges to actually participate in the decisions and resolution of the legal issues. Article 4 of the statute that eventually passed the IGC stated that the "Governing Council, if it deems necessary, can appoint non-Iraqi judges who have experience in the crimes encompassed in this statute, who shall be persons of high moral character, impartiality, and integrity." International judges would have changed the dynamics of the judicial deliberations in the Dujail trial without doubt.

Despite this concession to international image, no international judges ever agreed to serve on the tribunal bench, even though the Iraqis went to a number of governments around the world requesting such assistance.

The retention of the death penalty as an authorized punishment for the tribunal was, and remains to this day, the most controversial dimension of its legal structure. None of the UN-affiliated tribunals permit the death penalty, and the modern trend is toward its elimination in states around the globe. In Sierra Leone, the UN-affiliated tribunal banned the death penalty, which in time caused its elimination in domestic law. The IHT judges, however, must apply penalty provisions that are roughly equivalent to those provided under Iraqi domestic law. The death penalty was seen as an important aspect of the legitimacy of the process in the eyes of the Iraqi people. Though many Iraqis oppose capital punishment on a personal level, it has always been a part of the Iraqi legal tradition. Abolishing any possibility of a death penalty in the tribunal would have created domestic pressures because lower-level Iraqis subject to trial in normal Iraqi courts would be subject to the death penalty if convicted based on domestic law, while the more senior planners and those with overall authority for the crimes would expect a maximum of life imprisonment. Imagine the reaction from survivors of the Anfal mass graves or any of the dozens of other major regime crimes when they heard the news that the Iraqi judges had caved to international pressures and removed the death penalty from Iraqi law. One early draft of the statute did not specifically include or eliminate the death penalty as an authorized punishment in the hopes that "there is enough ambiguity in its formulation that could allow for the imposition of the death penalty if no one on the Security Council notices and specifically insists on the exclusion of that penalty."

Iraqi jurists are themselves divided and hold varying personal moral convictions on the issue; they are united in their commitment to comply with the law in applying the range of punishments permitted by law. When told of international skepticism that he would use the trial processes simply as a vehicle for vengeance and that a maximum of life imprisonment would increase the perception of legitimacy in other nations, one judge scoffed and said, "I am a judge, not a murderer." One Iraqi translator explained that "the law must help the people by taking away the bad men from among them." He supported capital sentences, but the United Nations and a number of

European nations would never have supported their appropriateness. In any event, rumors and innuendo floated across Iraq like an echo chamber. If the tribunal had any realistic hope of helping Iraqi society move toward a better future, the drafters felt, the death penalty must be an option. They believed permitting Saddam or the other Baathist leaders to remain alive even after conviction for the most grievous crimes known to humanity, and after being sentenced to death for those crimes by an Iraqi court, would lead to a permanent unease and insecurity and the ultimate failure of the entire enterprise.

## WHAT'S IN A NAME?

International law is clear that no accused should face punishment unless convicted pursuant to a fair trial affording all of the essential guarantees embodied in widespread state practice.[64] Article 3 of the 1949 Geneva Conventions states that only a "regularly constituted court" may pass judgment on an accused person.[65] Iraq became bound by the 1949 Geneva Conventions on February 14, 1956.[66] Interpreting the requirement of the Geneva Conventions in light of state practice, the International Committee of the Red Cross concluded that a judicial forum is "regularly constituted if it has been established and organized in accordance with the laws and procedures already in force in a country."[67] The Iraqis designed the tribunal from the ground up to apply general principles and specific norms drawn from existing Iraqi criminal law rather than simply supplanting those norms with externally mandated principles. The Iraqi Special Tribunal (IST) statute provided that the president of the tribunal shall "be guided by the Iraqi Criminal Procedure Law" in the drafting of the rules of procedure and evidence for the admission of evidence as well as the other features of trial.[68] Furthermore, the statute specifically lists the provisions of Iraqi law that contain the general principles of criminal law to be applied in connection with the prosecution and trial of "*any* accused person" (emphasis added to highlight the nondiscriminatory intent of the drafters).[69] Where there are substantive gaps that remain in the rules and procedures, they are automatically filled by resort to the underlying principles of Iraqi domestic law, even as the judges are charged with interpreting the substantive international crimes by "resort to the relevant decisions of international courts or tribunals as persuasive authority."[70] This represents an admirable attempt to harmonize international and domestic norms.

The allegation that the tribunal was a concrete manifestation of victor's justice in the wake of an illegal and aggressive war was far more than an esoteric concern for the Legal Affairs Subcommittee. It aspired to countermand Baathist efforts to use a charade of justice as a tool for subverting the people's rights. Like the Nazi regime before them,[71] the ruling regime in Iraq created "special" or "revolutionary" courts to impose political punishments at the hands of obedient minions rather than trained legal professionals.[72] Every day during the Dujail trial, Judge Awad al-Bandar sat in the front row at Saddam's immediate right elbow. Awad al-Bandar was figuratively Saddam's right-hand man in committing the crimes against the citizens of Dujail because he was the head of the Revolutionary Command Council Court that had sentenced them to die. He was the one that sent the death orders for innocent civilians to Saddam to be signed.

One of the major issues during the trial itself revolved around the defense by Judge Awad al-Bandar that he had merely been dispensing justice in accordance with the law. During the closing arguments, Judge Ra'ouf looked down in exasperation and exclaimed, "What kind of judge were you?" Awad al-Bandar's eyes flashed in anger and he snapped back, "I was the best kind of judge." When told of that exchange after the fact, one well-known Iraqi judge illustrated Awad al-Bandar's notion of "justice" by observing that he would often sentence Iraqis to death based only on his mood or the whim of the moment rather than the evidence.

Judge Dara had spent time in prison himself at the hands of the unjust regime courts, which had been created by Saddam as a way to bypass the ordinary and well-trained judges across Iraq who continued to resist his influence in ways both subtle and effective. As a deliberate amendment at the very last editing session, the authoritative Arabic text used a different word to make a clear distinction from the "special" or "revolutionary" courts run under Baathist authority. This resulted in a slightly off-kilter English translation of the statute adopted in December 2003. Although the statute created jurisdiction over war crimes, genocide, and crimes against humanity, as well as a small list of select crimes drawn from the Iraqi criminal code, the English translation of Article 1 of the original

Iraqi Special Tribunal statute stated: "a Tribunal is hereby established and shall be known as the 'Iraqi Special Tribunal for Crimes Against Humanity.' "[73] This subtle but powerful reminder shows the keen sensitivity of the Iraqi lawyers responsible for the drafting as well as their commitment to the long-term restoration of the rule of law within Iraq.

The Arabic name of the original statute itself served to illustrate the vast difference between the open and public process afforded to Saddam and his codefendants and the kind of politically driven "justice" that had been handed out by the regime. When the Iraqi parliament repromulgated and amended the statute in October 2005, they further refined the title to eliminate any ambiguity: the formal title of the tribunal became the Iraqi High Criminal Court (though it continued to be termed the Iraqi High Tribunal outside Iraq, and will be so denominated by the authors). The very difficult decision to televise the proceedings on a live basis (with a very short delay for security reasons) was further evidence of the intent to demonstrate a fair trial that would jump-start the rule of law within the region.

## THE DICTATOR'S DELUSION

On December 10, 2003, Judge Dara stood at the microphone to announce the adoption of the tribunal statute by the Interim Governing Council. He was flanked on both sides by members of the council as well as by some key members of the Legal Affairs Subcommittee. There were no Westerners at the front to respond to questions from the assembled world media. Judge Dara was calm and professional as he patiently answered questions. Though he was pressed repeatedly to concede that Saddam could be tried in absentia under Iraqi law, Judge Dara explained that the tribunal would have jurisdiction over all of the leading Baathists who had committed crimes against the Iraqi people. He patiently explained that the guarantees of the statute (which is the meaning of the word in Arabic; the English translation uses the word "rights") mean that the accused can only be tried while present. This provision reflected international practice. Saddam remained at large, but he cast a shadow over the announcement that was reminiscent of his seeming omnipotence while he had ruled Iraq for nearly three decades. He was like a mirage whose very freedom mocked the principles of law that Judge Dara exemplified and that the IGC sought to validate.

Days later, Iraq and the world would be abuzz after the special operations team had pulled Saddam from his underground hiding place near ad Dawr. Salem Chalabi, who stood as the last man on Judge Dara's left when the statute was publicly announced, confidently predicted, "We'll be ready soon—we're moving very quickly."[74] He told a group of Iraqi jurists that the work of the tribunal would move forward in only two to three months following the selection of qualified judges. Just hours after he was captured, Saddam received his first official visitors while in American custody. Ambassador Paul Bremer strode into his cell along with Lieutenant General Ricardo Sanchez, the top civilian and military Americans in the country. They were accompanied by four senior Iraqi politicians: Adnan Pachachi, Adel Abdul-Mahdi, Achmed Chalabi, and Mowaffak al-Rubaie. The mood was solemn; the Iraqis took their seats, while the Americans stood. The Iraqis began to ask Saddam poignant questions about why he had committed such crimes against his own people. "What other leader in the world used chemical weapons against his civilians?" "Why did the two hundred thousand Kurds have to die and five thousand villages be bulldozed during the Anfal campaigns?" "Why did you order my friend to be executed?" After about a half hour of exchanges, the Iraqis grew weary of Saddam's casual admissions and his nonchalance. The group stood to leave. Mowaffak al-Rubaie, who was serving as the national security adviser and would witness Saddam's execution some thirty-six months later, recounted that Saddam's mood shifted as they prepared to leave. "He expected to be tortured, to be hanged, or he expected Sanchez to pull out his pistol and empty three or four bullets into his head." That was Saddam's idea of justice . . . that's what he expected because that is how he ran Iraq."[75]

The record of the Dujail trial is one of missteps, misconceptions, and misstatements. Its process and political dimension were filled with controversy both inside and outside Iraq. There was very little about this first trial held by the Iraqi High Tribunal that was predictable, yet its very audacity is inspiring. The year 2004 would be one of preparation and perseverance as Iraqis suffered and the fathers of the tribunal began to prepare for the most important trial in the history of the Middle East. But Iraqis felt safer knowing that Saddam could not miraculously return to power.

# 4

# PROVING INCREDIBLE EVENTS

## COLLECTING THE EVIDENCE

Nuremberg's chief prosecutor, Robert Jackson, captured the challenge at the core of any major war crimes trial when he said, "We must establish incredible events by credible evidence."[1] For the Saddam trial, that challenge would be all the more difficult as the critical events had all occurred twenty-five years in the past. There is much truth to the adage "Justice delayed is justice denied." Over time, witness memories fade, documents disappear, and proving authenticity and chain of custody can become a nightmare.

In one respect Saddam's regime was very similar to Adolf Hitler's Third Reich: it was an established practice of the Baathist regime to record in minute detail the brutal repression of the Iraqi population by its security, intelligence, and even judicial apparatuses. Through a series of events, beginning with the Iraqi invasion of Kuwait in 1990, those documents would end up in the possession of the Iraqi High Tribunal's Secure Evidence Unit and would ultimately seal the fate of Saddam Hussein.

In the midst of the 1990–1991 Persian Gulf conflict, the UN Security Council adopted a novel resolution, Resolution 674, calling on "states to collate substantiated information in their possession or submitted to them" concerning Iraqi atrocities "and to make this information available to the Security Council." As the evidence began to pour in, the U.S. Congress enacted Public Law 102-138 on October 28, 1991, which stated that the president of the United States should propose to the Security Council that members of the Iraqi regime be put on trial for war crimes.

While the effort to bring Saddam to trial was blocked by other members of the Security Council who preferred inducing Saddam's cooperation through economic sanctions, Resolution 674 ended up achieving far more than its drafters could have dreamed. At the time, one of the authors (Scharf) was serving as attorney-adviser for UN affairs at the U.S. State Department. When Iraq-like atrocities were reported in Bosnia in 1992, he was asked to draft a Security Council resolution similar to Resolution 674 for the Balkan conflict. The result was Resolution 771, which called on states to provide information about Bosnian atrocities to the UN secretary-general and required him to prepare a report summarizing the information and recommending additional measures. A few months later this led to the adoption of Resolution 780 (another resolution Scharf drafted), which established a UN Commission of Experts to examine the evidence of atrocities in the former Yugoslavia. The commission, in turn, concluded that acts of genocide had been committed and recommended the establishment of an international tribunal modeled on Nuremberg. On May 25, 1993, the Security Council adopted Resolution 827, establishing the Yugoslavia Tribunal. This tribunal served as the model for the creation of the Rwanda Tribunal in 1994 and the International Criminal Court in 1998. And bringing the story full circle, in 2003, the drafters of the Iraqi High Tribunal statute would borrow heavily from the statutes and rules of these international tribunals in crafting a court to prosecute the Baathist regime leaders.

Meanwhile, in response to Saddam's brutal crackdown of the March 1991 Kurdish uprising in northern Iraq, the coalition forces imposed a no-fly zone over the northern third of the country, enabling the Kurds to obtain a status approaching full autonomy. Under the protection of the coalition's Operation Provide Comfort, relief workers, journalists, and human rights investigators were able to drive across the border from Turkey into the region without impediment. This new access to Iraqi Kurdistan meant that for the first time in decades independent researchers could begin to document and publicize the regime's most serious atrocities. Human Rights Watch spent over six months collecting testimonies from survivors of the Anfal campaigns and another two years studying eighteen metric tons of Iraqi government documents that the Kurds had captured during their short-lived uprising. In 1997, David Scheffer, then U.S. Ambassador-at-Large for War Crimes Issues, said that the number of documents obtained by Human Rights Watch amounted to over 5.5 million pages, which the U.S. government subsequently scanned and indexed into computer-readable form on 176 CD-ROM disks.[2]

At the same time, U.S. forces in Kuwait and southern Iraq during Operation Desert Storm captured thousands of files documenting a wide range of atrocities and war crimes committed by the Baathist regime. Army lawyers and investigators spent years compiling the evidence and organizing it for a future war crimes trial. Describing the American cache, Ambassador Scheffer said, "If you remember the final scene of the movie *Raiders of the Lost Ark*, where the Ark is being wheeled into a warehouse of crate upon crate, I should tell you that that warehouse does exist—it's in Suitland, Maryland."[3] Ambassador Scheffer's office also launched a program to review satellite imagery for use in war crimes prosecutions. For years, American spy satellites had focused their lenses on Iraq, producing high-resolution pictures of the destruction of Iraqi villages—including, it turned out, Dujail.[4]

Fast-forward to the 2003 invasion of Iraq: In the chaos that ensued with the fall of Baghdad on April 9, 2003, U.S.-led coalition forces, Iraqi opposition groups, and individuals seized hundreds of thousands of state documents from government buildings, Baath Party headquarters, offices of the intelligence agencies, and military barracks. Relevant documents were even found stashed in schools and private homes, apparently placed there for safekeeping and then abandoned as military defeat became imminent. While coalition forces were collecting as many documents as they could get their hands on, many others were pilfered, looted, or destroyed, resulting in the loss of potentially vital information. In one particularly tragic incident, British officials allowed the looting of Baath Party buildings in Basra, which housed important archives, as a means of showing the population that the party had lost control of the city.[5] Still other document collections were seized by Iraqi political groups and nongovernmental organizations. As it became clear that American authorities would pay to obtain them, a lucrative black market in "atrocity documents" formed, with documents going for as high as $2,500 for a few pages of material. Under these circumstances, many documents were poorly processed, reshuffled, and written on, and the possible presence of faked or forged material became a serious problem.[6]

The Coalition Provisional Authority's energetic Sandy Hodgkinson, whom we met in chapter 3, set about to gather all of the relevant documents in a single collection. According to her, the CPA received documents from the State Department, Department of Defense, INDICT (a London-based organization formed in 1996 to campaign for the establishment of an international tribunal for Iraq), and other organizations.[7] Meanwhile, the U.S. Congress appropriated funds in 2004 to build a Secure Evidence Unit (SEU) to house captured Baathist regime archives and hire expert staff to process the documents. Soon thereafter, Peter Boyles, who had prior experience organizing documentation for the Yugoslavia and Rwanda tribunals, was hired as "evidence custodian," and by February 2004 his office was scanning over one million pages of documents per month. By June 2004, fifteen staff members were working around the clock with Boyles to ensure that the process of scanning, indexing, labeling, and case tracking of the documents would be complete before the commencement of trials.[8] Documents were stored behind the steel doors of what had once been cells holding the regime's enemies. The importance of the evidentiary effort could never be ignored. The SEU conference room had hooks in the ceiling where prisoners had once been tortured. Sitting in that room to discuss the sufficiency of evidence as well as the required standards for authenticity under Iraqi law was a chilling reminder of the evil uses in the prior life of the SEU building.

As massive as it was, the effort to build a credible case against the Baath Party leaders was not just confined to documentary evidence. The U.S. Congress ultimately appropriated over $128 million in support of the Iraqi High Tribunal's investigations and evidence gathering. In addition to paying for the construction of the SEU and hiring and training its staff, this money covered mass grave exhumations, security and transportation costs for on-site investigations and thousands of witness interviews, safe houses for judges, prosecutors, witnesses, and defense counsel, and translation support to assist with cataloguing and analyzing documents.

## THE ARRAIGNMENT

On July 1, 2004, seven months after he had been captured, sixty-seven-year-old Saddam Hussein was brought before an IHT judge for arraignment. Under Western practice, the word "arraignment" can mean either the defendant's first appearance in court before a magistrate or a later appearance, in which the defendant is advised of the formal charge and called upon to enter a plea. The purpose in this case was to inform Saddam of his rights and that he was a defendant in a criminal case before the Iraqi High Tribunal. The timing was critical because the occupation was about to officially end and it was important that the Iraqis establish their lawful right to maintain Saddam and the others in custody following the return of Iraqi sovereignty.

The former leader of Iraq was flown from the detention center by helicopter to a hastily converted building at Camp Victory, a sprawling U.S. military base near the Baghdad airport. Flanked by two Iraqi prison guards and four Iraqi policemen, Saddam was ushered into the small courtroom in handcuffs and with a chain around his waist. Dressed in a dark suit, polished brown shoes, and a crisp white shirt buttoned to the collar, Saddam sported stylishly coifed hair and a neatly trimmed beard that was a far cry from his scraggly Ted Kaczynski/Unabomber look at the time of his capture in December 2003. The Arab world had never seen anything like this scene, which was broadcast repeatedly over the next twenty-four hours. In a region of the world accustomed to tyrants and despots, a seemingly invincible dictator was hauled before a court of his own citizens.

The television broadcasts of the event showed only the back of the judge's head and his name was not mentioned for security reasons, but a few months later the world would learn that the man who read Saddam his rights and summarized the charges on that July day in Baghdad was thirty-five-year-old Ra'id Juhi Hamadi al-Sa'edi. Built like a football player, the youthful judge was a graduate of Baghdad Law School. He was originally one of the investigative judges of the Central Criminal Court of Iraq (CCCI), Iraq's newly established criminal court for ordinary crimes. Judge Ra'id had come to the attention of American authorities in 2003 while serving in Najaf when he courageously signed an indictment for notorious Shiite warlord Moqtada al-Sadr, charging him with murder. The public revelation of the Moqtada al-Sadr indictment placed the young judge and his family in great danger, and they were relocated for their protection to the International Zone in Baghdad, where they resided until the end of the Dujail trial. Because of his solid command of English and his unflappable demeanor, Ra'id Juhi became an obvious choice to head the investigation phase.

When the authors asked him why he agreed to serve as the investigative judge for such a sensational, challenging, and dangerous case, Judge Ra'id answered simply: "This is my job, my responsibility, my duty to my society." He added, "Many Iraqi people thought that there was no law, no rules, no order, and we wanted to bring the rule of law and justice back to Iraq." In response to the follow-up question of how it felt to be face-to-face with one of the world's most ruthless dictators, Judge Ra'id merely shrugged his shoulders and said, "I just tried to think of him as an ordinary criminal defendant."

The guards removed Saddam's handcuffs and gently guided him to his chair across from Judge Ra'id, who sat behind a table. The dictator and the judge faced each other about eight feet apart, with a low railing separating them. The first moments were palpably tense. Saddam, who apparently thought he was about to be summarily executed, was visibly anxious. But in a preview of things to come in the later trial, during the twenty-six-minute session, Saddam went from being nervous and hesitant to being confrontational and belligerent, while at the same time displaying legal acumen and even a sense of humor. CNN correspondent Christiane Amanpour, who was one of three reporters permitted to observe the proceedings, described Saddam as looking like a shadow of his former self, alternately downcast and defiant.

Answering the judge's request to state his name for the record, Saddam said, "I am Saddam Hussein, the president of Iraq."

"Former president of Iraq," Judge Ra'id corrected.

To which Saddam insisted, "No. Present. Current. It is the will of the people."

As the hearing got under way, Saddam began to challenge Judge Ra'id, asking who he was and under what authority he was holding the hearing. Judge Ra'id proceeded to explain that the tribunal that would be trying him had been set up under the U.S.-led occupation. "So you are representing the coalition?" Saddam asked. "No," the young jurist replied, without showing emotion or raising his voice. "I am an Iraqi representing the Iraqi judicial system."

Next, Judge Ra'id summarized the general charges against the former dictator, which included gas attacks on Kurdish villages, mass murders in the suppression of uprisings, political assassinations, and the invasion of Kuwait. Saddam sat passively as the judge read the charges until Kuwait was mentioned, at which point he exploded: "How could Saddam [referring to himself in third person] be tried over Kuwait? He defended Iraq's honor and revived its historical rights over those dogs." And when Judge Ra'id told Saddam that Iraqi law would be governing the proceedings, the former dictator remarked, "So now you are using the law that Saddam signed against Saddam."

When Judge Ra'id asked him if he could afford a lawyer, Saddam sarcastically replied, "The Americans say I have millions hidden in Switzerland. How can I not have money to pay for one?" He then added with a smile, "I don't want to make you feel uneasy, but you know that this is all a theater by Bush, the criminal."

As the session drew to a close, Judge Ra'id handed Saddam a sheet of paper to sign, as required under Iraqi procedural law, indicating that he had been informed of the charges and understood his rights. But Saddam refused to put his name to the document, saying he would not sign anything without lawyers present. By this time, Saddam's wife and daughters had retained a team of twenty foreign defense lawyers, among the best money could buy.

The hearing ended with Saddam asking the judge, "Have you finished?" "Yes," Judge Ra'id answered. "*Khalas!* [meaning 'finished']," Saddam exclaimed. The scene was essentially repeated eleven more times that day, as Judge Ra'id arraigned each of the other senior members of the Baathist regime. Over the next several months, Judge Ra'id would interview the defendants (always with their lawyers present) and compile a dossier, called a referral file, against Saddam and the others, containing over a thousand pages of witness statements and incriminating documents—many bearing the former leader's signature. In the Iraqi system, the investigative judge serves to collect all available evidence, whether it tends to incriminate or exonerate a potential defendant. Judge Ra'id told the authors that during the Dujail investigation, he kept at least four copies of the entire referral file hidden in various places at all times because he was worried about things that could derail the investigation—bombs, rockets, fires. One was stored in the Secure Evidence Unit, one was kept in the IHT office building, and two more were kept in secret places that he changed from week to week.

## TRAINING THE JUDGES

While Judge Ra'id and the other investigative judges were busy poring over witness statements and documents, the Regime Crimes Liaison Office (RCLO) decided the time had come to begin to train the newly appointed Iraqi High Tribunal judges to preside over some of the most complex and challenging cases ever to be tried. First, the Department of Justice and Judge Advocate General's Corps lawyers who made up the RCLO held a series of afternoon sessions in Baghdad to familiarize the judges with the substantive offenses, unique defenses, and procedures that would govern their trials. Next, in a trip organized by the U.S. Institute of Peace, a dozen of the judges were transported to The Hague for three days of informal meetings with the international judges and prosecutors of the Yugoslavia Tribunal. The group especially benefited from the discussion of lessons learned from the plodding trial of Slobodan Milosevic, and from viewing the sophisticated software and monitors that the tribunal employed in its three high-tech courtrooms.

The third phase of their training would consist of several week-long sessions, featuring some of the world's foremost experts in international criminal law; these sessions were held in London and Stratford-upon-Avon. In early September 2004, the RCLO enlisted the authors to design and lead these sessions. (First-person references in this section are to Michael Scharf.) Although I had recently conducted a series of human rights training sessions for Iraqi judges and lawyers held in Dubai, UAE, I was quite surprised by the call from Baghdad.

"Professor Scharf, would you be willing to help us train and provide legal advice to the judges who will be presiding over the trial of Saddam Hussein?" Greg Kehoe, of the Regime Crimes Liaison Office, asked in a surprisingly clear voice. "I'm not sure you have the right guy," I replied. "Are you aware that I've taken strong public stands against the U.S. invasion of Iraq, and I have been highly critical of the Iraqi High Tribunal?" In fact, I had recently published an article in the widely read *Journal of International Criminal Justice* that advocated for an international trial for Saddam Hussein and opined that the Iraqi High Tribunal would be viewed as a U.S. puppet court and that the Iraqi judges would not be up to the challenge of prosecuting the former dictator.[9]

"Yes, we've done our homework," the voice from Baghdad answered. "We also know that you helped create the Yugoslavia Tribunal when you worked for the Department of State Office of Legal Adviser, that you've trained judges from all over the world in international humanitarian law, and that the War Crimes Research Office you run at Case Western Reserve University currently provides research assistance to the Yugoslavia Tribunal, the Rwanda Tribunal, the Special Court for Sierra Leone, and the International Criminal Court." He then told me that the content of my training sessions would be completely up to me to design, and that I could publicly say anything I wanted about the IHT when I returned from the training sessions. "Listen, Professor Scharf," he pressed, "do you want to stay on the sidelines and hurl criticisms at the tribunal, or do you want to get involved in an effort to make it a more fair and effective judicial process?"

I found this appeal hard to resist, as it reminded me of a favorite quote from President Theodore Roosevelt that Mike Newton had long ago shared with me—words upon which we have both endeavored to approach life's challenges. Roosevelt said: "It is not the critic who counts; not the man who points out how the strong man stumbles, or where the doer of deeds could have done them better. The credit belongs to the man who is actually in the arena, whose face is marred by dust and sweat and blood; . . . who at the best knows in the end the triumph of high achievement, and who at the worst, if he fails, at least fails while daring greatly, so that his place shall never be with those cold and timid souls who neither know victory nor defeat."[10]

A month later, on October 13, 2004, Mike Newton, four other international trainers, and I arrived at the Crowne Plaza London–St. James Hotel, where we were introduced to the forty-two newly appointed judges of the Iraqi High Tribunal. The other trainers included Geoffrey Robertson, an internationally recognized author in the field and a sitting judge serving on the Special Court for Sierra Leone; Professor Christopher Greenwood of the London School of Economics; Joanna Korner, former senior prosecutor at the Yugoslavia Tribunal; and Gabrielle Kirk McDonald, the former president of the Yugoslavia Tribunal. The judges were a mix of ethnic Shiites and Kurds (including some Sunni Kurds), but no former Baathists as the IHT statute precluded their appointment. They ranged in age from the youngest, thirty-five-year-old Ra'id Juhi, to Judge Ra'ouf Rasheed Abdel Rahman, who was thirty years his senior.

They were dignified and professional, and their sincerity was apparent even across linguistic barriers. But they knew that they were unprepared for the rigors that lay ahead. Saddam had prevented Iraqi lawyers from traveling abroad to learn the detailed provisions of modern international criminal law. Iraqis were often embarrassed that the regime had kept them from staying abreast of the latest developments of the integrated body of law that had developed since the end of the Gulf War in 1991. The trainers in London were notable experts in the complex body of international law that would need to be used by the Iraqis.

The judges were attentive both in large groups and in the small working groups. This week of training was followed by a mock trial held at Stratford-upon-Avon, as well as more training at the International Institute for Higher Studies in Criminal Sciences in Siracusa, Italy. The tribunal investigators had a special training session dedicated to their unique needs held in Bournemouth, England. The director of the RCLO at the time, Greg Kehoe, helped to arrange and fund these training events. Kehoe, an American, is a booming man with an imposing presence. He believed that the Iraqis could deliver a fair and independent trial. "The whole process is very important for reestablishing the rule of law in Iraq," he would say. "The trials not only have to be fair, but also have to be seen to be fair. A rush to judgment would do nothing to restore the Iraqis' faith in the rule of law." These aspirations would be put to the test in the Baghdad courtroom almost exactly two years later.

There were several women in the group, one of whom would later serve as one of the judges that presided over the Anfal campaign trial. Through an interpreter named Riyadh Wahiab Hamad[11] (who was tragically killed weeks later), the judge told me of her two children, ages nine and three. My own son was also nine, and it turned out that we had much in common. She choked up as she told me that she knew taking on this position would keep her away from her home in northern Iraq for months at a time. And it would put her family at risk, probably for the rest of their lives. But when I asked if she was having second thoughts, she did not hesitate to answer in the negative. "This is the most important thing I can do for my country," she told me. This was a sentiment I heard expressed again and again in my conversations with the judges.

Each morning during the week-long training session, the forty-two judges and six international trainers would cram into unmarked white minibuses, which would whisk us from our hotel, past Buckingham Palace, and deposit us ten minutes later at the Regus Training Room on the top floor of a government office building with a stunning view of Big Ben and the Houses of Parliament. It quickly became clear that training the Iraqi High Tribunal judges would present several daunting challenges. While judges selected to preside over international war crimes trials usually have some experience with trying complex cases, applying international criminal law, and adhering to the equivalent of international standards of due process, none of this was true for the Iraqis. In addition, language was going to be a problem since, with the exception of Judge Ra'id, few spoke English and the newly hired IHT translators were in no way comparable to those at the United Nations, with whom I was used to working from my time at the State Department. This required us to speak in slow motion so that they could keep up, which in turn meant that we would cover much less ground than we had planned in our lessons.

The pace of the translation was not the only challenge. We found that many American legal phrases did not have direct counterparts in Arabic. Even the translation of common metaphors could lead to misunderstandings. For example, at one point during the training session, one of the English-speaking trainers said that the Iraqi judges had to be like pit bulls when it came to enforcing the standards of due process. The translator stopped speaking, a puzzled look darkening his face. "What is this pit bull?" he inquired of the trainer. "It is the dog that bites the neck and does not let go," the trainer answered. "Do you really want me to say that?" the translator asked the trainer. "Because in my country, comparing someone to a dog is the worst insult of all," he explained. "It is far worse than all of your English four-letter words combined." For the first time, I understood the extent of the insult Saddam had made against the Kuwaitis during his arraignment.

We approached the sessions the same way I teach my law school courses. We would begin each session with a thirty-minute lecture by one of the trainers, followed by questions and answers, and then a simulation designed to provide experiential learning that would ensure that the Iraqi judges mastered the concepts. The sessions covered the elements of the substantive crimes (war crimes, crimes against humanity, and genocide), theories of liability (aiding and abetting, command responsibility, and joint criminal enterprise), unique defenses to international crimes (immunity, duress, superior orders, military necessity, reprisals), the investigative process, witness protection, plea bargaining, appeals, and effective courtroom management.

The simulations were based on a series of three-page scenarios that I designed with Eric Blinderman of the RCLO. One involved war crimes; one, crimes against humanity; and one, genocide. So as not to prejudge actual cases, we were careful to use fictional names of countries (the Republic of Alpha), towns (Omega), and people ("President Asayh," "Director of Security Saafir," "General Fawaz," and "Colonel Bakir"). We even included a made-up map to facilitate the discussion. Despite the fake names, it was obvious to all that the stipulated facts were akin to the most notorious of atrocities committed in Iraq, including the gassing of the Kurds, the attacks against the Marsh Arabs, and even the destruction of a town similar to Dujail. During the simulations, the judges would first read the scenarios and then participate in small group sessions led by one of the international trainers, in which they would discuss what, if any, crimes under the IHT statute were raised by the stipulated facts; what difficulties in proof would likely arise; what theories of liability were relevant to each potential defendant; and what defenses would likely be asserted.

The week's final session was to be a roundtable discussion, featuring a half dozen judges of the Yugoslavia Tribunal, who were eager to fly out to

London to work with the IHT judges. Though the RCLO had weeks earlier purchased their tickets and booked their hotel rooms, at the last minute UN Secretary-General Kofi Annan forbade them from participating in the training session on the grounds that the United Nations was not satisfied that the IHT would be a fair tribunal. Ironically, the IHT rules, which would codify the court's due-process standards, had not yet been finalized, and thus the secretary-general's judgment was at best premature. Although the incident cast a pall over the training session, the presence of Gabrielle McDonald, an African American jurist who had presided over the Yugoslavia Tribunal's first case and was later elected president of that tribunal, ensured that the IHT judges would receive the wisdom of a judge experienced in war crimes trials.

In the evenings after the sessions the judges were provided tours of London's top attractions and most famous sites, as well as the opportunity to shop at Harrods department store, while the international trainers caught the newest musicals in London's West End. None of the Iraqi judges had been to Europe before, and they took pictures of everything from double-decker buses to phone booths. For security reasons, the press was not informed of the existence of the training sessions, but it was hard to keep the presence of the three dozen traditionally robed Iraqi jurists secret as they toured all over London. Perhaps for this reason, a last-minute decision was made to move the venue of the second training session in March 2005 from London to Stratford-upon-Avon, the bucolic town north of London where William Shakespeare was born.

Whereas the London training session had been organized by the RCLO, the International Bar Association took the lead in organizing the Stratford-upon-Avon session, which was held at the Alveston Manor Hotel, a quiet inn on the edge of the historic town. One of the greatest public misconceptions about the Iraqi High Tribunal was that all of its international advisers were American members of the RCLO or former American State Department officials like Mike Newton and me. In fact, the International Bar Association, a professional association of seventy thousand lawyers from 150 countries under the leadership of executive director Mark Ellis, played an equally significant role in training and assisting the judges. In addition to organizing the March 2005 training session, Ellis recruited a noted Canadian expert in international criminal law to assist the IHT defense counsel and a distinguished British judge to assist the IHT judges during the trial.

To put together the Stratford-upon-Avon training session, Ellis tapped the British husband-and-wife team of Stuart Alford and Sylvia de Bertodano. I first met de Bertodano in 1996, when the then twenty-six-year-old barrister cut her honeymoon short to join the defense team for Dusko Tadic, the first person to be tried by the Yugoslavia Tribunal in The Hague. On the eve of the Stratford-upon-Avon session, Sylvia gave birth prematurely to twins, and in between shuttling back and forth between Alveston Manor and a London hospital to visit them, Stuart Alford served as the chair of the training sessions. We were also joined by a new trainer, Mischa Wladimiroff, a distinguished Dutch lawyer who had served with Sylvia de Bertodano as defense counsel during the first trial before the Yugoslavia Tribunal.

While the London session was conducted in a discussion format, the Stratford-upon-Avon session was conducted as a mock trial. Instead of stipulated facts, Sylvia and Stuart had come up with a realistic-looking case file, complete with fictional witness statements. The object of the session was to get the Iraqi jurists, including the prosecutors and investigative judges, to test-run the new IHT rules of procedure, which had been adopted by the judges a few weeks earlier, in the context of a simulated trial.

During the mock trial, the other trainers and I played the roles of defense counsel and prosecutors. We tried to provide a glimpse of what the judges could expect from the real litigants, including acting disrespectfully, shouting at and interrupting the judges, intimidating witnesses, and making speeches instead of asking questions during cross-examination. We would periodically suspend the proceedings to offer a critique on the judges' actions and to suggest other possible responses to such conduct. Regrettably, one thing we failed to rehearse with the judges was what to do in the event of a defense walkout and boycott, as that would become one of the most challenging tactics they would face during the real trial.

The mock trial was supplemented with sessions on use of international precedent and writing a reasoned judgment. This last point engendered one of the more unusual discussions between the Iraqi judges and the international trainers. The judges explained that Iraqi legal judgments tended to be quite brief, at most three or four pages. They fully understood that such brevity would not be appropriate for the IHT. The judges had recently read the Nuremberg Tribunal judgment and several opinions of the Yugoslavia and Rwanda tribunals, which the RCLO had translated into Arabic, and they wanted to know if their judgments had to be as long. We answered that the international tribunals had been criticized for writing overly lengthy, ponderous opinions that were difficult for experts, let alone ordinary people, to digest. We suggested that the IHT judges should instead try to write opinions that were easy for the Iraqi people to read and understand, since they would constitute the historic record of crimes committed during the rule of the Baathist regime. Though I specifically told them that sixty or seventy pages would be a good target, the Dujail opinion ended up being close to three hundred pages, and the Anfal campaign opinion was more than three times that long.

With one or two exceptions, who seemed to have been appointed for their political ties rather than their expertise, the Iraqi judges were very bright and quickly grasped most of the nuances of this unique body of law. The procedural law was another matter altogether. It became increasingly clear to the trainers just how different the Iraqi inquisitorial procedural approach to trials is from the common law adversarial approach that is employed by the several international tribunals. Since the IHT statute and rules were based largely on the provisions of the modern international tribunals, we tried to explain to the judges that they would have to depart in some ways from what they were used to in order to control their courtroom, protect the security of witnesses and the due process rights of defendants, and convince the people of the region and the world that their trials were fair.

As it turned out, we were not very successful in this endeavor. Though the Iraqi judges would nod in agreement, when the actual trials commenced they tended to go back to their legal traditions. For example, as described in more detail in subsequent chapters, the Iraqi judges failed to follow our advice that motions challenging jurisdiction, the legitimacy of the tribunal, the pretrial production of evidence, and the composition of the bench should be decided in written opinions at the beginning of the trial and subject to immediate review by the IHT appeals chamber. (They left them all until the end of the trial.) And they failed to follow our advice about preventing the defendants from speaking in the courtroom until they took the witness stand at the end of the trial. (As we'll see, interruptions were a near constant during the trial.)

Sometimes the training sessions would go off on unusual tangents, such as the day in Stratford-upon-Avon when the judges wanted to discuss the International Criminal Court. Though we were happy to indulge the Iraqis, the international trainers did not see the relevance of the ICC to their work since the ICC statute prohibits the court from trying any cases involving crimes that occurred before the treaty became legally binding on July 1, 2002, while the IHT statute prohibited the Iraqi tribunal from considering any cases that arose after March 2003. But with stories about American mistreatment of Iraqi detainees at Abu Ghraib and attacks on civilians by American military and contract personnel appearing in the news that week, the Iraqis were obviously interested in seeing more than Baathist officials brought to justice. On the second day of the Stratford-upon-Avon training session, the new Iraqi government announced that it was considering becoming a party to the ICC, which would potentially subject any war crimes committed in Iraqi territory after July 1, 2002 (including by Americans), to the court's jurisdiction. The next day, bowing to intense pressure by the United States, the Iraqi government reversed course. Paradoxically, as this book goes to press there is growing support in both the U.S. government and the Iraqi government for Iraqi ratification of the ICC statute, with some Americans hoping that this would help deter sectarian atrocities and help provide sustained assistance to the IHT during a U.S. military drawdown and eventual withdrawal from the country. U.S. forces in Afghanistan are protected from transfer to the ICC by an agreement between the two nations; more than one hundred nations have such agreements with the United States and American consent is thus the only legal way that the ICC can obtain custody over an American soldier for crimes committed in one of those nations. The potential advantages to the Iraqis of ICC assistance may outweigh the necessity for negotiation of a similar agreement in Iraq.

Much time during the training sessions was spent discussing the relevance of the international tribunal precedents of the Nuremberg Tribunal and the modern international tribunals to the work of the Iraqi High Tribunal. To facilitate their use of international precedent, subsequent to the training session the authors set up a consortium of five American law schools (Case Western Reserve, University of Connecticut, University of Texas, Vanderbilt University, and William and Mary) that provided over fifty research memos to the IHT on issues likely to arise during the trials. Along with the international cases they cited, the memos were translated into Arabic by the RCLO and provided to the judges. This was the first time that the leading case law in the field was available in Arabic. As one judge told Professor Newton, "I should know more about the international case than what the lawyers tell me." The focus on educating the Iraqi judges about the international precedents seemed to pay off, as the Dujail judgment ended up containing scores of citations to these international judicial authorities.

On the last day of the London training session, one of the IHT judges asked earnestly, "Professors, do you think one day, perhaps in five or ten years, judges in other war crimes trials will be discussing the precedent we set?" It was a heartwarming moment for us, as the question demonstrated the depth of the IHT judges' commitment to holding fair and legitimate trials. Unfortunately, much of this potential was squandered by events outside the control of the judges.

## THE DECISION TO BEGIN WITH THE CASE OF DUJAIL

Shortly after the conclusion of the training sessions in March 2005, the Iraqi High Tribunal judges decided to try Saddam Hussein and other former Baathist leaders in a series of discrete cases, rather than in one mega trial like Nuremberg or the Yugoslavia Tribunal's massive case against Slobodan Milosevic. And they decided they would begin with the case of Dujail. There are those who questioned the wisdom of this decision. After all, only a few hundred residents of Dujail were tortured and killed, while Saddam Hussein stood accused of murdering hundreds of thousands in the other cases. Moreover, there were plenty of crimes committed against Sunni citizens, and some advisers urged that such a trial would provide a vehicle for reconciliation between the warring factions. There were other cases under investigation that had far more victims, and arguably a more extensive impact on Iraqi society.

Quite simply, Dujail was selected as the first case to be tried by the IHT because it was the first investigation to be completed, and the first case file ready for referral. Initially, the Dujail case was going to be a warm-up to the later trial of Saddam Hussein, who would probably make his first appearance as a defendant in the Anfal campaign case. As originally envisioned, the Dujail trial would feature only subordinates, and would serve to establish a glimpse into the character, the modus operandi, and the command structure of the Baathist regime. But as the Dujail case file was being assembled by Judge Ra'id, it became clear to him that Saddam's fingerprints were all over the crimes related to the tragic village and its inhabitants. Under Iraqi law, there is far less discretion than under the American system. Once the investigative judge finds a prima facie case against a defendant, the individual must be brought to justice for those crimes. As it turned out, the decision to start with the Dujail trial was a good one for three reasons.

First, the evidence for the Dujail prosecution was extremely strong. The documentary evidence was overwhelming. Eyewitnesses (both victims and insiders) were available to testify. Incriminating videotapes existed of Saddam and the defendants at the scene. And satellite imagery was available to prove the destruction of the town and its farms and orchards. In addition, it is far easier to prove the elements of a crime against humanity (the charge in the Dujail case) than the elements of genocide (the charge in the Anfal campaign case). A conviction for genocide requires proof that the perpetrator had a specific intent to destroy an ethnic or religious group, while crimes against humanity require only a systematic or widespread attack against a civilian population.

Second, the Dujail case would not lend itself to as many defenses as would be available with respect to the other charges. If Saddam Hussein's lawyers argued that his subordinates acted without authority in Dujail, he could still be held responsible under the principle of command responsibility for failing to punish those subordinates for the atrocity. If the defense team argued that Saddam Hussein's actions were justified as self-defense in response to acts of terrorism, the prosecution could demonstrate that his response (razing the town, executing 148 townspeople, and destroying the surrounding orchards) was disproportionate and therefore unjustifiable.

Finally, it made a lot of sense to begin with a less important and less complex case because it enabled the tribunal to focus on the broad legal challenges to the process that were brought by the defense. Once these were disposed of in the Dujail case, the principle of res judicata would prevent the defense from relitigating them in subsequent trials, enabling the tribunal to focus entirely on the factual and legal complexities of those more difficult cases.

In another sense, however, the decision to begin with Dujail turned out to have a significant disadvantage. Initially, the authors and other international advisers believed that if Saddam was convicted and sentenced to death for the Dujail charges, the execution would be stayed to allow him to stand trial in the other cases. At a minimum, we believed that the appeal process would take long enough that Saddam would be available for the entire second case, which was scheduled to be the Anfal genocide trial. The casualty figures involving the Anfal campaign were more than one hundred times greater than the number of victims of Dujail. But as discussed in chapter 8, the appeal process was expedited and Saddam did not live to face the other charges. Though he was charged for the Anfal crimes against the Kurds, those charges against him were dismissed after his execution, and the Anfal trial continued against the remaining defendants. For a historic comparison, one might consider the 1931 trial of Chicago mob boss Al Capone, who was prosecuted and convicted for tax evasion rather than for the thousands of murders he orchestrated in a series of gang wars in the 1920s. While Saddam would pay the ultimate price for Dujail, his victims would be robbed of seeing him face justice for much greater atrocities. At the end of the day, though, the Iraqi jurists and politicians confronted the difficult balance between justice, accountability, politics, and perception to actually carry out the approved sentences on Saddam and the other Dujail defendants.

# 5

# TRIAL AND ERROR

**The judges of the** Iraqi High Tribunal assumed their seats at 12:05 on October 19, 2005, to call the first session of the Dujail trial to order. Just as it would during each of the trial days to come, the voice of the Iraqi bailiff barked out as they entered, and echoed off the marbled walls and high ceiling. Judge Rizgar Mohammed Amin assumed his seat in the middle of the bench, with two of his colleagues on his right and two on his left. Judge Rizgar is a handsome man with a sculpted, fine-boned face set against short silver hair. He wore a gray suit for the historic occasion along with judicial robes trimmed in white. The scion of a well-known and quite well-to-do Kurdish family, he has a refined and natural personal elegance, a habit of impeccable dress, and a manner of unerring politeness and seemingly effortless poise. Before coming to serve on the Iraqi High Tribunal, he was a sitting judge in Irbil. Among his peers, he is measured and reserved, but always engaged and warm. His smile is genuine and almost shy. Judge Rizgar had participated in all of the judicial training sessions and was notable for his pensive politeness, but also for his probing questions. He stood out among the group of judges in the training, and had been hand-selected to preside over Trial Chamber 1 in the most important trial in the history of his nation. That morning he was the face of justice to a breathless world audience as the long-awaited trial began.

Throughout the trial, the faces of the other four judges would never be revealed; for security reasons the camera focused only on the image of the presiding judge, and the world saw only his interchanges with the defendants. During the training leading up to the trial, the judges had a hard time accepting the notion that security precautions required their identities to remain hidden. The other judges would take notes, or often sit impassively and observe the proceedings. Apart from the events in the courtroom, the Dujail trial would include an unprecedented degree of turnover for a trial of such major international significance as judges suffered illness or battled charges that they had been members of the Baath Party and hence were ineligible to participate in the trial. Only one of the five judges who assumed their seats on October 19, 2005, would be present for the final judicial act of the Dujail trial on February 12, 2007.

The investigation and documentation of the crimes had required an intensive process, but the transfer of the investigative judge's report to Trial Chamber 1 for the Dujail case was only the beginning of the enormous effort needed to prepare for trial that October morning. Almost two years after adopting the first statute for the tribunal, the democratically elected Iraqi parliament had enacted a revised statute that made some notable amendments to the previous statute and gave the court a new name: Iraqi High Criminal Court. (It continued to be known as the Iraqi High Tribunal outside Iraq, however, and the authors will continue to use that term for the sake of consistency.) As is the practice in Iraq, the new statute took effect upon publication in the official gazette, *Al-Waqa'i al-Iraqiya*—on October 18, 2005, the day before the scheduled start of the trial. When Trial Chamber 1 convened that October morning, it did so under the authority of a law enacted by the freely elected representatives of the Iraqi people.

As with every other day of the Dujail trial, the proceedings in the courtroom represented only the visible aspect of an enormously complicated choreography of behind-the-scenes work. Trial seldom began at the precise time of day that had been scheduled, simply because the judges could not sit down while any detail was out of place. Behind the scenes, advisers would often wage friendly bets on the precise time that the judges would enter the courtroom. Television viewers would know only that trial was delayed or that the lunch break went on far longer than anticipated. A confluence of components had to be satisfactorily resolved each and every day of trial, and every time the court took a recess of any length: travel arrangements to and from court for witnesses, lawyers, judges, and distinguished visitors; the occasional illness or physical complaint of court personnel or of defendants that required attention by the on-site medical team; shifting security procedures; coordination of witnesses to and from Dujail; media inquiries; transfer of evidence to the courthouse and preparations for its use in open court; the malfunction of courtroom technology; defense matters such as communications with the judges and the mechanics of conferring with obstreperous clients; delivery of food to the courthouse; judicial conferences to debate pending legal issues; defense motions and frequent demands to the judges. The list went on and on, and new challenges seemed to arise daily. Almost any minor event could trigger extended delays.

For example, one day the most critical person for a timely judicial day was a cat catcher on contract to the Americans. Insurgents constantly probed the defenses of the International Zone. Though it was easy for some to become complacent as they roamed freely around the secured area in the heart of Baghdad, the steady drumbeat of attacks, random mortars, and rockets was accompanied by the occasional car bomb or other orchestrated attack. Insurgents learned that by releasing stray cats, they could sidetrack the dogs that were trained to detect explosives. The delays would cause chaos and snarl traffic at checkpoints, frustrate orderly schedules, and make tempers short. The release of cats demonstrated the art of asymmetric warfare perfectly; but the art of modern counterinsurgency requires adaption to a shifting enemy. The answer: bring in cat catchers. They were from Louisiana, and they were very good at what they did.

Security could never be taken for granted or shortchanged for the sake of convenience. The courthouse itself was barricaded behind rows of vehicle barriers and guardhouses, and security was at least three levels thick. For every day of trial, attorneys, media, and distinguished guests were met at a set time and location, early in the morning. They were driven to the nearby courthouse on black reinforced buses, known as Rhinos for their heavy side armor and the protuberance on their front, and then escorted through the layers of security and metal detectors as a group. The security arrangements for controlling access to the building took months to perfect; they were implemented by the Iraqi policemen who had been trained and directed by the disciplined professionals of the U.S. Marshals Service. The

Iraqi captain in charge of security was the living embodiment of physical and moral courage as he instituted the rigorous security protocol and maintained the discipline needed to make it accomplish its purpose. Every person who entered the courthouse the entire trial went through the security procedures—no exceptions, no deviations, no shortcuts. This occasionally meant that judges or attorneys were late and court was delayed.

The security environment in Iraq required stringent measures, and there were times during the trial when the conflict outside the courtroom seemed to be fed and sustained by the conflicts in court. Within minutes of entering the courtroom for the first time, Saddam tried to communicate the secret location of the courthouse to his supporters watching the broadcast. As Judge Rizgar began the procedural formalities for opening the trial session, Saddam interjected (incorrectly), "I have been here at the Military Industrialization premises since 0230." Iraqi officials arrested some insurgents on the second day of the Dujail trial after uncovering what was believed to be a plan to assault the courthouse. Such an attack would have been highly unlikely to succeed, and the defendants themselves were always under tight control. The security conditions outside the courtroom would prompt one court translator who was in her ninth month of pregnancy to schedule a cesarian section for midafternoon on a Saturday to ensure that she would not be stopped by sectarian roadblocks on her way to deliver her baby. Her daughter was safely delivered.

The preparations for this first day of the first trial came down to the wire. What had once been a marbled ornate Baath Party headquarters building had been reconfigured, rewired, and almost reengineered to become the most secure and modern courthouse in Iraq. It had cameras monitoring almost every corner of the building, and high-speed Internet lines running to the media area. One camera was mounted high in the corner facing the witness booth, and one would show the world the view from over the shoulder of the presiding judge. There was only one courtroom in the building after early plans for a second courtroom had to be scrapped in order to fit everything into one building. Once all of the trial participants were present for trial, the main courtroom felt surprisingly cramped despite its high ceilings.

Each group of participants in the process had specially designed and segregated areas. The press had a large open room with a number of cubicles and computers from which to file reports, while Arabic speakers could watch the proceedings on closed-circuit television. After going through the body scan machine, they would be escorted as a group to the press gallery directly behind the group of defendants sitting in the dock. The prosecution team had a large area close to the courtroom where they could gather to eat or prepare arguments. The distinguished visitors had a rather narrow rectangular room where they would sit on couches until it was time to be shepherded to their observation area. The observation gallery was a glassed-off area up one flight of stairs and located directly above the press gallery. The glass would eventually be tinted after one defense attorney complained about what he claimed to be "Iranian agents" showing him their feet from the observer gallery (which would have been a grave insult in Iraqi culture).

One of the main arguments in favor of holding trials in Iraq even in the midst of the deteriorating security situation had been to permit the attendance of ordinary Iraqis and ordinary victims. This goal quickly proved to be a fantasy because of the practical gap between the people of Iraq and the walled-off courtroom behind reinforced levels of security. No ordinary Iraqis were able to attend the trial, though they could watch the televised broadcasts on a twenty-minute delay from the real-life events in the courtroom. On the first day of trial, Judge Rizgar would explain to the defendants that "due to security conditions, it was not possible to summon the plaintiffs and witnesses in this first session of the court."

Fulfilling its mandate to provide independent and unbiased assessment of the trial, the International Center for Transitional Justice (ICTJ) would compile detailed and very professional observations through its representatives. The official ICTJ records indicate that the crowded VIP gallery had sixteen local observers in attendance for the beginning of the Dujail trial, including national security adviser Mowaffak al-Rubaie, government spokesman Laith Kubba, an official from the British embassy, representatives of international human rights organizations such as Human Rights Watch, several tribunal officials, and six Iraqi marshals. Miranda Sissons, the ICTJ Middle East deputy director, was in the gallery and recalls that the observers on that first day of trial were tuned to every nuance and reacted audibly to very subtle signals and comments from the courtroom. The ICTJ observer notes would in time provide one of the most important records of the Dujail proceedings.

The defense team was provided with secure transportation every time they wanted to enter Iraq to confer with their clients and for each trip to the International Zone in Baghdad for court sessions. The simple act of providing U.S. military helicopter transport to non-Americans requires extensive coordination and approvals. Defense lawyers were required to request access to clients or transportation sufficiently in advance to allow that approval process, though they were never denied transportation for their repeated failure to meet those time lines. The daughter of one defense attorney was escorted to safety after she heard about wanted posters with her father's name and face being hung in Sadr City during the trial. When court was in session, the defense team was lodged in a safe house and escorted to court each day. After going through security, they had a segregated area with Internet access where they could gather and talk freely. Phone lines were run to the area of the holding cells so they could confer with their clients in confidence. Only twelve defense attorneys were permitted in the courtroom at any given time, and the judge ordered that no more than five of those could be representing Saddam. Security procedures prevented the entire defense team from being in the courtroom at one time, so they would often rotate through the available seats and watch the closed-circuit broadcast from their area behind the courtroom. The defendants also had closed-circuit broadcasts in their holding cells so that even when they chose to boycott attendance in court, they could observe the proceedings and talk to their attorneys.

The judges had a small anteroom just to the rear of the courtroom, and the witnesses could gather before their testimony in a small area on the other side of the courtroom. During breaks in the trial, the judges' room would fill with smoke, and chai tea was never in short supply. Western advisers were often in this private area to respond to the questions of the judges, as the trial produced surprises almost by the minute. As the judges entered the courtroom up a small set of stairs, they came in single file through a narrow door onto the platform at the front of the trial chamber. There were many occasions when the judges would open the door and announce a decision that would in turn lead to more lengthy discussions and more delay. No one in the watching world ever saw these detailed debates as judges wrestled with the best way to handle the myriad legal and practical difficulties that arose.

An excerpt from the Koran was emblazoned in gold letters on the marble wall behind the judges' raised dais: "When you judge between people you judge with justice."[1] Attentive viewers could see it on the televised broadcasts. Many Iraqis were impatient to see Saddam humbled. One mother who had lost her son argued that rather than being prosecuted, Saddam and the others should be imprisoned without further proceedings: "I will go every day to personally punish them," she said. Many Iraqis prayed for justice to be done because they felt that their Muslim faith forbids revenge. Watching from the United States, Sheikh Fadhel al-Sahlani, who served as the imam of the Al-Khoei Islamic Center and lost twenty-five members of his extended family to the cruelty of the regime, spoke for many of his countrymen when he told the media that he never really thought that Saddam would face trial for his crimes. The televised broadcasts that began on October 19, 2005, would prove him wrong, to the unmitigated joy of the Iraqi street.

## THE BEGINNING

Despite a provision of Iraqi law requiring that the defendant attend court "without restraint or handcuffs," the first defendant entered the courtroom in handcuffs, prompted by a nod from Judge Rizgar. Defendants had gathered in the holding room and waited for the judge to call their names, and shuffled into the courtroom one by one. The beginning of the trial was delayed due to technical difficulties with the equipment used to broadcast the images and sounds of the trial to a waiting world. RCLO officials joked that this in itself should serve as proof to a skeptical public that the Iraqis were in control. The members of the press from around the globe were packed into the gallery overlooking the courtroom; the time passed slowly as their emotions alternated between boredom and nervous tension. Mohammed Azawi Ali el-Marsoumi was the first defendant to enter; he was an elderly man who had to be helped to his seat by the Iraqi policemen. Iraqi courtrooms, like civil law courts around the globe, have a wooden framed area where the defendant sits by himself during trial proceedings. American courtrooms are typically arranged so that the defendant sits at a table alongside the defense attorneys. The original dock that had been built in the Dujail courtroom had barely been large enough to hold one person, but had to be scrapped in favor of a larger area that encompassed three rows of seats that could seat up to fifteen if needed. In this courtroom, the rows of defense lawyers were to the right of the group of defendants, who were in the middle of the open courtroom in the wooden dock with a waist-high rail built for the occasion. They faced the judges, who sat on a raised dais at the front of the room. The witness box was to their front right.

As Mohammed Azawi sank down into the leather chair at the rear of the dock, farthest away from the judges, he had no way of knowing that when the final judgment was rendered, he would be the only one of the eight to receive a full acquittal from the trial chamber. Next came the other three low-level officials from Dujail fated to stand trial with the most powerful leaders of Baathist Iraq. Ali Diyah Ali was a low-level Baath Party official in the Ministry of Education whose father was the mayor of the Dujail area in 1982. He had returned home the evening of the assassination attempt, and the evidence would show that he participated in the roundups of local citizens. He was joined in the dock by the oldest of the defendants, Abdallah Kasim Ruwayyid (commonly spelled Roweed in the Western media) al-Mashari, over eighty at the time the trial began. His son Mizhir Abdallah Kasim Ruwayyid al-Mashari entered the courtroom next and sat at his father's right side, where he would remain throughout the trial.

One by one, the lower-level defendants were joined by the more prominent defendants. At the very rear corner of the dock, to the right of the trial chamber (which was the upper-right-hand portion of the screen for those watching the trial from the camera angle directly behind the judges), sat Barzan Ibrahim al-Hassan al-Tikriti. Barzan was the half-brother of Saddam Hussein and headed the Iraqi secret police. He commanded the regime forces that descended on Dujail to punish the town in the wake of the failed assassination attempt, though he might well have been charged in several other cases. Barzan would display some of the most disrespectful behavior toward the bench, such as the day he wore his long underwear to court in protest and sat with his back toward the bench throughout the testimony. At times, he would also be active and quite effective in his own defense.

The second of the four prominent defendants was Taha Yassin Ramadan, who had been captured by Kurdish forces after the fall of Baghdad and was the former vice president of Iraq.[2] In July 1982, he was serving as the head of Iraq's largest militia, known as the Popular Army, and was the official responsible for overseeing the destruction of Dujail's fields and bulldozing the palm groves and date orchards. Taha was sentenced to life imprisonment by the trial chamber, but that sentence was summarily reversed with no explanation or legal reasoning by the appeals chamber (known in Iraqi practice as the Court of Cassation). A reconstituted trial chamber of new judges convened on February 12, 2007, to hold a pro forma session at which Taha's punishment was summarily increased from life imprisonment to death.[3] Of the many controversies associated with this first trial held by the Iraqi High Tribunal, the execution of Taha Yassin Ramadan on March 20, 2007, caused perhaps the most international outrage and represented the final act of the Dujail trial.[4]

Only two defendants would sit in the front row throughout the trial. Awad Hamad al-Bandar served as the president of Saddam's Revolutionary Command Council Court. He was a glowering presence at Saddam's side through the months of trial. The Revolutionary Command Council Court had jurisdiction over any case directed by Saddam, in particular national security matters.[5] Defendants in the Revolutionary Court could expect little or no due process and their verdicts could not be appealed, although Saddam Hussein had to personally approve death sentences. Some of the most potent evidence against Saddam and, by extension, Awad al-Bandar would be the signed death warrants that were introduced into evidence. When the Iraqi Special Tribunal had been announced in December 2003, Adnan Pachachi, then serving as the rotating leader of the Interim Governing Council, specifically said that the intent from the very beginning was that trials "be open and just, and it will be possible for all defendants to have attorneys. It will not be like the courts [under the regime] that would sentence and execute within minutes." Iraqis had no way of knowing that the Dujail proceedings would take more than fourteen months to conclude, but they certainly sought to demonstrate a sharp contrast to the summary justice imposed by the judges under Saddam's political control. One of the ironies of the Dujail trial was that its very length and the often chaotic atmosphere that was caused by the effort to protect the due process rights of the defendants were primary reasons why ordinary Iraqis became increasingly skeptical and disillusioned.

On May 27, 1984, Saddam referred 148 men and boys from Dujail to the Revolutionary Court for "trial," whereupon Awad al-Bandar dutifully sentenced them to death. One of the critical issues of fact for Trial Chamber 1 would be to weigh the available evidence to decide whether Awad al-Bandar even held a hearing before sentencing the Dujailis to die. In the Dujail judgment, the trial chamber noted that Judge Awad al-Bandar characterized the civilians as "ravaging traitors" in the papers for the case, and described the sham proceedings as a legal fig leaf to cover the crime of murder. One of the most important conclusions of the trial chamber would be that Awad al-Bandar's legal action was sufficient to permit his conviction for crimes against humanity because the required element of a "widespread or systematic attack directed against the civilian population" need not be a military attack.[6] Although Iraqi law permits only a maximum life sentence for the attempted commission of a crime, Awad al-Bandar decided that an unsuccessful assassination attempt merited death.[7] Awad al-Bandar sentenced all 148 civilians to death despite the fact that documents introduced during the trial showed that 46 had already died in the custody of the intelligence services,[8] some of the named persons had been released instead of being executed, and others not on the list were executed by mistake. More than two dozen defendants were minors, some as young as fifteen.[9]

At precisely 12:21 P.M., Saddam Hussein entered the courtroom in Baghdad to stand trial for the crimes committed against the citizens of Dujail. The beginning of the long-awaited trial was a major media event that made headlines in every news outlet across the globe that day. The expectations of the Iraqi people had been raised to a fever pitch in the months leading to trial. Abdul Rahman al-Rashid wrote in the pan-Arab *Al-Asharq al-Awsat*, "It is certainly not a trial of Saddam himself, but of his regime and of its history."[10] Richard Dicker, the head of the international justice program for Human Rights Watch, was in Baghdad at the time. "I think it was very stirring to see Saddam Hussein in the dock as a defendant in a criminal trial," he said. "There were horrific crimes that occurred in Iraq over three decades of Baath Party rule. And I think it's been a long time coming that those most responsible be brought to book before a court of law in determining guilt or innocence. So I think it was very stirring. At the same time, it's crucial this tribunal get it right."

Saddam was the last one of the eight defendants to enter, and the only one whose handcuffs had been removed before he stepped into the courtroom. As he came into view, the scene sent a visible thrill through the galleries; the onlookers were surprised to see the other defendants and the defense lawyers rise to their feet in respect for the fallen leader. His presence in the dock brought the proceedings immediate electricity and an almost palpable gravity. During one break in the proceedings that day, Taha Yassin Ramadan would go over to Saddam and kiss his head as a sign of loyalty and respect. Court officials decided thereafter that Saddam would always be the first to enter the courtroom in order to prevent the symbolic gesture of respect from ever recurring. Behind the scenes, Saddam would come to dominate his codefendants at every opportunity. The men were held separately at the Camp Cropper detention facility, but on trial days, they could meet in a designated smoking cell. On more than one occasion, Saddam would berate his codefendants for something they had said in court that he disapproved of.

As Saddam passed close to the chief prosecutor, Ja'afar al-Moussawi, he muttered an ethnic Iraqi slur, *shrugi*, under his breath in a tone of contempt and condemnation. Prosecutor Ja'afar is a robust man who sports a gray-sprinkled beard and a proud manner. Ja'afar has a large personality and an imposing personal presence. In the eyes of the Iraqi people he would assume something akin to rock-star status during the course of the trial. *Shrugi* is a slang term that Iraqis use to describe the people who originate in the region to the south and east of Baghdad. That area of Iraq abuts the Iranian border and is largely inhabited by Shia Muslims, who make up the majority of Iraqi citizens. The Sunni-dominated regime often used *shrugi* as a phrase to belittle its Shiite enemies. It is a term of derision and discrimination that carried connotations that Ja'afar was uncivilized, uneducated, and inferior. Saddam sought to psychologically bully Ja'afar through the ethnic insult, and he almost succeeded. Ja'afar was incensed at the slur and nearly refused to return to the courtroom until Saddam could be forced to apologize. Only behind-the-scenes cajoling by the RCLO attorneys persuaded Ja'afar to take the high ground and ignore the insult. To his great credit he recognized that the entire trial would be derailed if he directed his anger at the deposed dictator in its opening moments. He gave no outward indication of being disturbed and kept his composure to make a far-ranging and, by Iraqi standards, lengthy opening speech to the row of judges.

Saddam joined the other defendants in the wooden holding area that had been built in the middle of the courtroom. As he sat, he was a criminal defendant like any other defendant. In the nation where his word and will had been the equivalent of law, he was under the authority of the statute and the trial chamber charged with applying the law. The scene was one that thousands of Iraqis had only imagined as they suffered and often died. In contrast to the other defendants, who wore traditional robes, he wore a dapper blue suit. Guards did not allow him to wear a tie or a belt, presumably to prevent any attempt at suicide while in his holding cell. His thick black hair was combed carefully, and he walked with an erect stance and a confident glide. His appearance riveted Iraqis to their televisions, and many were emotional in the opening moments of the trial. It was a scene of high drama.

He carried a Koran to cultivate the image that he was united with the believers across the Muslim world, which caused howls of scorn from the thousands of families who had been victimized by the cruelty of his regime. During open court on December 14, 2005, observers would roll their eyes when Saddam raised his hand to interrupt the testimony of a witness from Dujail to ask for a prayer break. Judge Rizgar denied the request. Saddam was a secular leader to the core, and the reality of his regime made a mockery of Muslim principles. He nonetheless sought to quote passages from the Koran in order to create the illusion of unity with the watching Arab street. In fact, when Judge Rizgar asked him for his name, the first words that Saddam spoke in open court came from a Koranic verse. The ICTJ observer notes record that Saddam's first message to a listening world, after nearly two years in custody, was "In the name of God, the compassionate, the merciful. Men said to them, 'A great army is gathering against you' and frightened them. But it only increased their Faith. They said: 'For us, Allah sufficeth . . .' "[11]

Judge Rizgar had been selected in part for his even keel and calm demeanor. As Saddam challenged his authority from the very first moments of the trial, the judge drily interrupted him and restated his question: "Mr. Saddam, we want to record your identification information." Saddam doggedly continued the Koranic verse: " 'And he is the best disposer of affairs.' " Rizgar persisted: "Your full name, please." Saddam began again, and the judge interrupted him yet again. This opening salvo embodied the struggle between law and power that would run throughout the entire trial. The aspiration of the Iraqis was that the Dujail trial would serve as a defining moment of clarity and purpose in the newly freed nation. Kanan Makiya, who had published the seminal account of life under Saddam in

1989 entitled *Republic of Fear*,[12] told CNN host Soledad O'Brien, "It was a remarkable moment, one almost difficult to put into words. The sight of the man, close-up, there is a shuffle with the guards that took place. This is a truly historic moment, and the opening shot in something that promises to be very large and of great consequence to the whole region."

The scene in open court was a stark contrast to Saddam's actions in 1979 when he purged the president, proclaimed himself leader, and organized a show trial similar to Stalin's trials in the 1930s.[13] Throughout the modern history of Iraq, leaders who lost power were executed by their successors in short order. In Baghdad in 2003, the founders of the Iraqi High Tribunal sought to establish a new pattern. The dream that the Dujail trial would serve as the defining moment to generate momentum toward peaceful democracy in Iraq immediately came up against the reality of a defiant defendant who would stay true to his narcissistic nature rather than admitting any shred of remorse or shame for the cruelty he displayed toward his own people. Commenting on the fact that he had not been permitted to carry a pen and paper, Saddam used a characteristic saying from his political speeches: "It seems these are scary items these days. Well done, people of Iraq!"[14]

Saddam refused to simply provide his name, but Judge Rizgar persisted with patience and politely asked Saddam to identify himself yet again. Saddam then articulated the legal issue that would resonate through the entire trial and would only be resolved in the trial chamber judgment and in the appeal. "But in respect of the will of the Iraqi people who chose me, I must say that I don't recognize this so-called court despite my respect for its members. I reserve my rights as the President of Iraq . . . let me finish . . . no, I won't be long . . . I just want to comment on what you said about the fact that these are court formalities." Rizgar interrupted him again with the comment "Yes, you are knowledgeable of the law." In Arabic, this phrase is literally understood as "You are a man of the law" *(anta rajul qanuni)*. The observers in the gallery grumbled their dismay that the judge would speak to Saddam in such a respectful way. Saddam pressed on in what would be his most quoted statement around the world that day. "I do not recognize the party which appointed you, nor do I recognize the aggression against Iraq, because what is based on falsehood is falsehood."

This confrontation was a microcosm of the entire trial process. The gap between the aspirations of the Dujail trial and its actuality would prove cavernous. The defense sought to create a perception of illegitimacy that took hold of the Iraqi consciousness and was independent of the process followed in the courtroom. In truth, the legal principle of individual responsibility is clearly stated in the IHT statute, and is based almost word for word on the standards found in every other tribunal applying international law. Article 15 embodies the will of the Iraqi people that Saddam and the other leading Baathists could be charged for their crimes despite their positions of power and privilege. "The official position of any accused person, whether as president, prime minister, member of the cabinet, chairman or a member of the Revolution Command Council, a member of the Arab Socialist Baath Party Regional Command or Government (or an instrumentality of either) or as a responsible Iraqi Government official or member of the Baath Party or in any other capacity, shall not relieve such person of criminal responsibility nor mitigate punishment. No person is entitled to any immunity with respect to any of the crimes stipulated in Articles 11–14 of this law." The challenge for the court would be to correctly apply the complex principles of crimes against humanity in open court with the world watching. That first day revealed the inherent difficulties that would haunt the process to its climactic moments.

## PUBLIC OUTREACH

As early as July 2004, Mowaffak al-Rubaie recognized that the success of the Iraqi High Tribunal would rely in large measure on its ability to be a transparent forum, but also one that Iraqis understood and appreciated. He predicted that Saddam would "turn the trial into a military showdown."[15] "This is going to inflame the Arab world. We have to start a huge public campaign to educate Iraqis what to expect. Otherwise, he will steal the whole show."[16] Saddam's persona was far more powerful for Iraqis than the Western experts who helped the judge prepare for trial understood, and the court was caught in a delicate balance. As we've seen, during the mock trial held at Stratford-upon-Avon, experts had attempted to prepare the Iraqi judges for a defiant Saddam who would act along the lines of the Milosevic model. When a Western journalist in Baghdad asked what measures the court had taken to prevent Saddam from using the court to address the Iraqi people and the Arab nations, Judge Ra'id replied that "Saddam Hussein is like any other defendant. He can defend himself. And as for the organization of the trial, it is related to the Iraqi laws and according to the laws of trials. And the head of the session can use these regulations to keep the trial legal."[17] Judge Ra'id was correct, but also assumed incorrectly that the decision to televise the proceedings was itself a guarantee that the public would understand and support the work of the court.

The most successful and internationally acclaimed model for public education had been provided by the war crimes tribunal in West Africa, called the Special Court for Sierra Leone. The founding chief prosecutor of that court, David M. Crane, describes the importance that he placed on reaching out to the victims and citizenry in the war-torn region served by his court.

> During the first four months our goal was to visit every district and every major town within that district. We accomplished this task just before Christmas of 2002. In my mind it was imperative that Sierra Leoneans see their Prosecutor, to tell me what took place in their town, district, or village, and to ask me questions about my work and the work of the Special Court. Additionally, the town hall meetings allowed me to get a sense of the horror that was Sierra Leone in the 1990's. Though planned and developed well in advance, a typical event was a day-long affair. An outreach team arrived a day prior to talk to various chiefs and elders and to brief them on the next day's events. The outreach team usually was present and ran the program. The day of the event, the outreach team set up the venue and briefed the audience on the program and talked to them about the Special Court in general. I would arrive, and after brief remarks, open up the floor for comments and questions. My focus was never on the indictees, but on the Court, the process, and the organization of the Court. The central themes generally were that the rule of law is more powerful than the rule of the gun, no one is above the law, and that the law is fair. After I left there would more discussion with the outreach team.[18]

In the context of the burgeoning insurgency in Iraq, such an approach was impossible. The need to demonstrate that the trial was based on internationally acceptable standards of due process and fairness was more than a legal technicality. If the Dujail trial was to accelerate the healing of the societal divisions within Iraq, then it had to be understandable to ordinary Iraqis. The reliance on television created difficult trial management problems for the presiding judge that had been inadequately addressed when the trial began. An Iraqi government official privately told the authors that the judges had learned much in preparation for the trials, but did not appear to be "ready for the bright lights." The lack of an effective outreach strategy to explain to the Iraqi people what was really happening or to clarify the legal misconceptions as they arose meant that the visual images were the only way to measure the work of the court.

On the one hand, if the judges simply muzzled Saddam, the image would reinforce perceptions that the trial was nothing more than a dance to reach a prearranged conclusion. The transparent demonstration of a fair trial could never be accomplished if the judges did not give Saddam and the other defendants the full rights to participate in their defense and speak in open court. At the same time, the Iraqis naïvely clung to the belief that the Dujail trial would be a "pure Iraqi trial," in the words of one judge. Iraqi law provides that the court has power to "prevent the parties and their representatives from speaking at undue length or speaking outside the subject of the case, repeating statements, violating guidelines or making accusations against another party or a person outside the case who is unable to put forward a defense."[19] The court statute simply states, "The Criminal Court shall ensure that a trial is fair and expeditious and that proceedings are conducted in accordance with this Statute and the Rules of Procedure and Evidence annexed to this Law, with full respect for the rights of the accused and due regard for the protection of the victims, their relatives and the witnesses."[20] Relying on these precepts, the court created an inadequate Web site and never provided a designated and knowledgeable court spokesman to clarify the misperceptions of press and populace.

The actual legal substance of the first day took about three hours, and was not complex. Judge Rizgar followed the formula laid down by the third paragraph of Article 20, which states: "The Criminal Court shall read the indictment, satisfy itself that the rights of the accused are respected and guaranteed, insure that the accused understands the indictment, with charges directed against him, and instruct the accused to enter a plea." The court informed the defendants that they were charged with crimes against humanity for the murder, imprisonment, and torture of the Dujailis. Before their selection for the Iraqi High Tribunal, and the multiple training sessions, both in Iraq and overseas, the Iraqis had no way of prosecuting crimes against humanity, or of correctly distilling the complex body of principles entailed by those charges. All eight of the defendants pleaded not guilty, essentially telling the trial chamber that it would be required to comb through the referral file and to listen to the testimony of complainants and witnesses and establish every element of the crimes against humanity charges beyond a reasonable doubt if they were to be convicted. After taking the "not guilty" pleas, Judge Rizgar read aloud the entire article of the statute listing the legal rights of the defendants to a fair trial.[21] One of the defense attorneys prefaced his comments that day with the acknowledgement that "we see that your Excellency and esteemed members of the court are making relentless efforts to render the trial a fair one, and to give the defendants the right to defend themselves, for which we thank you, even though this is a legal duty." Judge Rizgar listened to complaints made by the defense attorneys about the legibility of some of the documents provided to them prior to trial, and most significantly, he granted their request for delay until November 28, 2005. Foreshadowing the persistent failures to communicate with the public audience, none of the legal principles that were inherent in the crimes against humanity charges were explained to the Iraqi people.

## INDEPENDENT AND IMPARTIAL?

The failure of the court to develop an outreach strategy prior to the start of the Dujail trial is even more significant because its credibility as a neutral and impartial judicial body had been debated from the time of its announcement. Before the court was even announced, one Western expert told the Associated Press, "Any Tribunal established on behalf of the Coalition Provisional Authority will not be able to rid itself of the perception and the fact that it is an instrument of American power. Any justice it dispenses will be of dubious legality and questionable legitimacy."[22] Allegations of so-called victor's justice have haunted virtually every major international trial since Nuremberg. When given a copy of his indictment before the International Military Tribunal at Nuremberg, Hermann Göring scrawled the phrase "The victor will always be the judge and the vanquished the accused" across its cover.[23] There is a visceral power in the concept of victor's justice that threatened to corrode every facet of the trial, and Saddam intuitively exploited that power at every opportunity.

The Iraqis recognized that authentic justice is not achieved on the wings of societal vengeance, innuendo, or external manipulation; rather, the very essence of a fair trial is one in which the verdict is based on a regularized process and on the quantum of evidence introduced in open court. The very first defense objection in the trial came during Prosecutor Ja'afar's opening comments the first day of trial as he described the range of crimes committed by the regime. Ja'afar opened with stinging and blunt oratory: "The Iraqi people and mankind have been waiting for you impatiently to witness the fair sentence you will pass on those who committed these odious crimes against mankind." Judge Rizgar cautioned him immediately against an excess of emotionalism: "Mr. Ja'afar, let us not carry out slander."[24] When Ja'afar launched into a wide-ranging excoriation that began to outline all of the major crimes committed during the thirty-five years of Saddam's regime, the defense interrupted.

One defense attorney said, "Mr. President, the court is looking into a case, the case of Al Dujail. We believe the public prosecutor has exceeded his rights that are enunciated in the bylaws of the court. The public prosecutor has become an adversary, for he has taken sides." The other defense lawyers shouted out their agreement. Fighting to keep the trial focused on a complete and dispassionate presentation of the available evidence, Judge Rizgar asked Ja'afar to confine his comments to the specific events surrounding Dujail. This early interchange is ironic because the defense strategy of obstruction and obfuscation led by this same attorney, Khalil al-Dulaimi, later sought to redirect attention away from the evidence throughout the rest of the trial.

The entire defense strategy was obvious to close observers from the first day. They sought to delegitimize the process by creating the impression that the trial was not about the events and evidence from Dujail, but was instead a showcase for political interests. If the Iraqis had intentionally created a tribunal under the sway of political influence and based on populist revenge, they would have had no greater moral authority than the Baathists. The very first provision of the statute accordingly provided that "a court is hereby established and shall be known as the Iraqi Higher

Criminal Court (the 'Court'). The Court shall be fully independent."[25] Belying this line of logic, the Iraqi High Tribunal was set up as an autonomous legal entity beyond the control of the normal Iraqi Ministry of Justice channels, even though the pay and perks of tribunal personnel would flow from the government. In practice, this meant that the tribunal was in almost constant contact with political officials in order to obtain the funding, housing, and other necessities for its operation.

To illustrate the transformation of justice in a free Iraq, the statute also specified that "no officer, prosecutor, investigative judge, judge or other personnel of the tribunal shall have been a member of the Ba'ath Party.'[26] The first CPA order decreed that the Baath Party was dissolved and that the future of representative democracy in Iraq would not be undermined by those who served in positions of power under Saddam.[27] CPA Order No. 1 limited its effects to the four highest levels of officials.[28]

> Full members of the Ba'ath Party holding the ranks of "Udw Qutriyya" (Regional Command Member), "Udw Far" (Branch Member), "Udw Shu'bah" (Section Member), and "Udw Firqah" (Group Member) (together, "Senior Party Members") are hereby removed from their positions and banned from future employment in the public sector. These Senior Party Members shall be evaluated for criminal conduct or threat to the security of the Coalition. Those suspected of criminal conduct shall be investigated and, if deemed a threat to security or a flight risk, detained or placed under house arrest.[29]

Despite its superficially laudable intentions, the de-Baathification provision in the tribunal statute was broader than that mandated by the CPA. On the one hand, it dramatically limited the pool of potential candidates for judicial or prosecutorial service. At the same time, there were no procedures specified for certifying candidates for service on the tribunal, and it was silent about the procedures for ensuring that political interests outside the tribunal did not use the de-Baathification requirement as a pretext for exercising undue control over the judges and prosecutors. The de-Baathification requirement hung over the heads of those who served the tribunal, and they could never be completely confident that it would not be used to remove them. The fact that Achmed Chalabi controlled the de-Baathification commission only amplified the potential problems.

In essence, this provision created a black hole of politicized influence that would later haunt the operation of the tribunal.

Radio Free Iraq quoted Abd al-Aziz Hakim, who served as rotating president of the Interim Governing Council in December 2003, as terming it "the Court of Justice and Fairness" at the time of its creation. The ninety-three Iraqis who assembled in the Convention Center in December 2003 were the first to have the chance to review the newly adopted statute. When Salem Chalabi discussed its provisions with them, the very first question from one of the lawyers was whether the court would truly operate free of political influences. Judicial salaries and appointments would flow through Iraqi political channels. In purely legalistic terms, authentic justice must be the product of an "impartial and regularly constituted court respecting the generally recognized principles of regular judicial procedure."[30] Seeking to establish a viable and fair process that would meet the expectations of the Iraqi people but also satisfy the standards of international justice, the Iraqis were caught in a virtual whirlpool of competing legal and political dynamics. They had to select and train judges who were free of personal bias, but also knowledgeable of both the relevant international law and the key components of Iraq law and procedure.

More importantly, the judges would need to be tough-minded and independent enough to withstand the inevitable perception of political pressures. To be truly independent, the judges would need to stand on their own expertise and instincts, though of course they could rely on the international advisers that the statute specifically required. Neither the Iraqi government nor the American government could have any voice in the proceedings. Justice is by definition apolitical and impartial. The chief investigative judge's admonition that "only the evidence speaks" captures the essence of his view that neither the Iraqi government nor the Americans had any legitimate influence in the actual decisions inherent in the trial proceedings. The trial chamber had to walk a tightrope.

Cherif Bassiouni exemplified the skepticism of the outside world when he warned in 2004 that "the trial could be an extraordinary opportunity to send a message to the tyrants of the Arab world. But the deck is being stacked, and it's going to be obvious. . . . Where in the world can you say that this is an independent judiciary, with U.S. proxies appointing and controlling judges, with U.S. gift-wrapped cases?" The reality of the complex interdependence between RCLO and the Iraqi jurists was far more than external observers could fathom. Judge Zuhair al-Maliki echoed the criticisms from a different perspective after Salem Chalabi persuaded the Interim Governing Council to accept the first six nominees to serve the newly formed tribunal. Seeing Chalabi and the Iraqi National Congress as an extension of Washington politics, he complained, "This tribunal is not ours; it is somebody who came from abroad and created a court for themselves. Chalabi selected the judges according to his political opinions." Salem Chalabi, on the other hand, vigorously maintained that he merely identified potential candidates and that the properly appointed political channels made the decisions about judicial nominations. This process would have been very similar to those followed in many parts of the world. Of course, the selection of qualified lawyers with the right temperament and experience to serve as judges in the midst of an ongoing insurgency against the backdrop of three decades of oppression and political polarization would be difficult in the very best of circumstances. Behind the scenes, the selection and nomination of judges was completely opaque to American advisers. This meant that the United States would be blamed for the appearance of political bias, but had no actual voice or influence in the identification and nomination of judges or other officials.

The truth is that, as in many nations around the world, the selection of judges to serve the Iraqis was an inherently political and delicate process. The statute provides that nominees shall be "of high moral character, integrity and uprightness. They shall possess experience in criminal law and shall fulfill the appointment requirements stipulated in the Judicial Organization Law No. 160 of 1979 and the Public Prosecution Law No. 159 of 1979."[31] The statute sets out a deceptively simple process. "The Supreme Juridical Council shall nominate all judges and public prosecutors to this Court. The Council of Ministers after approving their nomination shall issue their appointment order from the Presidency Council and will be classified as class (A) judges, in an exception to the provisions of the Judicial Organization Law and the Public Prosecution Law. Their salaries and rewards shall be specified by guidelines issued by the Council of Ministers."[32]

Of course, in the circumstances of Iraq, judges also needed enormous personal courage and the support of their families. There is one account of a judge who called to ask Eric Blinderman of the RCLO what he should do because his neighbors had called to tell him that killers were waiting for him and his family in front of his apartment. Rather than calling the military, Blinderman commandeered an unarmed car and sped to the rescue. The family hastily gathered its belongings, and Blinderman took them to the safety of the International Zone. The entire family lived in cramped conditions in the Al-Rasheed Hotel for an extended period of time until safe housing could be arranged. The pool of qualified and courageous jurists was simply not deep enough.

Before he was forced to resign as administrator of the court, Salem Chalabi of the Iraqi National Congress succeeded in getting six people nominated and confirmed for service on the tribunal. Judge Dara, who had been so instrumental in drafting the early statute, and who was perhaps the most respected judge in Iraq, declined to serve because of the appearance of bias caused by his own imprisonment at the hands of the regime. One of Chalabi's first appointments would prove to be fateful. Muneer Haddad was a lawyer at the time of his selection, but he had no judicial experience. Three of his brothers had been jailed by Saddam's forces, and then executed. His family was deported because of alleged ties to Iranian influences. He was approved for service initially as one of the investigative judges. At a time when the nominees were under strict guidance to keep their identities secret, an Iraqi judge who was never affiliated with the IHT remembers Judge Muneer coming up to him and introducing himself with a swagger. During that first introduction, the Iraqi judge recalls how Muneer made no secret of his appointment to the tribunal (as an investigative judge at the time), and expressed the hope that, as this judge recalls, "I will be the one to execute Saddam." More than two years later, Judge Muneer had been elevated to the appeals chamber of the renamed Iraqi High Criminal Court. He was in the room when Saddam died on December 30, 2006, and made a number of statements to world media outlets as an official observer of the execution.

## THE PERCEPTION OF POLITICS, NOT PROCESS

After the defendants said that they were innocent, the defense lawyers made a series of requests to Judge Rizgar to end the first day of the Dujail trial. One defense lawyer said flatly that "the government interferes with the court's duties." Judge Rizgar responded that there was no external interference with his judicial decision making, but the defense persisted. As evidence of an unseen and inappropriate political hand guiding the trial chamber, he said that it was widely known that it is the duty of the court to set the date for trial, inform the parties, coordinate the attendance of complainants, and convene the trial on the selected day. "But what happened is that it was Mr. Laith Kubba, spokesman for the Prime Minister, who set the date for the trial."[33] Laith Kubba was present that day in the observer gallery and laughed out loud when he heard the accusation. He had indeed been the one to announce the specific date for the beginning of the Dujail trial in September, but he did so at the request of the tribunal. The tribunal had no press spokesman and no public outreach strategy, so instead relied on the information channel of the prime minister's office to make the long-awaited announcement.

This small incident illustrates one of the truisms that would resonate throughout the trial and the appeal process. The viewing audience, as well as visiting human rights lawyers, Western political officials, UN officials, and citizens from around the world, would often have no way to distill the real truth from the barrage of misstatement and misconception. In its judgment at the end of the trial, the trial chamber voiced its indignant response to assumptions that the judges were politically driven. In response to the constant insinuations that they were "propelled by others" as a result of the occupation, the judges wrote that the defense allegations constituted "degrading statements" amounting to an "indecent attack" on their character. The Iraqi Judicial Law specifies that the judge shall be bound to "preserve the dignity of the judicature and to avoid anything that arouses suspicion on his honesty."[34] Judge Rizgar's performance that first day was measured and fair. It was obvious that a long and difficult trial lay ahead.

Judge Rizgar responded to the defense complaints with poise, and no small degree of optimistic prophecy. "In order not to have meaningless arguments, we should work in accordance with the law. God willing, the trial will be fair, and everything will be all right." Time would tell.

# 6

## DISORDER IN THE COURTROOM

**This chapter provides** the first full gavel-to-gavel account of what transpired during the trial of Saddam Hussein. Although the media devoted a great deal of attention to the trial, the coverage was surprisingly incomplete, especially during the several days that Saddam boycotted the proceedings. While, like the media coverage, this chapter focuses on trial highlights, we do so in hindsight with a better understanding of what ended up being significant to the disposition of the case and to the public perception of the trial. Any deviations from the actual record, which will someday be released in Arabic, are due to translation errors and the authors' efforts to edit the account down to a manageable length. The numbering of trial sessions in this chapter may differ from the numbers used by news accounts and other sources because we only count days of actual trial sessions in the courtroom, and have excluded brief hearings and proceedings held outside of the courthouse.

The trial of Saddam Hussein will no doubt be remembered as one of the messiest trials in legal history. As detailed in this chapter, during the nine months of televised proceedings, Saddam, his seven codefendants, and their dozen lawyers regularly disparaged the judges, interrupted witness testimony with outbursts, turned cross-examination into political theater, and staged frequent walkouts, boycotts, and hunger strikes. None of this should have come as a surprise to the IHT judges. As the authors explained during the judicial training sessions in the fall of 2004 and spring of 2005, because of the political context and widespread publicity, former leaders on trial such as Saddam Hussein are more likely than ordinary defendants to perceive that they do not stand a chance of obtaining an acquittal by playing by the rules. Instead, we warned the judges, the defendants will attempt to derail the proceedings, hoping for a negotiated solution such as a pardon or an amnesty. They will try to hijack the trial, hoping to transform themselves through their political diatribes into heroic martyrs in the eyes of their followers. And at the same time, they will seek to discredit the tribunal, hoping to provoke the judges into inappropriately harsh responses that will make the process appear patently unfair. While the international trainers and advisers armed the judges with an arsenal of ways to respond to such forms of disruption, things did not go quite as we had hoped.

## SADDAM'S BLUEPRINT FOR DISRUPTION

Former leaders on trial, like Saddam Hussein, Slobodan Milosevic, and Charles Taylor, seem to have a playbook on all the ways to wreck the proceedings. If such a book actually existed, its first chapter would no doubt be about the Chicago Eight (later, Seven, when Bobby Seale's case was severed) conspiracy trial of 1969–1970, the most notorious disorderly trial in American history. In that case, leaders of the anti–Vietnam War movement—Bobby Seale, David Dellinger, Abbie Hoffman, Jerry Rubin, Rennie Davis, Tom Hayden, Lee Weiner, and John Froines—were charged with conspiring, organizing, and inciting riots during the 1968 Democratic National Convention in Chicago. The trial drew considerable public notice because of the notoriety of the defendants and their courtroom antics. The Chicago Eight trial is particularly relevant to the Saddam Hussein trial because Saddam's chief American lawyer, former U.S. attorney general Ramsey Clark, had also been an adviser to the defense team in that notorious trial three decades earlier.

On the first day of the Chicago Eight trial, when the presiding judge, Julius Hoffman, declined to issue a postponement so that Bobby Seale's attorney would have time to recover from a gallbladder operation, Seale said to the judge: "If I am consistently denied this right of legal defense counsel of my choice who is effective by the judge of this Court, then I can only see the judge as a blatant racist of the United States Court." This brought a strong rebuke from Judge Hoffman. That same day, Judge Hoffman reprimanded Tom Hayden for giving a clenched-fist salute to the jury and Abbie Hoffman for blowing kisses at the jurors. A few days later, the defendants tried to drape the counsel table with a North Vietnamese flag in celebration of Vietnam Moratorium Day, drawing another round of sharp words from the judge.

Throughout the trial, the defendants refused to rise at the beginning or close of court sessions. On two occasions, defendants Abbie Hoffman and Jerry Rubin wore judicial robes in court onto which was pinned a yellow Jewish star, meant to imply that Judge Hoffman was running his courtroom like the courts of Nazi Germany. The defendants frequently called Judge Hoffman derogatory names, accused him of racism and prejudice, and made sarcastic comments to him, such as asking, "How is your war stock doing?" The most serious disorder occurred two weeks into the trial, when Judge Hoffman learned that a few minutes before the commencement of the court session, Bobby Seale had addressed the audience of his supporters in the courtroom, telling them that if he was attacked, they "know what to do." Judge Hoffman responded by having Seale bound and gagged. Defense counsel William Kunstler then scolded the court, saying, "This is no longer a court of order, Your Honor; this is a medieval torture chamber. It is a disgrace."[1]

At the conclusion of the trial, Judge Hoffman issued a total of 159 citations to the defendants and their lawyers for contempt in response to these incidents of disruption and disrespect. The Seventh Circuit Court of Appeals, however, reversed the contempt convictions on the ground that a judge cannot wait until the end of the trial to punish the defendants and their lawyers for misconduct. It also reversed the convictions on the substantive charges, in part due to the prejudicial remarks and actions by the trial judge and the inflammatory statements by the prosecutor during the trial.[2] It should come as no surprise that the Chicago Eight trial is universally seen as a low point in American courtroom management. Rather than viewing Judge Hoffman as a brave hero fighting anarchy, history remembers him more as an accomplice who unwittingly fanned the flames of disorder. This is exactly what Saddam and his defense team wanted to accomplish in the Dujail trial.

If the Chicago Eight trial provided Saddam and his defense team their inspiration, it was the international war crimes trial of Slobodan Milosevic (2001–2005) that provided them with a detailed game plan. Not coincidentally, the former Serb leader was also represented by Ramsey Clark. On the eve of the Milosevic trial in September 2001, the Coalition for International Justice faxed one of the authors (Scharf) a draft brief reportedly prepared by Clark, which he had distributed to the press and human rights organizations. This document—which contained bombastic argument headings, such as "Creation of the International Criminal Tribunal for the Former Yugoslavia Was a Lawless Act of Political Expediency by the United States Designed to Demonize and Destroy an Enemy," "Powers That Create Ad Hoc International Criminal Tribunals Divert Attention from Their Own Offenses," and "The Violence and Division Within Yugoslavia Since the Collapse of the Soviet Economy Was Caused by U.S.-Led Acts Designed to Balkanize the Federal Republic of Yugoslavia with the International Tribunal as Principal Weapon"—was never filed in court. Rather, it was designed for the court of public opinion.

Building on the theme of Clark's brief, the Milosevic defense began with a Hollywood-quality video and slide show presentation showing the destruction wrought by the 1999 NATO bombing campaign—though the acts of NATO were not relevant to any of the charges or defenses. Although he was assisted behind the scenes by an army of defense counsel, Milosevic decided to assert his right to act as his own lawyer in the televised proceedings before the Yugoslavia Tribunal, as this would enable him to make lengthy opening and closing statements and turn cross-examinations into opportunities for unfettered political diatribes. As the trial unfolded, Milosevic skillfully exploited his right of self-representation to treat the witnesses, prosecutors, and judges in a manner that would have earned ordinary defense counsel expulsion from the courtroom. He often strayed from the specifics of the case into long vitriolic speeches and he was frequently strategically disruptive.[3]

On numerous occasions, the presiding judge, Richard May of the United Kingdom, tried to rein in Milosevic with little success. A defendant who is represented by a lawyer is ordinarily able to address the court only when he takes the stand to give testimony during the defense's case-in-chief; the defendant is usually limited to giving evidence that is relevant to the charges, and is subject to cross-examination by the prosecution. While a judge can control an unruly lawyer by threatening fines, jail time, suspension, or disbarment, there is little a judge can do to effectively regulate a disruptive defendant who is acting as his own counsel.

Although Milosevic's antics were not winning him points with the judges, they were having a significant impact on public opinion back home in Serbia. Rather than discredit his nationalistic policies and educate Serbs about the atrocities that were committed in his name, the trial had the opposite effect. Milosevic's approval rating in Serbia doubled during the first weeks of the trial, and two years into the trial he easily won a seat in the Serb parliament in a nationwide election. In addition, opinion polls indicated that a majority of Serbs felt that he was not getting a fair trial, and that he was not actually guilty of any war crimes.[4] Culminating with his untimely death just before the conclusion of the trial, the judicial proceedings at The Hague transformed Milosevic from a disgraced politician who had been ousted by a popular revolt into one of the most esteemed public figures in Serb history.

Saddam is reported to have obsessively followed the Milosevic trial, as he saw Milosevic's tactics as providing the blueprint for the approach he would take if he ever found himself in a similar position.[5] When the media reported that Saddam had retained Milosevic's lawyer Ramsey Clark to serve as one of his lead counsel, one noted criminal law expert told CNN's Anderson Cooper: "Saddam Hussein deserves to get a fair trial and to be represented by good lawyers. I'm not sure he deserves Ramsey Clark. Clark will often go into a case as an attorney and use the case as a vehicle to criticize the United States. That's not necessarily representing your client."[6]

## THE PROSECUTION'S CASE

*Day 1 (October 19, 2005)*

The authors spent much of October 19, 2005, viewing the live televised proceedings of the first day of the Dujail trial and providing commentary for a variety of American and other foreign news media, including CNN, Fox News, ABC News, MSNBC, and the BBC (London). Altogether there would be thirty-seven days of trial spread over a nine-month period. Each session would have its share of memorable moments, and looking back to that first day (which is described in chapter 5), there were three developments that stood out in particular.

First, the world was introduced to the judge selected to preside over the Dujail trial—Rizgar Mohammed Amin, whom we met in the preceding chapter. In contrast to most of the other Iraqi jurists that the authors have known, who tend to be animated and forceful, Judge Rizgar had a uniquely low-key temperament, an infectious smile, and a patient demeanor. The word that perhaps best describes Judge Rizgar would be "avuncular." From our perspective, Judge Rizgar's demeanor was perfect for the Saddam trial. Unlike the stern British judge, Richard May, who tried to shout down Slobodan Milosevic when he acted in a disrespectful or disruptive manner at the Yugoslavia Tribunal (making the trial process seem unfair), Judge Rizgar handled Saddam's outbursts and refusal to answer his questions on that first day of trial and the days that followed in an extraordinarily calm and tolerant manner. Moreover, Judge Rizgar's first decisions in the trial were to order that the defendant's handcuffs be removed while in the courtroom and to grant the request of three of the defendants to allow them to wear their Islamic head coverings in court, demonstrating that he was committed to being respectful of their fundamental rights. The approach seemed to be working. By the end of the first trial session, Saddam Hussein had transformed from defiant to cooperative, entering a plea of not guilty (rather than refusing to enter any plea, as Slobodan Milosevic had done in The Hague).

The second development of note was that Judge Rizgar indicated that the judges had decided to broadcast the proceedings gavel-to-gavel on live television, with a twenty-minute delay to handle witness protection and security concerns. This decision had been hotly debated for months by the IHT. The authors had suggested during the training session that on balance televising the proceedings might be more trouble than it was worth, and up until a few weeks before the Dujail trial the judges were about evenly split on the issue. Not only did Judge Rizgar insist on televising the Dujail trial, but he decided not to have his own visage electronically obscured even though televising his identity would put him at great risk of assassination by Saddam's supporters. This did not surprise the authors, as Judge Rizgar had told us during the training session in London that he was interested in achieving "transparency" and showing the "face of justice" so that the IHT would not be subject to the kind of criticism leveled at some Latin American courts that have employed hooded judges. While Judge Rizgar was fully aware of the risk that Saddam and his lawyers would try to use the televised trial as a political stage, in the end he convinced the other members of the Dujial trial bench that the importance of transparency outweighed this hazard.

Third, despite some glitches with the video equipment that temporarily delayed the start of the proceedings, the first day of the trial was a very well choreographed event, with a great deal of symbolism that was apparent to the Iraqi people, if not the Western media. For example, in beginning the proceedings by asking Saddam to identify himself and state his former profession, Judge Rizgar demonstrated that in his courtroom Saddam was an ordinary criminal defendant, entitled to no better or worse treatment than any other criminal defendant. The defendants were seated in a traditional Iraqi dock, which resembled a cattle pen with three rows of chairs surrounded by a four-foot-high wooden railing, as opposed to the "cage" that some media outlets had reported would be used. The judges decided that the defendants should be seated in order of their importance. The back row consisted of the lesser defendants. Seated in the middle row was the fifty-four-year-old Barzan al-Tikriti, the white-mustached former chief of Saddam's intelligence agency, who wore army fatigues and a red-checkered kaffiyeh. Next to Barzan sat Taha Yassin Ramadan, the gray-bearded former commander general of the People's Army and vice president of Iraq; he wore a dark suit and a black-and-white checkered kaffiyeh. A now-bearded Saddam occupied the first row, dressed in a dark suit and a starched white shirt buttoned to the neck without a tie, with a copy of the Koran clasped tightly in his hand.

It was particularly significant that the person seated next to Saddam was sixty-year-old Awad Hamad al-Bandar, who had been the chief judge of Saddam Hussein's Revolutionary Court, since at the core of the Dujail trial was the question of whether the 1984 Revolutionary Court proceedings had been a sham. According to the prosecution's opening statement, under Saddam Hussein, the Revolutionary Court was used as a weapon against Saddam's political opponents, and Judge Awad al-Bandar himself allegedly signed the warrant to execute the 148 victims of Dujail. In this way, the Dujail trial would be similar to the famous *Altstoetter* ("Justice") trial at Nuremberg, which we'll return to in chapter 8. This was said to be one of the most important of all of the Nuremberg trials, since it established the precedent that judges who participate in a court system that perverts the law can be held responsible as accomplices to crimes against humanity—a precedent that had not been employed in the sixty intervening years, until the Dujail case.

After Judge Rizgar had the defendants identify themselves, he established that each was represented by counsel, and then took thirty minutes to explain to them their rights before the IHT. Judge Rizgar used this opportunity to demonstrate to the defendants and the world that the IHT was governed by stringent standards of due process, modeled on the rules of procedure of the Yugoslavia and Rwanda tribunals.

This was followed by the prosecutor's recitation of the charges and the main facts that the prosecution intended to prove at trial. The most significant revelation was that the prosecutor intended to enter into evidence written orders, signed by Saddam himself, for the retaliatory actions against the town of Dujail and its citizens. In this way, the world learned that Saddam might be convicted on the strength of his own records, much like the Nazis were at Nuremberg.

As the three hours of proceedings drew to a close, Judge Rizgar announced that the tribunal had decided to grant the defense motion for a temporary adjournment of the trial to give the defense team forty more days to prepare its case, to give the prosecution time to guarantee the safety of reluctant witnesses, and to give the Iraq government a chance to publish the new (August 11, 2005) revised version of the IHT statute in the *Official Gazette* (similar to the U.S. *Congressional Record*), which was necessary for it to come into force.

Former State Department peace negotiator Richard Holbrooke told CNN that when the Dujail trial begins, "the Iraqi people will discover how pathetic a creature Saddam is, just as we discovered on December 13, 2003, when we found him in a spider hole, that this is just a pathetic, small man."[7] But in the months to come, the world saw a very different

Saddam. He was cunning, arrogant, forceful, at times petulant, but rarely pathetic, and never small.

*Day 2 (November 28, 2005)*

Despite a decent start, the credibility of the Iraqi High Tribunal immediately suffered a severe blow. The morning after the Dujail trial opened, defense counsel Saddoun al-Janabi, who was representing defendant Awad Hamad al-Bandar, was dragged from his car, kidnapped, and found dead from a gunshot to the head. Awad al-Bandar's son would step in to serve as his father's lawyer for the remainder of the trial. A few days later, on November 8, a second member of the defense team, Abdel Muhammed al-Zubaidi, who was representing former Iraqi vice president Taha Yassin Ramadan, was fatally shot while driving in his car. The two dozen surviving defense lawyers, joined by representatives of human rights organizations, made statements to the press, forcefully arguing that the tragic deaths, amid the rapidly expanding sectarian violence in Iraq, demonstrated that the Iraqi High Tribunal did not have the capacity to guarantee a fair trial, and that the trial should be terminated or moved to another country.

For the Iraqi High Tribunal and its international advisers, the situation was particularly frustrating. According to one member of the Regime Crimes Liaison Office, "the security options offered to the defense counsel before trial were at least as good as those being offered to other participants in the trial." The first time that he met Khamees al-Obeydi, Marine Major Lawrence Lee specifically remembers warning him that his safety could best be protected by moving into the protected International, or Green, Zone. The IHT and its international advisers felt the deaths could have been avoided if the defense lawyers had only agreed to have their faces obscured from the television broadcasts and their identities withheld from the press, following the example of four of the five judges, three of the four prosecutors, and most of the witnesses—all of whom survived the trial. But the defense counsel chose not to follow their lead because they wanted to be able to try the case in the court of public opinion. In fact, the day before he was killed, defense lawyer Abdel Muhammed al-Zubaidi had given an extensive interview to *The New York Times*.

Immediately after the murder of the first defense lawyer, the U.S. government, via the Regime Crimes Liaison Office, offered again to relocate the two dozen other defense lawyers and their families into the Green Zone or locations outside of Iraq. The security arrangements had been put into place for defense attorneys well before trial. Some members of the defense team complained that they would actually increase the danger to them and to their families by moving into the Shia-dominated area. This rationale overlooks the reality that the area was protected by coalition military units. The RCLO also offered to give them around-the-clock guards for their temporary homes and offices and to provide armed escorts for the remainder of the trial. After being warned of the possible personal threats, some of the defense lawyers chose to remain outside the Green Zone at their own homes. They gave various reasons for declining the complete safety offered by the International Zone, among them that they still had practices and clients in Baghdad. Short of forcibly relocating them, the IHT could not have protected them better.

This was not the first trial in the world in which there was a high risk to the safety of the trial participants. The same types of concerns have been successfully dealt with in the trials of war criminals in Sierra Leone, major drug lords in Central America, and major terrorists in Europe and Latin America. The difference here was that defense attorneys wanted their faces and identities to be broadcast and then refused to accept protection, creating a recipe for disaster. The deaths of defense attorneys created a lasting impression reinforced by many pundits that the circumstances of the Dujail trial would not permit a fair and equitable defense. However, on the issue of attorney access and safety, RCLO officials point out correctly that every defendant was represented by at least one counsel of his choice every single day of investigation and trial. In fact, there was never a single occasion when the security environment prevented defense counsel from seeing their clients, though not always at the precise time they requested.

Judge Rizgar began the second day of the trial by expressing the court's deep regret for the deaths of the two defense lawyers. Behind the scenes the judge was able to work out a compromise with the defense team, in which the IHT would pay for them to hire private security guards of their choice, while some of them accepted the previous offer to relocate to the

Green Zone or outside of Iraq. At least one of the defense team families was safely relocated outside Iraq.

Next, two of the defense counsel—Najib al-Nu'aymi, former minister of justice of Qatar, and Ramsey Clark, former U.S. attorney general—asked to speak about the competence and legality of the court, with al-Nu'aymi declaring, "We will reserve the right not to listen to witnesses or do anything before the court settles whether it is competent to look into criminal cases, according to international law and local law." Judge Rizgar gently responded: "We will reply to the points you made in your motion in writing at the proper time." While it is the practice of international criminal tribunals to issue written opinions on preliminary issues regarding legitimacy at the start of the trial, the IHT judges decided they would wait until they wrote the judgment, which would include a section analyzing the issue. Waiting to the end of the trial to address such matters was consistent with Iraqi law, but the failure of the IHT to issue a written opinion on this important issue at the start of the trial did not sit well with the defense counsel, who continually raised the question in an increasingly shrill manner during subsequent trial sessions, culminating in their decision to boycott the end of the trial. Had Judge Rizgar and his colleagues instead followed the international practice, and definitively decided the legitimacy issue in a written opinion at the start of the trial, it would have forced Ramsey Clark and the other lawyers to focus on the evidence rather than on the question of legitimacy for the remainder of the trial.

For Ramsey Clark, this seemed to be the primary reason he had signed on to defend Saddam Hussein. Clark was the founder and current chairman of the International Action Center, one of the largest antiwar movements in the United States. A vocal critic of U.S. military actions around the globe, in op-eds and newspaper interviews he had called U.S. government officials "international outlaws," accusing them of "killing innocent people because we don't like their leader." Clark wrote that rather than Saddam Hussein, it was the United States that should be on trial, terming the invasion unlawful and pointing to the subsequent destructive siege of Fallujah, torture at Abu Ghraib, and the U.S. military's role in the deaths of Iraqi civilians. Though his demeanor is always genteel, Clark is known for turning international trials into political stages from which to launch attacks against U.S. foreign policy, and the IHT judges' decision not to permit extensive oral argument

LEFT: Ali Shakir al-Khuzaii with his foot on Saddam's throne shortly after his return to Iraq in December 2003. In Iraqi culture, this is one of the most insulting gestures possible.

RIGHT: Saddam Hussein's half-brother Barzan Ibrahim al-Hassan al-Tikriti. Barzan was more disruptive than Saddam on many occasions and frequently made long-winded speeches. Barzan was responsible for some of the most bizarre moments during the trial, such as sitting with his back to the bench or wearing his long underwear to open court; Judge Ra'ouf often ignored Barzan's behavior. *(Courtesy of the Iraqi High Tribunal)*

LEFT: Six of the eight defendants as they looked in the first moments of the trial. Judge Rizgar's first decision was to grant their request to wear traditional coverings, but Saddam appeared in Western dress throughout the trial. *(Courtesy of the Iraqi High Tribunal)*

LEFT: On the Iraqi five-dinar notes, issued during Saddam's rule, the Code of Hammurabi is prominently displayed next to the Monument to the Unknown Soldier that Saddam built to glorify the martyrs of the Iran-Iraq War. What looks to some like a flying saucer frozen in midair was intended to represent a traditional Iraqi shield *(dira'a)* dropping from the arm of a dying Iraqi warrior. *(Courtesy of Jenny Mandeville)*

BELOW: The Adolf Eichmann trial concluded in Jerusalem in May 1962. Here, Eichmann is seen in a glass enclosure similar to what some recommended for the Baghdad courtroom. (The former Baath Party headquarters would not have supported the weight of such an enclosure, hence the more traditional Iraqi dock was built.) Eichmann was tried and executed for serving as the Third Reich's foremost facilitator for what was euphemistically termed "the Final Solution to the Jewish Problem." *(Courtesy of the U.S. Holocaust Memorial Museum)*

RIGHT: Rizgar Mohammed Amin, the Kurdish judge who began the trial as the presiding judge. *(Courtesy of the Iraqi High Tribunal)*

LEFT: Judge Ra'ouf Rasheed Abdel Rahman, who presided over the trial and was one of the driving forces behind the lengthy opinion, had the experience and judicial presence to battle with Saddam and the other disruptive defendants to retain control of the courtroom. *(Courtesy of the Iraqi High Tribunal)*

RIGHT: The announcement of the tribunal statute by Judge Dara Nur al-Din. Achmed Chalabi is to his right; Chalabi's nephew Salem Chalabi, who played a key role in drafting the statute, is on Judge Dara's far left.

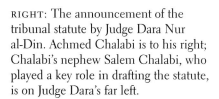

LEFT: Munqith Takleef Mibdir al-Firaoon with Professor Newton. Prosecutor Munqith was the deputy prosecutor for the Dujail trial and later assumed the lead in prosecuting the Anfal genocide case. He was also present during Saddam's execution; his voice is heard on the execution video, pleading for dignity and respect during the dictator's last moments.

LEFT: Judge Aref Abdul Razaq al-Shahen with Professor Scharf. Judge Aref served as the president of the tribunal and the head of the appeals chamber.

BELOW: All of the defendants present in the dock. The glare of Awad Hamad al-Bandar, sitting to Saddam's right, was typical throughout the trial. *(Courtesy of the Iraqi High Tribunal)*

BELOW: Ramsey Clark at the Baghdad airport en route to the courtroom, escorted by Marine Major Lawrence Lee.

ABOVE: This never-before-published photo shows Saddam Hussein as he appeared shortly after his capture by American forces.

RIGHT: One of the death sentences that was entered into evidence, showing Saddam's approval for the judicially imposed murder of citizens without a trial. (*Courtesy of the Iraqi High Tribunal*)

BELOW: The entrance to Saddam's Republican Palace in Baghdad. Originally, it was built to house the British embassy; Saddam later added large ornate wings on either side of the building and decorated it with his initials on almost every wall and fixture.

LEFT: One of the cast heads of Saddam Hussein being removed from the roof of the Republican Palace in December 2003.

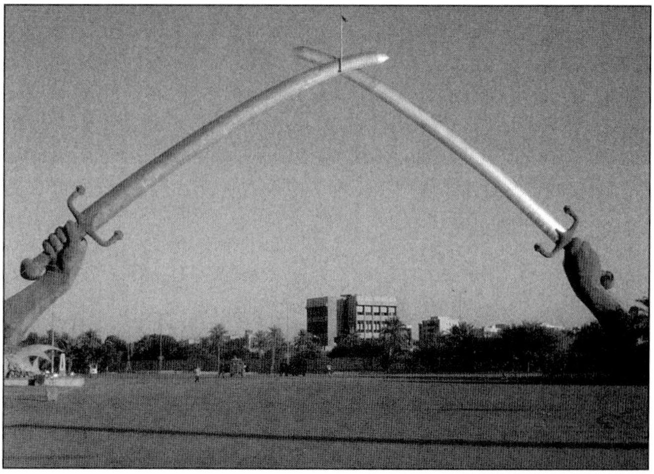

ABOVE RIGHT: Hands of Victory in Baghdad, reputedly based on castings of Saddam's hands. The speed bumps around the base of the monument, made from the helmets of dead Iranian soldiers, were worn down by the treads of the American First Armored Division.

BELOW: The phrase emblazoned on the front wall of the IHT courtroom is an excerpt from the Koran: "When you judge between people you judge with justice." Here Professor Newton is accompanied by Judge Abdullah al-Amiri, who presided over Trial Chamber 2 as the Anfal genocide trial began. Charges against Saddam Hussein were dismissed in the genocide case following his execution on December 30, 2006.

INSET: Ja'afar al-Moussawi, chief prosecutor of the Iraqi High Tribunal.

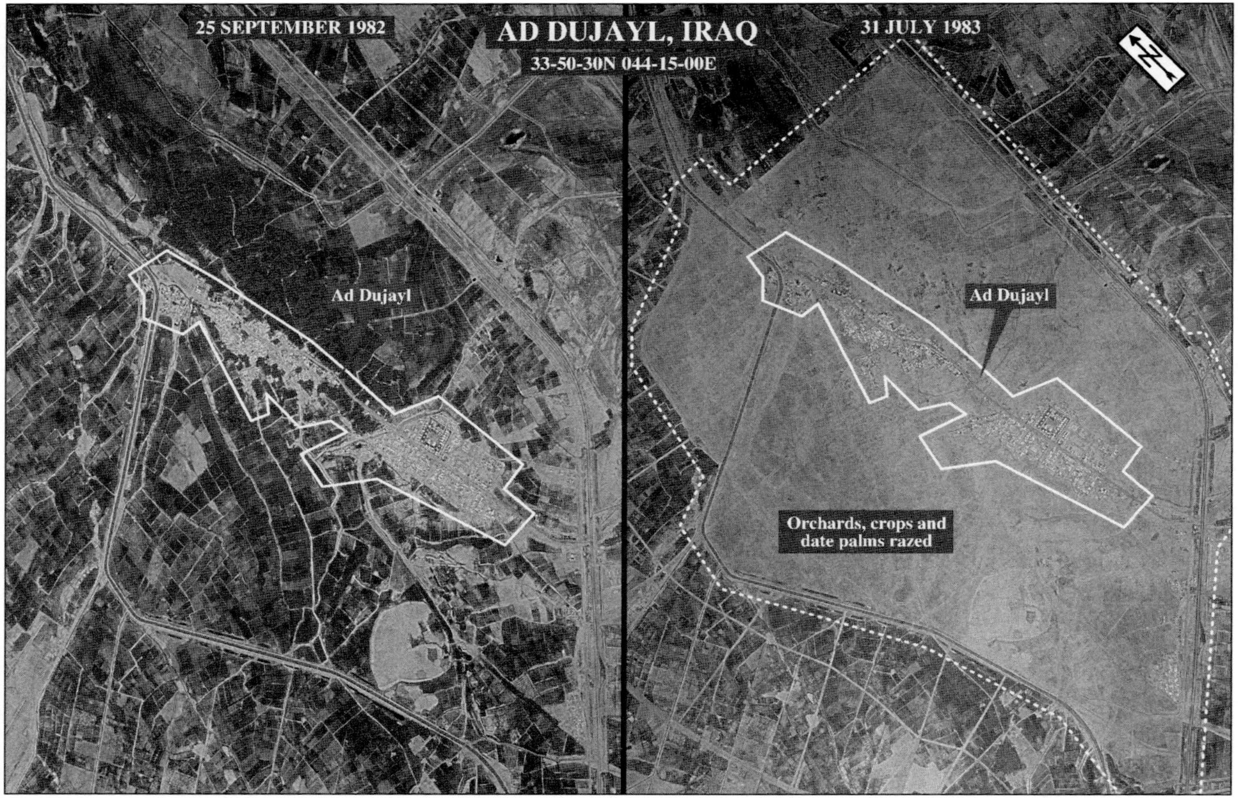


The destruction of 5,000 acres surrounding Dujail is seen from this before-and-after image introduced during the trial. The date palms and crops were bulldozed along with the homes built in their shade. Those held responsible during the trial were convicted of the crime against humanity of inhumane acts for what the tribunal termed "collective punishment" against the people of Dujail.

The International Military Tribunal sitting in Nuremberg, Germany, rendered its judgments on September 30 and October 1, 1946. Judges from the victorious Allied nations found nineteen of the twenty-two defendants guilty on one or more counts of the indictment, and acquitted three. Twelve defendants were sentenced to death by hanging, three to life imprisonment, and the other four to imprisonment of ten to twenty years. In his opening statement, Supreme Court Justice Robert Jackson, serving as the American prosecutor, foreshadowed the Nuremberg legacy: "That four great nations, flushed with victory and stung with injury, stay the hand of vengeance and voluntarily submit their captive enemies to the judgment of the law is one of the most significant tributes that Power has ever paid to Reason." *(Courtesy of the U.S. Holocaust Memorial Museum)*

RIGHT: Ra'id Juhi Hamadi al-Sa'edi was the first Iraqi judge to confront Saddam in July 2004. He managed the transfer of eleven high-value detainees (including Saddam Hussein, Barzan al-Tikriti, Ali Hassan al-Majid, and Tariq Aziz) from coalition custody as prisoners of war, subject to the laws of war, to the legal custody of the Iraqi criminal justice system. Judge Ra'id served as the chief investigative judge for the IHT, and later as the official spokesperson of the tribunal. His work prepared both the Dujail case and the Anfal genocide case for trial. (*Courtesy of Ryan Durdella*)

about the legitimacy of the tribunal robbed him of his chance to do so in the Saddam trial. For that he would make the judges pay.

As the second day of trial got under way, the lead prosecutor, Ja'afar al-Moussawi, displayed a video of Saddam interrogating the citizens of Dujail immediately following the July 8, 1982, assassination attempt. Thus, the prosecution sought to begin its case by establishing through video images the high degree of personal involvement Saddam had in crafting the regime's retaliatory response to the attack on his life.

Next, Judge Rizgar read the testimony of the trial's most important eyewitness, a high-level Baathist regime insider named Waddah Ismai'il Khalil, who had recently succumbed to a terminal illness and was therefore not available to testify in court. Judge Rizgar explained that the five judges, along with the prosecutors and two members of the defense team, had questioned and cross-examined Waddah on his deathbed in a U.S. military hospital during the recess, and that Waddah's statement had been transcribed for use at trial.

"On the date of the incident, 8 July 1982, I was director of the investigation department at the [Mukhabarat] Intelligence Service which was headed by defendant Barzan at the time," Waddah's statement began. "He told me that defendant Saddam Hussien's convoy had come under fire in Dujail during his visit over there. I went to Dujail along with a number of directors of the intelligence service," Waddah explained. "I then went to the site of the incident, which was adjacent to the Dujail court. It was a mud wall. In my view, the individuals, who numbered about seven to twelve, opened fire from behind the wall," he continued. "Shortly after my arrival there on the day of the incident, defendant Barzan showed up at the Baath Party headquarters, accompanied by the interior minister, Sa'dun Shakir. The security, intelligence, and military forces received orders from Barzan, and proceeded to arrest more than four hundred people in the town. The detainees were moved to the Mukhabarat headquarters in Baghdad by Mercedes cars belonging to the intelligence service."

According to Waddah's statement, after the Dujail residents had been interrogated by "our intelligence officers," the detainees were moved to Abu Ghraib prison. Waddah added, "I was very sure, through the examination of the place, that the number of individuals who had opened fire on the motorcade was not more than twelve. I established that in the report I submitted to Barzan. I don't know why they arrested this large number of citizens." Turning to the role of defendant Taha Yassin Ramadan, Waddah said that "a committee was formed under Taha about a month later. The main role of the committee was to raze the groves in Dujail."

Throughout the trial, the defendants and their lawyers would refer back to Waddah's statements as completely fabricated, since Waddah's dependence on American authorities for medical aid in his dying days had rendered him extremely vulnerable to suggestion. The prosecution, on the other hand, said Waddah was perhaps the only witness who had nothing to lose by telling the truth since he knew his days were numbered.

The second trial session ended with a colloquy between Barzan and Judge Rizgar about Barzan's health, which provided an early indication of the IHT's administrative lapses. Barzan told Judge Rizgar that three weeks earlier his lawyers had provided a written request to the tribunal for his release because he was suffering from cancer and needed tests and aggressive treatment without delay. When Judge Rizgar said that he had not yet received the correspondence, Barzan shot back: "This is indirect murder, Your Honor. For a year and six months, I have been asking for tests while they ignore my request. Are they going to carry out the tests only after my situation has deteriorated, then diagnose the disease, and after that you will receive my letter?"

Although Barzan would continue to complain about his health on numerous occasions, what the media did not report was that he and the other defendants were under American health care for the entire period of their detention before and during the trial. The last thing the Americans wanted was a repeat of the Milosevic fiasco, where the Serb leader died of a heart attack just a few months before the conclusion of his four-year-long trial, requiring dismissal of his case. Consequently, the defendants' health was closely monitored and there was a medical team on standby at the courthouse whenever court was in session. Saddam even had a hernia operation during the summer of 2004.

*Day 3 (December 5, 2005)*

Judge Rizgar began the third session with a surprising announcement: The judges had decided to allow the defense counsel to present a brief oral argument on the legality of the court, after all. With Ramsey Clark whispering in his ear, defense counsel Najib Al-Nu'aymi rose to present three arguments challenging the legitimacy of the proceedings. First, he said that "according to international law, a court is considered illegal if it is established under occupation." He read paragraphs from the Fourth Geneva Convention, which stipulate that "the occupation force should not change the status of state officials or judges in the occupied territories," that the penal laws of the country must remain in force, and that the occupation force cannot try people for actions that occurred before the occupation. Second, he noted that according to international law, special courts should not be established. He added that he felt the IHT was not independent, and was being influenced by government officials. Finally, he argued that the IHT was not competent to retroactively try Saddam for acts that occurred in the 1980s, when he had been arrested on December 13, 2003, and the law establishing the IHT and enumerating the crimes under its jurisdiction had not been issued until October 18, 2005. Judge Rizgar did not, however, deny these motions until the issuance of the written judgment in December 2006, leaving the unfortunate impression throughout the trial that the arguments about legitimacy had simply fallen on deaf ears.

Next, Judge Rizgar called in Ahmad Hassan Muhammad al-Haideri, a forty-year-old resident of Dujail who had witnessed the mass arrests and destruction of plantations following the July 8, 1982, assassination attempt. This was the first live witness from Dujail to address the court, and he literally spoke on behalf of the thousands from many tribes and many towns throughout Iraq who had suffered under the Baathist regime. After taking the tribunal's oath, Ahmad told the court that subsequent to the attack on Saddam's convoy he and about five hundred other Dujail townspeople were taken to the Interrogation Department of the Mukhabarat Intelligence Service in Baghdad, and added that several of his friends (whom he named) had died during interrogation. He also identified defendant Taha Yassin Ramadan as the person who supervised the destruction of the farms around Dujail after the incident. Barzan rose to his feet and scoffed at Ahmad's "fabrications," in particular that five hundred people could have been taken to the Intelligence Service building. "Judge, go to the building to see if it could accommodate five hundred people. It simply cannot," he said.

This witness was particularly important because he was one of the very few to testify openly during the trial, with his face shown on television and his name appearing in the newspapers. His testimony was powerful and memorable. Defense counsel Khalil al-Dulaimi pointed out eleven reasons why the court should not believe Ahmad's testimony, starting with the fact that he had been only fourteen at the time his family was allegedly sent to the torture center and their home was destroyed. Barzan remarked afterward that the witness "should have sought a career in television, given his good acting skills." Sadly, Ahmad paid a terrible price for his courageous decision to testify on camera: subsequent to his courtroom appearance, two of his cousins were kidnapped, a nephew was killed, and a brother was shot through the legs and permanently crippled.[8]

*Day 4 (December 6, 2005)*

Judge Rizgar opened the fourth session by noting that based on the witness protection provisions of the IHT statute, most of the witnesses' names would not be made public and they would testify from behind a curtain. Such witnesses would be identified in court by an initial, starting with A. This drew an immediate protest from Saddam, who asked, "How can we address the witnesses, explore their credibility, if we can't see them and only know them by initials?" While the outside world will never know the true identity of the "letter witnesses," the judges, prosecutors, and defense counsel were all privy to their real names and backgrounds. However, as a security measure, the identities of such witnesses were not provided to the defense counsel until the morning of the day they were to testify, prompting human rights organizations to argue that this procedure did not give the defense timely information necessary to prepare for their cross-examination of witnesses.

Witness A began to testify from behind a curtain, hidden from the public gallery, television cameras, and defendants but visible to the judges, prosecutors, and defense counsel. Saddam, who had himself been trained as a lawyer, again interrupted: "According to the rules of this court, the defendant and the witness must face each other." "Yes," Judge Rizgar answered, "they will face each other. By that I mean they will hear each other's voice."

Witness A provided some of the most emotionally compelling testimony of any witness. Crying throughout, she described how, during her detention at the Mukhabarat Intelligence Building, she had been beaten with hoses and prodded and tortured with electricity to force her to confess that she was somehow involved in the assassination attempt. When the interrogation was concluded, she said she was taken with the other Dujail detainees to Abu Ghraib. "The prisoners there had envied donkeys for enjoying their freedom, while they were kept in the worst conditions imaginable and treated inhumanely," she said. She told the court that she was one of the few from Dujail to be returned home to the village, and that she had lost everything, her family, her property, her future.

Several other individuals, identified as Witness B, Witness C, Witness D, and Witness E, gave similar eyewitness accounts from behind the curtain of the mass arrests, torture, and retaliatory destruction of Dujail. At the end of the final witness's testimony, Saddam asked for and was given permission to question the witness. "In the name of God, the merciful, the compassionate," he began. "The Americans came to Iraq under a lie. To remain in Iraq for the duration they want, they produced this theatrical piece of trial," he stated. "The Americans and the Zionists want to execute Saddam Hussein, and they will be smaller than a bedbug if they do not see him executed," he added. "My people ask me, and I am ethically bound to call them to fight and to keep fighting. Therefore, these testimonies, Brother Judge, are meant to disparage a march of thirty-five years. During that time, we built great Iraq with our tears. This march is being disparaged. Therefore, the people are being disparaged. I do not believe that any true Iraqi, and you are a true Iraqi, accepts this." Finally, Judge Rizgar lost patience and instructed Saddam, "Please ask the witness the question that you want to pose to him." When Saddam threatened to boycott the proceedings if he was not permitted to say his piece, Judge Rizgar adjourned the day's session.

Like many observers of the trial, the authors were stunned to see that Judge Rizgar had permitted Saddam to question the witnesses. There had been much concern prior to the trial that Saddam might try to emulate Slobodan Milosevic by asserting a right to act as his own lawyer, thereby enabling him to appear on the nightly news throughout the Middle East, railing against the illegal U.S. invasion of Iraq, insisting that the United

States was complicit in Iraqi war crimes against Iran, and encouraging his followers to step up the acts of violence against the United States and new Iraqi government. To avoid this, at the authors' urging, when the Iraqi Transitional National Assembly promulgated the IHT statute anew on August 11, 2005, it replaced Article 20(d)(4), which stated the accused has a right "to defend himself in person or through legal assistance of his own choosing," with a new provision, Article 19(4)(d), which states only that the accused has a right "to procure legal counsel of his choosing." This amendment was meant to ensure that Saddam would not be able to speak at his trial until the end, when he could take the stand in his own defense. What we did not at the time comprehend, however, was that this legislative change would not accomplish the goal if the judges decided to follow the unique Iraqi legal tradition of permitting a defendant to cross-examine each witness after his lawyer had done so.[9] By importing this tradition into the Dujail trial, Judge Rizgar had opened Pandora's box. Perhaps more than any other decision, this would lead to the chaos in the days to follow.

It is noteworthy that Saddam's diatribe came after the emotional testimony of witnesses who had described in vivid detail the horrible acts of torture they endured at the hands of Saddam's subordinates. Saddam knew that this moving testimony could be extremely damaging to his standing within the Iraqi Sunni community unless he could find a way to quickly distract media and public attention from it. In this he succeeded, as the media devoted far more attention to Saddam's outburst than to the substance of the compelling witness testimony. Sixty years ago, Nuremberg chief prosecutor Robert Jackson had a similar experience with defendant Hermann Göring, who at the height of the prosecution's case was seen "thumbing his nose" at another defendant. Jackson described this as an "irrelevancy that was conveyed to the American reader as the important and sensational event of the day." Throughout the trial Jackson felt that the media tended to "emphasize to the reader what had no importance to the legal case."[10] This was exactly what Saddam was counting on.

*Day 5 (December 7, 2005)*

The fifth trial session began with Judge Rizgar explaining that Saddam had elected not to attend the session and that the court would inform him of what took place during his absence, in accordance with the Iraqi Criminal Code. Consistent with international standards of due process, Judge Rizgar could have ordered Saddam brought to the courtroom by force, and even placed in a glass booth as happened in the Israeli trial of Adolf Eichmann, to prevent Saddam from further disrupting the trial with his tirades. But that would only add to the appearance of injustice, which Judge Rizgar was desperately trying to avoid. So instead, arrangements were made for Saddam to follow the trial by video link from the detention center, a strategy that other international trials have successfully employed. The international advisers believed that Saddam would quickly choose to come back to court once he realized that his absence did not derail the trial.

The session featured the testimony of Witness F, who spoke from behind a curtain with his voice electronically distorted. Like those before him, the witness was a resident of Dujail who described the events of July 8, 1982, and the interrogation and torture that followed. During the testimony, defendant Barzan repeatedly interrupted Witness F, asking about certain details. After a while, Judge Rizgar told Barzan that he should pose his questions through the presiding judge and stop disrupting the testimony. In the interest of more efficient courtroom management, the judges would have been wise to insist on such a practice, which is how most civil law countries handle questioning of witnesses. Instead, both the lawyers and the defendants continued to be permitted to ask questions directly of witnesses throughout the remainder of the trial.

### *Day 6 (December 21, 2005)*

During the sixth session, Saddam had returned to the courtroom only to interrupt the proceedings with the shocking claim that he and his codefendants had been tortured by American prison guards several months before the start of the trial. "They claim they were tortured," he said, referring to the testimony of the previous several witnesses. "What about how we've been treated by the Americans?" Saddam asked. To which prosecutor Ja'afar responded: "Did they beat you? Did someone truly beat you?" And Saddam shot back, "Yes, many times, all over my body." This allegation was shocking on its face, and if true, would have overshadowed every other aspect of the due process protections of the IHT. The allegation was ludicrous and completely unsubstantiated, but Saddam knew how to play to the popular Iraqi consciousness, particularly in the backlash over the graphic pictures and accounts emerging from Abu Ghraib.

In the first four sessions of the trial (October 19, November 28, December 5, and December 6), Saddam had taken advantage of the opportunity to freely air his grievances on several occasions, but so far his sole complaints of mistreatment were that he had not been provided a pen and paper with which to take notes, that he was given only six cigarettes a day (and did not like the brand), that he was required to wear the same suit for several days without a clean change of clothing, and that he was forced to walk up stairs rather than take an elevator to reach the courtroom. Had he really been subject to acts of torture, he certainly would have mentioned it then, rather than confine his complaints to these minor inconveniences.

In this context, Ja'afar responded sarcastically: "I visited the detention places in July when it was very hot and saw that the defendants all had air-conditioned cells even though Baghdad was without electricity. But if you have been mistreated by the Americans, we can ask that you be transferred into Iraqi custody," something Ja'afar knew Saddam would want to avoid at all costs. Before the two sides could get into a shouting match, Judge Rizgar wisely indicated that the defendant's claims would be fully investigated before the trial resumed again on January 24, 2006.

From a legal standpoint, the reader might be wondering what would have happened if the investigation had revealed that Saddam had in fact been subject to "serious mistreatment" at the hands of his jailers. This was a weighty charge that could have had considerable consequences. According to Article 17 of the Iraqi High Tribunal statute, the judges may refer to the precedent of the international criminal tribunals for the former Yugoslavia and Rwanda for guidance. The issue was addressed by the appeals chamber of the Yugoslavia and Rwanda tribunals in the case of Dragan Nikolic. The appeals chamber stated that in cases in which pretrial treatment of the defendant rises to the level of serious human rights violations (torture or cruel, inhuman, and degrading treatment), the tribunal must dismiss the case since "it would be inappropriate for a court of law to try the victims of these abuses." But the appeals chamber found that the mistreatment in the Nikolic case was not serious enough to merit dismissal (he had been abducted in the middle of the night and roughed up but not permanently injured), stating that apart from the most "exceptional of cases," the remedy of setting aside jurisdiction would "usually be disproportionate" with respect to a defendant charged with crimes against humanity. Although it found no evidence to substantiate Saddam's claims of mistreatment, the IHT never issued a written report to that effect, once again leaving the unfortunate impression that it had failed to take an important issue seriously.

According to one of the lawyers responsible for overseeing Saddam's treatment in custody, he was "probably the most well-treated, best-cared-for, and most heavily guarded prisoner in the world." As Saddam left the courtroom that day, he was reportedly overheard joking with his American guard: "I know you've treated me very well; it was just something I said for the court."[11] In fact, it turned out that the American army officer overseeing the detention facility was later charged in a general court-martial for aiding and abetting the enemy because of his generous treatment of detainees. According to public reports, the officer used government funds to buy hair dye and Cuban cigars for Saddam Hussein, and was alleged to have permitted detainees to use his official cell phone to make calls to unknown parties with no oversight or authorization. During the court-martial, the defense argued that the officer was merely trying to treat the detainees under his authority, including Saddam Hussein, "with dignity and respect." Though he was acquitted of the aiding and abetting charges, the officer was convicted of the improper handling of classified information, conduct unbecoming an officer, for providing special privileges to an Iraqi interpreter with whom he had an "inappropriate relationship," and failing to obey a lawful order. Despite his twenty-eight years of service and favorable reports from the International Committee of the Red Cross related to the management of the facility, the military judge sentenced him to confinement for two years, forfeiture of all pay and allowances, a reprimand, and dismissal from the service. The officer is serving time at Fort Leavenworth, Kansas, as this book goes to press.

In the Camp Cropper meeting room, Saddam got to smoke cigars and eat with his lawyers. He also had plenty of gifts brought to him—allowed were factory-packaged food items, packaged cigars, clothing, and books.

Each item was inspected in front of Saddam's attorney, and if it was approved, the lawyer then gave it directly to Saddam. It was policy to do whatever was needed to facilitate meetings with his lawyers. When his entire group of defense lawyers was present for a meeting, they were allowed to use the Camp Cropper courtroom. As there were no conference tables, American troops hauled the large tables up from the second floor to the fourth floor in order to accommodate the defense team. There could be no doubt that Saddam was treated very well during his captivity, but the mere allegation was designed to appeal to an Arab street that spread rumors with a relentless and invariable swiftness.

*Day 7 (December 22, 2005)*

Several witnesses testified during the seventh session of the trial about the attack on Dujail and the presence of the Popular Army forces (which defendant Taha Yassin Ramadan had commanded) in the aftermath of the assassination attempt. The first of these testified that he had been thirteen at the time of the Dujail incident. He and his family had been taken to the local police station, and then transferred to Abu Ghraib prison, where each male member of his family was taken out of the cell in succession and tortured. His father and older brother never returned from the torture session. He and the remaining members of his family were then sent to Layya prison in the desert, where they endured several months in the harshest conditions imaginable. When they were finally permitted to return to Dujail, they found that their homes and orchards had been demolished.

In the midst of this heartrending tale, defendant Barzan rose to point out to the judges that under Iraqi law, the testimony of someone who was a child when he witnessed a crime cannot be used in court. Shouting at the prosecutor, he exclaimed: "There were thousands of people in Dujail in 1982. Why can't you bring us witnesses who were adults?"

The next witness, who had been a young mother back in 1982, described how her children were imprisoned with her at Abu Ghraib for several years following the Dujail incident. To which Saddam interjected: "When we put women in prison they wish to take their children with them because otherwise there would be no one to take care of them, so we let them take their children with them. Where's the crime in that?"

When the chief prosecutor, Ja'afar, asked one of the witnesses to tell the court about the torture and deaths of the Dujail detainees that occurred during interrogation, defense counsel Khamees al-Obeydi interrupted: "Our role is to find and obtain justice. Prosecutor, your role is a consultative one." To which Ja'afar retorted, "You don't assign our roles." This exchange reflected the trial participants' struggle to understand their functions under the IHT statute, which was modeled upon the more adversarial approach of the statutes of the international tribunals and therefore diverged somewhat from what they were accustomed to under Iraqi law. While American readers may view Ja'afar's approach as legitimate for a prosecutor, the perception that Ja'afar was somehow inappropriately "against them" would later prompt the defense team to file a motion for his dismissal from the case.

*Day 8 (January 29, 2006)*

When the trial resumed a month later, a new face was sitting on the bench. In the place of Judge Rizgar was a newly appointed presiding judge, Ra'ouf Abdul Rahman, a stout, balding, sixty-four-year-old Kurd from the town of Halabja, where Saddam Hussein's security forces reportedly killed more than five thousand Kurdish Iraqis in a chemical gas attack in 1988. Judge Ra'ouf graduated from Baghdad University's law school in 1963. He worked as a lawyer in Baghdad, then in the city of Sulaymaniyah, and was appointed as the chief judge of the Kurdistan Appeals Court in 1996.

Judge Ra'ouf began the session by explaining that he had been selected to replace Judge Rizgar, who had resigned "for administrative reasons." There are many different stories about why Judge Rizgar stepped down. Some believe he was pressured by Iraqi government officials, who were not happy with his leniency toward Saddam and Barzan. Some believe it was the negative media coverage. Judge Rizgar had been mercilessly attacked in the Iraqi media, which fully exploited its new journalistic freedoms. His closest friends have confirmed that he was quite upset that the president of the IHT, Judge Jamal Mohammed Mustafa (who died of natural causes during the Dujail trial), would not speak out publicly to defend his management of the case. Still others think he was afraid for his life and the safety of his family. But the authors have reason to believe Judge Rizgar's resignation was at least in part due to the fact that, as a Kurd from northern Iraq, Rizgar's command of Arabic was shaky and he felt that he was not following everything that the Shiite witnesses, Sunni defendants, and their lawyers were saying in the courtroom. This also may explain his repeated failure to cut off Saddam's microphone in a timely manner when the former dictator would launch into one of his frequent diatribes. Whatever the reason, this changing of the guard midway through the trial further eroded the international perception of the IHT's legitimacy.

Judge Rizgar was originally to be replaced by Judge Sa'eed al-Hammashi, who was one of the four other members of the panel trying the Dujail case. But just hours after the IHT had announced that Judge Sa'eed would be assuming Judge Rizgar's position as presiding judge, Iraq's Higher National Commission for De-Baathification accused Judge Sa'eed of having been a member of the Baath Party. Under Article 33 of the IHT statute, "No person who was previously a member of the disbanded Baath Party may be appointed a judge" of the court. The commission, which was led by Achmed Chalabi, never provided any evidence of Judge Sa'eed's Baath Party membership, however, and Judge Sa'eed continues to maintain to this day that he was never a member of the party. Nevertheless, to avoid further diminution of the reputation of the IHT, Judge Sa'eed was quickly removed from the Dujail trial chamber, and Judge Ra'ouf was appointed in his place. It was never clear to the authors just who at the De-Baathification Commission had targeted Judge Sa'eed, but this incident indicated that the commission was being used as a tool of some party to interfere with the IHT. Judge Sa'eed later told one of the authors that his removal from the trial "was like being put into deep freeze." He wanted to serve, he was still a member of the IHT, but the tribunal's president never assigned him to another trial panel. (As this book goes to press, the IHT is on its fourth trial and Judge Sa'eed is still on the sidelines.)

Judge Ra'ouf had originally been appointed to Trial Chamber 2, which was about to try the Anfal case, a case involving allegations that Saddam and his henchmen had murdered over one hundred thousand Kurds in northern Iraq in the late 1980s. As it turned out, the shuffling of judges meant that a Kurd would preside over the rest of the Dujail trial, which concerned Shiite victims, and a Shiite judge would preside over the Anfal trial, which concerned Kurdish victims, thereby avoiding what would surely have been a perceived source of bias.

By judicial temperament, the stern and uncompromising Judge Ra'ouf was Judge Rizgar's polar opposite, a fact hammered home by the judge's pronouncement that he intended to bring far more discipline to the proceedings. But at the same time, Judge Ra'ouf assured the defendants that all of their rights would be preserved. "The defendants will be safe in our hands; for as Imam Ali said, 'If you have the ability to oppress people, then you should remember the power of God over you.'" With respect to the lawyers, Judge Ra'ouf announced a new approach designed to cut down on disruptions. "The defense lawyers," he said, "will have the right to ask questions, but not to make speeches, and questions must be via a lead Iraqi lawyer."

At that point the newest member of the defense team, Saleh al-Armuti, the head of the Jordanian Bar Association, stood up and said, "I want to address the court." Judge Ra'ouf hissed in response: "Sit down. Not now. Do not interrupt the court," and banged his gavel repeatedly until al-Armuti was seated. Then Barzan jumped to his feet, saying, "I need to explain my medical situation. My illness requires medical treatment that I can't get in this prison. Why don't you release me?" Judge Ra'ouf responded, "Listen, make this demand through your lawyers, and when we get it we'll refer it to the medical committee. Now, sit down!" But Barzan remained standing, bellowing, "I will not sit down," and added, "This court is illegal and the daughter of adultery." Judge Ra'ouf had had enough and ordered the guards to remove Barzan from the courtroom without further discussion.

Saddam then stood up and shouted, "Down with America! Down with the traitor! Long live Iraq!" He was followed by defendants Taha Yassin Ramadan and Awad Hamad al-Bandar and attorney Armuti, who all began to holler curses at the judge. Judge Ra'ouf banged his gavel repeatedly. "Sit down. Sit down." Then, turning to Armuti, he roared, "How can you do this? You are a legal man, in a court of law, not a circus. You are inciting the defendants. I can hold you in contempt for this. You are inciting them. Can you do this in your country?"

Attorney Armuti shouted back, "Yes, I do this in my country. We have our rights," and he walked out of the courtroom. Saddam's chief counsel, Khalil al-Dulaimi, then told the judge, "If he leaves, we all leave." To this, Judge Ra'ouf replied, "Okay, but if you go, you cannot come back." Saddam then interjected, "How can you conduct the trial without our lawyers?" To which Judge Ra'ouf answered, "They exceeded the limits of the court. We will use the court's standby defense lawyers."

Saddam then told the court that the defendants rejected the standby lawyers, and Saddam and Awad al-Bandar rose to their feet in an attempt to leave the courtroom. "You are removed," shouted Judge Ra'ouf in response. "The court takes this decision according to Article 158 of the Code of Criminal Procedure, which permits the judge to do what is necessary in order to control the session." Now all the retained lawyers and the primary defendants had departed, leaving just the four lesser defendants in the dock. At this point, defendant Mizhir Abdallah Ruwayyid softly addressed Judge Ra'ouf: "We are subject to the court, we respect the court, but we need our lawyers." Judge Ra'ouf turned to Mizhir and said, "The court lawyers will defend you and your rights," pointing to the six court-appointed lawyers in the room. He then took a deep breath, slowly exhaled, and said, "Call the first witness."

The media focused almost entirely on the chaotic exchanges that ensued as the new judge asserted his authority, but the fireworks only took up the first hour of the four and a half hours of the day's proceedings. Following the unceremonious departure of Barzan, Saddam, Awad al-Bandar, and their lawyers from the courtroom, the trial proceeded quite smoothly, with four of the eight defendants sitting quietly in the courtroom while three more witnesses completed their testimony.

### *Day 9 (February 1, 2006)*

Judge Ra'ouf began the ninth session of the trial by explaining that the defendants and their lawyers had violated the rules of the court by their insistence on boycotting the trial, compelling the tribunal to proceed with this session *huduran*—meaning in the absence of defendants who had waived their right to be present. Prosecutor Ja'afar interjected that despite his best efforts, he could not persuade the absent defendants to attend the session of their own accord, and that under these circumstances the court should compel the defendants to attend. To this, the head of the court-appointed defense lawyers responded, "The prosecutor requests to bring the defendants by force, but Iraqi law does not allow for this." Judge Ra'ouf said that he would conduct the day's session without the missing defendants, and then decide afterward whether to require their presence for the next session.

The first witness of the day described the role that the lower-level defendants Mizhir and Ali Diyah had played in the roundup of the Dujail detainees after the assassination attempt. "It was Mizhir who led the soldiers who took my husband and nephew. And later Ali Diyah came with more soldiers and took my brother," she said.

The next witness told the court that she had been taken with hundreds of Dujail residents to the Mukhabarat headquarters in Baghdad, where she was stripped naked, hung by the arms, and tortured. "And then a guard shouted, 'Mr. Barzan is here!' And Barzan said, 'Did she confess?' The guard said no. And Barzan told him to 'change her position.'" The witness added that, "they attached electrical wires to my fingers and toes and used electricity on me. They beat me. I still have scars." If believed, this testimony implicated Barzan in direct participation in acts of torture.

### *Days 10 and 11 (February 2 and 13, 2006)*

On February 2, the trial resumed with none of the eight defendants in court. After hearing from two witnesses, Judge Ra'ouf adjourned the trial for eleven days so he could travel back to the Kurdish area of northern Iraq to see his family. The presiding judge was separated from his family and away from his home the entire trial, and on this day he admitted privately that he was "very tired."

On February 13, the judges had decided to order the attendance of all of the defendants against their will, setting the stage for one of the most chaotic days of the trial. It was clear that things would not go smoothly when Barzan entered the courtroom in his long underwear. No sooner did the session begin but Saddam began to chant, "Long live Iraq! Long live the Arab nation! Down with the traitors! Down with Bush!" Then, turning to Judge Ra'ouf, Saddam said, "Are you a judge? Use your authority and proceed with the trial in absentia. You want to make what's in your chest feel good. You brought me here with force, why? Shame on you, Ra'ouf." At this point, Barzan jumped to his feet, shouting, "You are not Ra'ouf, you are not Ra'ouf"—a play on words since the judge's name means "kind" in Arabic.

Judge Ra'ouf shouted back, "Enough! Sit down!" He warned, "Political speeches will be rejected. I want to emphasize that we are going to implement the law if anyone tries to disrupt the process of the trial." Saddam then inquired, "I want to talk about a legal point: should the defendants be forced to attend the court without their lawyers?"

"Articles 145 and 158 say, 'The defendants must attend the trial,'" Judge Ra'ouf answered. "Your retained lawyers have abandoned you, but the court has arranged for you to be represented by court-appointed counsel," he added.

"Our lawyers didn't withdraw. You fired them," Saddam replied.

"We removed only one because he continued to make inappropriate political speeches despite our warning. The rest withdrew," Judge Ra'ouf explained.

To this, Saddam replied, "You are ignorant. We are not criminals. How can you say, 'No politics'?" Meanwhile, Barzan slid down to the floor beside the dock, where he now sat cross-legged with his back facing the judges' bench. Seeing that Barzan was at least behaving calmly, Judge Ra'ouf ignored the insult and proceeded to read the testimony of twenty-three short "complainant statements."

In Iraq, as in many other countries with a civil law system, most witnesses testify only before the investigative judge prior to the trial. The investigative judge is obligated to protect the defendants' rights by questioning such witnesses about possible bias, hostility, or prejudice that might have influenced their testimony. Such statements are provided prior to the trial to the defense and the prosecution as part of the case file, or dossier, and are usually not read in open court. When this approach was explained to the international advisers during the training sessions, a discussion ensued about how long the trial had to be in order to gain international respect and serve an educative function. We suggested that the court would be wise to depart somewhat from the Iraqi tradition by bringing witnesses in to retestify in open court. In that light, the IHT judges chose to read the twenty-three statements for the benefit of the public, since they provided further cumulative evidence of the victimization of the people of Dujail.

Next, the judges called Ahmed Hussein to the stand. "You were head of the President's Office. What do you know about the Dujail case?" Ja'afar asked the witness.

"I was deputy foreign minister in 1982. I didn't know much about Dujail," the witness replied.

"I will show you some documents and ask you for some explanation about some issues," Ja'afar told the witness as a document appeared on the television monitor, while a physical copy was provided to Ahmed. Ja'afar read the document aloud. It indicated that the Revolutionary Court had mistakenly executed two people who were not implicated in the Dujail assassination attempt, while the two who were supposed to be executed had mistakenly been set free.

"Is that your signature, as head of the President's Office, there?" Ja'afar asked. Ahmed responded with a yes. "And at the bottom of the document there is someone else's handwriting, which says, 'Coincidence should not be more merciful than us, even for people who do not deserve mercy.' Whose signature is that?" Ja'afar inquired. Ahmed answered, "That is the president's signature." "You mean the defendant, Saddam?" Ja'afar interjected. "Yes," replied the witness. This confirmation would turn out to be significant, as the defendants later claimed that virtually all the documents submitted at the trial were forgeries.

"Now here is another document," Ja'afar continued. "It says that the Dujail case is a case of a special nature. What's the meaning of this term, 'special nature'?" Ahmed answered reluctantly, "I don't know the meaning of this expression, but it seems that it's a special case, completely different from other cases. It's an assassination attempt against the president, so for sure it's a special thing."

"What about the handwriting at the bottom of this document? What does it say?" inquired Ja'afar. "It says 'Criminals sentenced to death and the sentences will be implemented,'" Ahmed replied. "And is this your handwriting?" Judge Ra'ouf interjected. "Yes, it looks like my handwriting," the witness acknowledged.

Then, becoming agitated, Ahmed said, "I refuse to answer any more of your questions." He added, "You dragged me to be a witness here. I don't accept this." Saddam and Barzan appeared to be delighted, shouting from the sidelines, "Well done! You are brave." In frustration, Judge Ra'ouf dismissed the witness.

*Day 12 (February 14, 2006)*

The twelfth trial session saw the final three witnesses for the prosecution. The defendants filed into the courtroom, chanting "God is great. God is great. Victory for the mujahideen. Down with the traitors." Saddam then announced, "We have been on hunger strike for three days because of the bad treatment by you and by your masters, the Americans."

Saddam's announcement that day must be viewed in the context of his other attempts to disrupt and discredit the trial, for example, his allegation that U.S. prison guards had tortured him, his attempt to take prayer breaks in the middle of witness testimony, and his frequent offensive outbursts (including calling the judge at various times "a son of a whore," "a traitor," and "a homosexual"). Indeed, the lead prosecutor, Ja'afar al-Moussawi, immediately told the press that Saddam and the other codefendants had eaten breakfast that very day. But later in the trial, Saddam would undertake a more rigorous hunger strike, causing his health to seriously deteriorate and prompting the IHT to order his hospitalization and force-feeding over the objections of human rights organizations that felt this violated his right to bodily autonomy.

The hunger strike can be a potent strategic weapon for a defendant determined to disrupt his trial, especially if it renders the defendant too ill to participate in the proceedings. Faced with that prospect, courts in the United States and several other countries have determined that force-feeding can be justified based on concerns for the defendant's life, for the orderly administration of justice, and over the administrative costs and burden precipitated by the defendant's hunger strikes.[12]

Judge Ra'ouf, who was not overly concerned by Saddam's announcement, ordered the defendants to sit, and promptly called the first witness. As the first witness took the oath from behind a curtain, Barzan interrupted, "Why do you change his voice? We know who this is. It's Khaled al-Amary. There's no need to change his voice." Responding to questions from prosecutor Ja'afar, the witness told the court that he was a member of the Mukhabarat at the time of the Dujail incident, and that Barzan was the head of the Mukhabarat and also in charge of Saddam's personal security. He added that Barzan was put in charge of the investigation following the assassination attempt at Dujail.

Barzan then rose to his feet and said, "I want to ask this witness about the building. Can the Mukhabarat building take four hundred persons?" To this, the witness replied, "No, it couldn't take that many; it's not so big." Growing emotional, Barzan then roared, "You see. This is what I told the investigative judge Ra'id Juhi. He only spent four hours with me, while I spent three years in a cell. This is injustice!"

Judge Ra'ouf ordered Barzan to "focus on the questions to the witness." But Barzan was just getting started, and began a self-incriminatory rant: "After I had heard from one of the president's guards about what had happened, I went to Dujail with about twenty members of the Mukhabarat. Saddam did not ask me to go there. When I arrived and saw that they had detained about eighty persons on mere suspicion, I ordered them released. And then I left. And the file on Dujail was in the hands of the general security agency, not the Mukhabarat, which is the intelligence agency. So the general security agency was responsible for the Dujail case, and I am being blamed only because I am the brother of Saddam." Barzan did not seem to understand that his diatribe was only helping to build the prosecution's case by confirming that he was in a position of command in Dujail following the assassination attempt. Judge Ra'ouf finally cut him off and ordered him to be seated.

The next witness was Fadil Tawfij, who had served as the deputy head of the Mukhabarat in 1989. Returning to the issue discussed during the testimony of Ahmed Hussein on February 13, Fadil testified that "Husayn Kamil, the head of the al-Hakimiya Special Security Force, came to me and said there was a problem. There were two Iraqis sentenced to death for the Dujail incident, but they had not been executed. And there were two that had not been sentenced to death but were mistakenly executed. So I said, 'Let's write to the president with a suggestion to amnesty the two who weren't executed.' And the President's Office answered us saying that they had the approval of the president to release these two people, and the two people who had been executed in error would be considered as martyrs and their families would receive martyr's rights."

The final prosecution witness was Hamed Yusuf Hammadi, who had been secretary to Saddam at the time of the attack in Dujail and had risen to the rank of culture minister before the 2003 American invasion. Ja'afar asked the witness if the Mukhabarat conducted the Dujail investigation, to which Hamed answered, "Yes, and then a committee headed by [defendant] Taha Yassin Ramadan took the responsibility for the investigation."

"Now let me show you a memo," Ja'afar said, as he handed Hamed a hard copy and displayed it on a large screen. "This is a memo issued by the Mukhabarat and addressed to the Revolutionary Command Council. The subject is 'Promotions and honors—secret.' And the memo mentions that according to the braveness of some members of the Muhkabarat when they faced Dawa Party members in Dujail after the assassination attempt that we are asking the president to promote them and give them awards because of their efforts. It is signed by the president of the Mukhabarat." He then asked, "There is handwriting on the memo dated July 26, 1982, and a signature. Whose signature is that?"

When the witness answered that it was defendant Barzan's signature, the court-appointed defense lawyer rose to address the court. "Since my client was the head of the Mukhabarat and he suspects the signature is a forgery, I submit the memo should be referred to experts for authentication." Judge Ra'ouf promised to discuss authentication during the upcoming documentary phase of the trial, and adjourned the court.

*Day 13 (February 28, 2006)*

February 28 and March 1 would turn out to be by far the most important two days of the trial. At the start of the thirteenth session, Judge Ra'ouf announced that the defense team's request for the dismissal of the presiding judge and the chief prosecutor for bias had been rejected by the court. Once again, no written decision was issued, though the judges would ultimately devote several pages of their judgment to the question.

This trial session was devoted to the submission of twenty-two documents, the most important of which are described below. The prosecution team spent many hours practicing the use of courtroom technology that enabled documents to be shown on the large screen. They hoped the display of documents in open court would serve as an important and tangible symbol to the Iraqi people, who could see Saddam's and the other defendants' signatures for themselves. As one observer in the courtroom put it that day, "An unaccustomed hush fell over the courtroom as Ja'afar leafed through page after page in which mass executions are discussed as calmly as purchase orders."[13]

Ja'afar began by reading a report from Barzan, who was then head of the Mukhabarat, to Saddam Hussein, dated July 13, 1982, five days after the Dujail incident.[14] The report states that the Mukhabarat managed to reach the "final results" of the investigation into the assassination attempt, and provides the names of ten people implicated in the attack. The report notes the arrest of a person named Burhan Ya'qub Majid, who confessed under interrogation that he was a member of the Dawa Party and that he was involved in the attack. The report ends with the comment, "We will let your honor know in a final and detailed report about the final steps in the case." It was signed by Barzan. The prosecutor specifically called the court's attention to three handwritten comments that, he said, Saddam made after reading the report: "Above-mentioned persons must be taken from the Min. of Interior Security and questioned; the party elements who did not ID the criminals must be questioned; the Mukhabarat must follow up those who fled." This document therefore confirmed both Barzan's supervision of the response to the Dujail incident and Saddam's knowledge that only ten people were involved in the assassination attempt.

Next, Ja'afar read a "secret" letter from Barzan to the Revolutionary Command Council (which included the president and vice presidents of Iraq), dated July 31, 1982.[15] This was the same letter that Ja'afar had asked Hamed about in the previous session. The letter requests that the council give awards and promotions to several named intelligence officers for their efforts in confronting elements of the Dawa Party in the aftermath of the Dujail incident. A handwritten note at the bottom, which Ja'afar said was written by Saddam, states "approved, July 26, 1982." In the context of other evidence indicating that these intelligence employees had tortured and killed several citizens of Dujail during their investigation, this letter suggested that, rather than discipline subordinates for criminal acts, Saddam rewarded them.

Ja'afar then read a third letter, dated September 23, 1982, from the Investigation Section to the head of the Mukhabarat, defendant Barzan, asking for guidance on what to do with the orchards of those detained from Dujail in the aftermath of the attack on Saddam's convoy.[16] The letter includes a lengthy list of the Dujail detainees. Ja'afar followed this by reading

"Revolutionary Command Council Decision No. 1283," issued on October 14, 1982, pertaining to the confiscation of orchards and agricultural lands of the Dujail detainees.[17] The decree noted that the ownership of the land was now transferred to the Ministry of Agriculture and included a list of individuals excluded from compensation. The signature on the document, Ja'afar pointed out, was that of Saddam Hussein. These two documents indicated that plans for land confiscation began well before the supposed "trial" took place in 1984 and tied Saddam directly to the land confiscation.

Next, the prosecutor read a letter sent by Sad'un Shakir, then minister of the interior, on December 28, 1982, to the secretariat of the National Security Council on the detainees from Dujail.[18] The letter, which indicated the mass scale of the roundup of Dujaili citizens, states that the number of detainees was 687, including 294 women and children.

Getting to the heart of the case, Ja'afar presented a decree dated May 27, 1984, to refer the cases of 148 persons from Dujail to the Revolutionary Court, signed by Saddam.[19] He also read the verdict issued by the Revolutionary Court on June 14, 1984, convicting all 148.[20] The verdict, which was signed by Awad al-Bandar, states that all the defendants appeared in the court, that they were all represented by attorneys, and that the accused all confessed. Next, Ja'afar read the verdict issued by the Revolutionary Court dated June 14, 1984, sentencing all 148 to death by hanging.[21] This document, too, was signed by Awad al-Bandar. Ja'afar then read Presidential Decree No. 778, dated June 16, 1984, endorsing the death sentence for the 148 convicted residents of Dujail; it was signed by Saddam.[22] The prosecutor followed this by reading an official letter, issued on March 23, 1985, by the administrator of Abu Ghraib prison, confirming the implementation of the death sentence against the 148.[23] The letter notes that they were all hanged in fulfillment of the presidential decree. Later, the prosecutor would introduce documents establishing that twenty-eight of the people executed were juveniles, including some eleven- and twelve-year-olds.

Turning to the subject that he had discussed with witnesses Ahmed Hussein and Fadil Tawfij during the February 13 and 14 sessions of the trial, Ja'afar next read a letter dated July 5, 1987, from Colonel Husayn Kamil, head of the Special Security Force, to Saddam Hussein, entitled

"Reasons for Nonimplementation of the Death Penalty Against Two Individuals." The letter noted that some of the 148 Dujail defendants had actually died in the course of the investigation and were therefore not available for hanging. It also stated that four others, who were not tried by the Revolutionary Court, were executed "by mistake," along with those whom the court had convicted. In addition, it stated that two of those who had been convicted by the court had been released in error. An annotation appears at the bottom of the letter, stating, "Fate should not be more merciful than we are," signed by Saddam Hussein. Ja'afar next read a related memo from the President's Office to the Mukhabarat, which stated that the four individuals who had been executed erroneously would be categorized as having died in detention. The memo was signed by Saddam, with a notation that a copy was to be sent to the Ministry of Health.

Following Ja'afar's lengthy presentation, one of the members of the defense team (now composed only of the court-appointed lawyers) asked for copies of these documents. Ja'afar noted that all of these documents had been included in the dossier that was provided to the retained lawyers and their clients forty-five days before the first trial session, but added that he would send additional copies to each of the court-appointed defense lawyers before the end of the day.

As the session drew to a close, Barzan rose to say that he questioned the authenticity of these documents, especially those written from his office, since, he noted, they lacked the Mukhabarat's logo and were not printed on the department's official stationery.

*Day 14 (March 1, 2006)*

The retained lawyers were back in the courtroom for the fourteenth session of the trial. They said that they had been forced to miss the previous session because they were meeting in Geneva with the high commissioner for human rights, where they were lodging a complaint about the unfair trial proceedings.

The prosecutor told the court that he had several additional documents he wanted to read for the record. First, he read an intelligence court document, dated September 23, 1987.[24] The document, which concerned disciplinary action against the officers responsible for failing to execute two of the Dujail convicts, noted that 46 of the 148 Dujail residents who were referred to the Revolutionary Court for trial had died during interrogation. This added weight to the suggestion that the trial was a sham because the Revolutionary Court was evidently not aware that a third of the defendants it allegedly tried had actually died before the trial.

Ja'afar next read a document from the Legal Affairs Department of the President's Office; it had been issued on April 19, 1987, and was titled "Dujail Event Results." The document, which is a final report on the Dujail investigation and response, states that on July 8, 1982, Saddam's motorcade was fired on by a "criminal group." It notes that "148 criminals were convicted and that death sentences were issued against them by the Revolutionary Court." It further notes that the death sentences were endorsed by Presidential Decree No. 778 in 1984. It states that a number of the convicts had died during interrogation and that the rest were executed. The document notes also that 399 family and relatives of the convicted persons who were detained in Muthanna Governorate had been released and returned to their homes.

The prosecutor then read three letters from the lower-level defendants that indicated that a few hours after the assassination attempt, each had written to the interior minister, informing on villagers with familial connections to a Shiite opposition group known as the Dawa Party. The first letter was from defendant Abdallah Kasim Ruwayyid, dated July 8, 1982, to Interior Minister Sad'un Shakir. In it Abdallah stated that due to extraordinary events in Dujail, he had been asked to present the names of all the families in Dujail who were members of the Dawa Party. Prosecutor Ja'afar then compared the names in Abdallah's letter to those tried and executed, suggesting that eight people were killed as a result of this document. Ja'afar then read a similar letter from defendant Mizhir Abdallah, also dated July 8, 1982, and also addressed to Interior Minister Sad'un Shakir. Mizhir's letter stated that "criminals of the Dawa Party" attacked Saddam and included a list of names of the families known to be opposed to the Baath Party. Ja'afar then read the names of four people on Mizhir's list who were subsequently executed as a result of the letter. Finally, Ja'afar read a handwritten report dated July 8, 1982, from defendant Ali Diyah addressed to Sad'un Shakir, also containing a list of suspects, several of whom ended up being executed.

These three were obviously small fish compared to the three primary defendants. But the evidence presented in court that day was meant to remind the world that tyrannical regimes do not succeed without the sycophantic support of such underlings. Several of the post–World War II war crimes trials confirmed that civilians and low-level officials could be held criminally liable for informing on neighbors who were opposed to the Nazi regime or were part of the underground resistance, where such neighbors were immediately thereafter arrested, tortured, and executed without trial.[25]

Next, the prosecutor displayed an easel on which a large poster showed full-color before and after satellite images of the destruction of the orchards, farms, and houses of Dujail. The photos, dated April 1982 and July 1983, provided graphic evidence of the tragedy that befell the town as a result of the government's retaliatory response to the assassination attempt. The extent of the destruction captured on these photos reminded the authors of a cataclysmic event in the nature of Mount St. Helens, Hurricane Katrina, or the Indonesian tsunami.

Ja'afar then played two audio recordings for the court that provided important proof that the attacks against Dujail were part of a broader series of attacks against the civilian population. The first was a recording of Saddam's voice, speaking to Abd al-Ghany Abd al-Ghaffur, a leading member of the Baath Party. Discussing how best to respond to the uprising in the city of Basra in 1991, Saddam says in the recording that he "will demolish it just like Dujail." In the second audio recording, also dated 1991, Saddam can be heard comparing the regime's destruction of the southern marshes in Iraq to the destruction of Dujail: "The nature of landscape sometimes encourages crime and transgression. Without that action in Dujail we would have fallen into trouble." With that, the prosecutor concluded the evidentiary portion of the case.

Just before the close of the Iraqi High Tribunal's proceedings on March 1, Saddam asked to address the court. The next five minutes were the most important of the entire trial. In a scene reminiscent of Jack Nicholson's self-incriminating tirade at the end of the film *A Few Good Men*, Saddam stood and told the court that he had ordered the destruction of the orchards and homes, and that he had ordered the arrest, interrogation, trial, and execution of the townspeople. "If I hadn't wanted to, I wouldn't have sent them to the Revolutionary Court. But I did," he said of the villagers. "And they were charged according to the law, just like you charge people according to the law. . . . When the person says he's responsible, why go to others and search? Saddam Hussein was a leader and says, 'I'm responsible.' "

## THE DEFENSE CASE

*Day 15 (March 12, 2006)*

In the fifteenth trial session, the defendants were given a chance to comment on the testimony they had given to the investigative judge, Ra'id Juhi, a year before the start of the trial. During their sessions with Judge Ra'id, each of the defendants had been informed of their right to remain silent, and each was represented by counsel. Nevertheless, they had all given detailed and largely self-incriminatory statements. Now they were provided an opportunity to clarify or disavow their earlier testimony if they wanted to do so.

The session began with defendant Mizhir Abdallah Kasim Ruwayyid, who insisted the transcript of his pretrial testimony was full of erroneous statements and claimed that he signed the document without reading it because he didn't have his glasses. Judge Ra'ouf asked Mizhir, "In a previous session there was a document, written by you to Sad'un Shakir, naming families, some of which were later executed. How do you explain this document?" Mizhir responded, "I did not sign such a document. It was not my handwriting or signature."

Next, the judge questioned defendant Ali Diyah Ali about his pretrial testimony. Echoing Mizhir, Ali Diyah Ali disavowed the transcript, saying: "My sight is not good. And when the investigative judge asked me to read before I signed, I said, 'No, I will sign it based on trust.' "

Defendant Abdallah Kasim Ruwayyid was the next to address the court. He denied having submitted any reports on the Dawa Party, insisting that the document submitted on March 1 was a forgery. Similarly, defendant Mohammed Azawi Ali el-Marsoumi denied the substance of his pretrial testimony, saying, "Whenever I uttered a single word, they wrote four lines. Trust me, I am telling the truth."

The next defendant to take the stand was Awad Hamad al-Bandar, who was determined to take full advantage of this opportunity to set the record straight about the legitimacy of the 1984 trial of the Dujaili defendants. Awad al-Bandar began by acknowledging that he presided over the 1984 trial, and that he sentenced all 148 Dujaili defendants to death after a trial that, he said, lasted two weeks. "They attacked the president of the republic and they confessed," he told the court. He said that their confessions were verified by the intelligence department's investigative judge, and added that the Dujaili defendants also admitted their responsibility on radio and television. Moreover, Awad al-Bandar said that the case file had established that weapons and incriminating documents proving the Dujail defendants' affiliation with the Iran-allied Dawa Party were found in their hideouts in the Dujail orchards. He insisted that the Dujaili defendants were represented by court-appointed counsel, and that his court issued the ruling in accordance with the law and without the interference or influence of any side. He admitted that the trial was a short one given the number of defendants, but said that owing to the war with Iran and the defendants' confessions, the trial could not be delayed, stressing that "these were extraordinary events, as the president was targeted."

When confronted with the document showing that 46 of the 148 Dujail defendants had actually died during interrogation before the 1984 trial, Awad al-Bandar replied, "Is it so strange for someone to die during interrogation?" asserting that five of his fellow former Baath Party leaders had died in U.S. custody since 2003. Awad al-Bandar then read from a prepared statement, saying, "According to the law, a judge cannot be arrested or tried unless he carries out a proven crime." He added that at the time of the 1984 Dujail trial, Iraqi law stated that any member of the Dawa Party was to be executed, and also required the death sentence for any person who attempted to kill the head of state. "Therefore, the court had no choice but to sentence the Dujail defendants to death."

Awad al-Bandar's argument was eerily similar to that of the defense attorney in the Academy Award–winning movie *Judgment at Nuremberg*, which was based on the real-life *Alstoetter* trial in which Nazi judges were tried before the Nuremberg Tribunal in 1947. In the movie, the attorney, played by Maximilian Schell, stated: "If the defendant is to be found guilty, certain implications must arise. A judge does not make the law. He carries out the laws of his country, be it a democracy or a dictatorship. The statement, 'My country right or wrong,' was expressed by a great American patriot. It is no less true for a German patriot. Should the defendant have carried out the laws of his country? Or should he have refused to carry them out and become a traitor?"

The final defendant to testify on March 12 was Taha Yassin Ramadan, who was in a quarrelsome temper. When Judge Ra'ouf asked him to state his name for the record, Taha said petulantly, "I won't say it because I don't approve of the legitimacy of this court." Taha's retained lawyer, Bushra Khalil, then interjected, "It is clear that my client wishes to invoke the right to silence." Judge Ra'ouf responded, "If he keeps silent, then we will have only his previous testimony to go on. Do you want to keep silent?" "No," Taha answered sulkily. "I need to talk about all my testimony."

Then, launching into an angry speech, Taha said, "First, I want to talk about the torture I endured during the first three weeks after my arrest. My arrest was on August 17, 2003, in Mosul and within three hours they moved me to Baghdad airport and I was handcuffed from behind, a black hood on my face. And then they took me to a room. One of them was in civilian dress and one a translator. They asked me, 'Where is Saddam?' I said, 'I don't know.' Then they beat me and asked me to crawl and they kept beating me and I started bleeding." Taha then described in detail a regime of sleep deprivation, extreme temperatures, and forced positions, which only halted when his health began to dangerously deteriorate.

Losing his patience, Judge Ra'ouf told Taha, "You are subject to serious criminal accusations, but you are giving us your biography. You need to prepare your defense in this case. You are a defendant and we are giving you the chance to defend yourself." In a surprising twist, Ja'afar interrupted the judge, saying, "According to what the defendant said regarding torture, these are crimes and the prosecutor asks the court to investigate these things." To which Judge Ra'ouf responded, "But this is not subject to the court's jurisdiction."

"The second thing I want to talk about," Taha pressed on, "is the false witness Waddah Ismai'il Khalil." Waddah, whose deathbed testimony had been read on day 2 of the trial, had stated that Taha was in charge of the destruction of the groves of Dujail. "Waddah said that I went to Dujail and headed a committee to destroy the farms. I don't have any connection to the security forces. I was the leader of the Popular Army. It was a domestic force. It guarded electrical facilities, machinery. Local official business was not our business." Taha added, "One of the witnesses said that he saw me in Dujail, but he was only five years old at the time. I wasn't there." Then, turning to the question of the destruction of farms, Taha said, "The whole issue is faked. Saddam did not ask me to undertake such a mission."

*Day 16 (March 15, 2006)*

On March 15, Barzan and Saddam were given their chance to comment on their pretrial testimony to the investigative judge. Both were combative and strayed from the task at hand in order to make political speeches, but Barzan, who like Saddam had been a lawyer, made some important legal points that cut to the core of the case against them.

Barzan began his testimony by asking the judge to give him enough time to present all his arguments. Weary of Barzan's distractions, Judge Ra'ouf replied, "I will give you your required chance to speak, but be specific. Keep within the limits of the case."

The first point Barzan made was that although he was Saddam's brother, he was not in fact a major figure in the regime, as the Americans seemed to believe. "I resigned my post as head of the intelligence services in October 1983, and never worked in the government after that." Barzan insisted that he had been arrested and was now being prosecuted under the mistaken belief that he was one of Saddam's close advisers and his banker. To substantiate the point, Barzan said that during his lengthy interrogation "they asked me about the whereabouts of weapons of mass destruction. Were they transferred to a neighboring country? They asked me about the whereabouts of $36 billion belonging to Saddam. They asked when and how did Osama bin Laden come to Iraq, and how and where he was received by Saddam." Barzan told the court that the Americans had frozen his bank accounts, throwing his children who had been living in Switzerland "into the street." "Is this humane behavior? Is this part of human rights and dignity?" he asked.

Next, Barzan inquired once again why he had not been released, given that he was suffering from cancer, saying that the Geneva Conventions, which were signed by both Iraq and the United States, stipulate that any person suffering from a serious disease should be released. "Where are human rights? Where is the Geneva Convention that regulates this matter? Where are the head of the Human Rights Commission and the head of the Red Cross? Where is Amnesty International? Where is the law, which some people claim exists in the new Iraq?"

Barzan then began to defend himself against the charges of involvement in the events in Dujail. "Your Honor, in the case of Dujail, I did not order the arrest of anyone. Nor did I interrogate anyone. I did not supervise the investigation and I did not see any memorandum by the spiteful Waddah Ismai'il Khalil." Barzan then repeated his assertion that when he visited Dujail after the assassination attempt he ordered the release of hundreds of people detained at the Baath Party headquarters because they were arrested without clear evidence. Barzan added that he never visited Dujail again after that day. "All of this evidence is faked to convict me. Waddah Ismai'il Khalil, faked," he shouted.

Changing tack from denial to justification, Barzan said, "The prosecutor showed papers that Dujail was one of the important places for the Dawa Party and they were using the orchards as a hiding place. There were explosives, guns, canned food, and typewriters. All these had been found by security, military, and police. And these people of the opposition were Dujailis." Focusing in on the attempt on Saddam's life by members of the Dawa Party, Barzan said, "With its action, this group endangered Iraq's security. The group's members carried out their action at the behest of a foreign power that was at war with Iraq." Then Barzan asked, "Where is the error in the president's endorsement of the court verdicts, in his exercise of his constitutional powers, or, before that, in incarcerating those arrested for their participation in these heinous actions? Wouldn't any government punish such assailants?" He added, "The group that masterminded and carried out the attack used the shelter of the orchards and palm groves. Where is the mistake in the measures taken by the state, including the uprooting of trees that served as hideouts for the group that jeopardized security?"

To drive home his point, Barzan compared the response to the assassination attempt at Dujail to that of the United States after the "alleged attempt" on the life of President George H. W. Bush in 1993. "Iraq was said to be implicated. There was no investigation, no trial, no wait to clarify the issue. Iraq was hit with missiles. Institutions, buildings, and houses were destroyed. Hundreds of civilians were victimized." He added, "And how is this different than what the Americans have done to Fallujah?"

Judge Ra'ouf interrupted, "Fallujah? This does not have anything to do with our case. It is another time, another place, another region." Judge Ra'ouf's comment indicated that he thought Barzan was making a tu quoque defense. Latin for "you also," this is a defense in which the defendant argues that since the other side committed the same crimes, it is not legitimate to prosecute the defendants for those crimes. The International Criminal Tribunal for the Former Yugoslavia stated in *Prosecutor v. Kupreskic* that the tu quoque defense has been "universally rejected" and that "there is in fact no support either in State practice or in the opinions of publicists for the validity of such a defense."

However, Barzan was not suggesting that it would be unfair to try him for crimes the United States was also committing, but rather that the conduct of the United States indicated that responding to terrorism in this manner was acceptable under international law. At Nuremberg, Grand Admiral Carl Doenitz succeeded with a similar line of reasoning. He argued that he should not be convicted of waging unrestricted submarine warfare in the Atlantic since the U.S. admiral Chester Nimitz had admitted that the United States had done the same thing in the Pacific, indicating that it was not really against international law. The Nuremberg Tribunal was persuaded by this argument and did not convict Doenitz of the charge.

After a short pause in the proceedings, Saddam Hussein took the stand. Unlike Barzan, who spoke extemporaneously and made some compelling legal arguments, Saddam merely read a prepared speech that was pure political rhetoric: "The Iraq people were my shield and sword under the banner of great Iraq, the banner of God is great. We were united in building and confronting enemies, the covetous, and the saboteurs. The Iraqi people decided to elect me to consecutive terms in accordance with the constitution in a democratic and free election."

He continued: "The invaders, criminal dwarfs and infidel slaves of foreigners, have sullied our pure land, believing that our people will be deceived by phony speeches and statements and rash decisions under the umbrella of the occupation. From this premise, I deliver this deposition on the occasion of my appearance before what has been called a court to shed some light on the tendentious slander and to expose the occupation, its slaves and lackeys that would have become alien and lethal snakes had the Iraqi people, God forbid, not been aware of the invaders, their lackeys, and treacherous plans."

Saddam then praised the Iraqi resistance to the occupation, saying: "Thus, the invader occupiers and their aides who helped them in the ugly crime inside and outside Iraq will realize that they are on their way to being swept away and sent to the dustbin of history. Their defeat is inevitable."

At this point, Judge Ra'ouf cut off Saddam's microphone, chiding: "What has any of this to do with the subject of this trial? You are a defendant in a criminal case. Defend yourself." To which Saddam answered, "I am the president," and then resumed reading his speech. Judge Ra'ouf again switched off his microphone, but Saddam read on. Finally, to deter Saddam from continuing his political diatribe, Judge Ra'ouf ordered that the court go into closed session.

### *Day 17 (April 5, 2006)*

The seventeenth session will be remembered mainly for the tussle that ensued between Judge Ra'ouf and defense counsel Bushra Khalil. Trial observers noted that the Lebanese lawyer was always well dressed, "almost as if she was going to a polo match." One court insider felt that she was more enamored with the cult of personality of Saddam than with her role as an attorney. But on day 17 she was the main event.

As the session began, Ja'afar attempted to ask Saddam to authenticate his signature and notations on several of the documents that were admitted into the record. Saddam refused to do so, saying, "If it is my signature, the document is mine. If not, it is not mine. It is so easy to forge documents these days." Ja'afar became quite agitated, grumbling, "I don't understand the answer. Is it your handwriting or not?" Saddam responded by suggesting the formation of an international committee of experts from China, Egypt, Germany, and France to come to Iraq and determine the validity of the documents.

To this, Judge Ra'ouf declared, "This is a national Iraqi court. The court does not see a need for bringing in forensic experts from outside

Iraq." He added that the court would call in Iraqi forensic experts to examine samples of the signatures of the defendants who denied their signatures on the documents that were produced in the previous sessions.

There was one other particularly noteworthy exchange between Ja'afar and Saddam that day. When the prosecutor asked Saddam if he was aware that there were 28 juveniles among the 148 people whose death sentences he had endorsed, the former dictator replied: "I would not order the execution of a young Iraqi, even if you take out my eye." When Ja'afar then began to read a list of names and dates of birth of minors who were executed and showed the identity cards for each person, Saddam remarked: "It is not the responsibility of the head of state to know their ages." He added, "In any event, I think the identity cards are forged."

At the end of the session, Ja'afar played a videotape of a speech in which Saddam declares: "Anyone who stands in the face of the revolution, even if they are one thousand, two thousand, three thousand, ten thousand, I will cut off their heads without raising a hair or my heart beating for them." The video then shows officers beating people with sticks. Saddam is then heard saying, "If a person dies in interrogation, he has no value."

A heated argument immediately erupted between the prosecutor, the presiding judge, and the defense team about the relevance of the video and its connection with the case. Saddam accused the court of corruption. His lawyer Bushra Khalil held up large photos of American abuses at Abu Ghraib prison and hurled her robe at the judge. In response, Judge Ra'ouf ordered her removed from the courtroom and promised to initiate disciplinary action against her, although no charges were ever pursued.

### *Day 18 (April 6, 2006)*

The eighteenth session of the trial was devoted to the testimony and cross-examination of defendant Awad Hamad al-Bandar, former head of the Revolutionary Court.

Prosecutor Ja'afar began his cross-examination of the defendant by presenting a document signed by Awad al-Bandar, sent to the President's Office, recommending that if a person slandered the president, he should be referred to the Revolutionary Court and get the death penalty. In response, Awad al-Bandar pointed out that the document had nothing to do with the

Dujail case. Though Awad al-Bandar's objection was on target, the document certainly suggested the character of Awad al-Bandar's judicial temperament.

Next, Ja'afar zeroed in on the legitimacy and fairness of the 1984 trial, asking, "Did the Revolutionary Court try the Dujail residents based on the charges outlined in the investigative documents without reviewing them?" Awad al-Bandar explained that the Revolutionary Court had reviewed the charges, but didn't examine the individual confessions since they had been reviewed by the National Security Department. When Ja'afar asked if the defendants were brought before him during the trial sessions, Awad al-Bandar insisted that every one of them was present and represented by assigned counsel. Next, Ja'afar asked about the imposition of the death penalty on minors. Awad al-Bandar responded that every one of the Dujail defendants was over the age of twenty, adding that it was his practice to verify the age of defendants based on the way they looked. If he was not sure about the age of a defendant, he would refer him to the Forensic Medicine Department to calculate the age.

Awad al-Bandar then requested that the court provide the defense the complete copy of the 1984 Dujail trial file. "The file is proof of my innocence," he maintained. "The case file was 360 pages long. Why don't you have them? You seem to have everything else?"

Awad al-Bandar had a valid point. The documents that Ja'afar had presented earlier in the trial made a fairly compelling circumstantial case that Saddam had retaliated against the town of Dujail by destroying its farms and sending those affiliated with the Dawa Party to a sham trial followed by execution. But without the missing case file, how could the court determine that the Revolutionary Court proceeding was really nothing but a fraud to facilitate Saddam's revenge?

According to Eric Blinderman, the Revolutionary Court case file was finally discovered among thousands of pages of uncollated papers in the IHT Secure Evidence Unit two months later, in June 2006, and was promptly provided to the defense lawyers, who signed a written document acknowledging receipt. "Importantly," Blinderman told the authors, "the disclosure of this document occurred while the defense portion of the Dujail trial was ongoing and—despite Awad al-Bandar's protests in open court that the document would prove that the trial he had conducted was fair—the document was not utilized because of the incriminating nature of the evidence therein."

*Days 19 and 20 (April 17 and April 19, 2006)*

Judge Ra'ouf began the session on April 17 by noting that the IHT appeals chamber (which he referred to as the "cassation committee") had ruled against the several motions submitted throughout the trial by the defense, seeking dismissal of Judge Ra'ouf for bias. Judge Ra'ouf added his own thoughts, stating, "I can say strongly there is no bias of any kind against defendants. I do not have any political or personal attitude regarding the defendants as a group or as individuals. I emphasize that this case will be decided on the evidence and in application of the valid law. There is no other external influence on my role as a judge. I emphasize again no one will be convicted unless enough evidence is available to prove the crime without reasonable doubt." This last comment was especially important as the defense lawyers and human rights organizations had criticized the IHT for the absence of a provision in its statute requiring proof beyond reasonable doubt, and Judge Ra'ouf had just publicly confirmed that the court would in fact use that standard. Indeed, the judgment that would be issued seven months later would use the phrase "beyond reasonable doubt" some two dozen times.

The session was also noteworthy because the judge announced that all of the documents read and displayed during the previous sessions had been referred to a committee of three court-appointed independent and professional handwriting and forensic experts for authentication. Judge Ra'ouf then read the report of the experts, which had been submitted to the court on April 12.

According to the report, the handwriting experts took samples from several of the defendants, but Barzan and Saddam refused to provide samples. For them, the experts compared the signatures to those on historic documents that were not in dispute. The experts concluded that all of the documents were authentic, with the exception of the letter signed by Mizhir Abdallah Kasim Ruwayyid, whose contemporary signature was found to be different from his signature in 1982; no other documents were available to compare with his 1982 signature.

Ja'afar then said that the prosecution would provide another document signed by Mizhir for the committee to examine. Saddam's lead Iraqi counsel, Khalil al-Dulaimi, then rose to say that the defense challenged the report on four grounds. "First, the experts are employees of the Ministry of the Interior, which is part of the government formed by invasion forces. Second, the case is a political case, and the government in power is against our clients. Third, we repeat our demand to assign the task of authenticating the documents to international experts who are well known from any country except Iran." Saddam then interjected, "Iran and Israel." To which Khalil al-Dulaimi responded, "Israel is not a real state, so I did not mention it." Finally, Dulaimi said, "We need to know the date of the papers and writing, since all the official stamps that bear the signatures of President Saddam and some of the other defendants had been stolen after the occupation of Baghdad."

On April 19, the defense counsel continued to attack the authentication of the documents. Judge Ra'ouf said that the court had decided to resubmit the documents to another panel of five experts, in accordance with Iraqi law. At the end of the session, Judge Ra'ouf instructed the defense to provide a list of witnesses they would seek to call, including full name, ages, profession, and addresses. In the days to follow, the defense team would submit list after revised list of proposed witnesses, prompting Judge Ra'ouf to complain, "You have submitted ten lists and not just one—ten lists. You are not allowed to submit a list every day. It is not allowed at all." Altogether, the court would permit fifty-six witnesses to testify on behalf of the defendants, whereas twenty-eight witnesses had been presented by the prosecution.

### *Day 21 (April 24, 2006)*

On April 24, Judge Ra'ouf began the trial session by presenting the findings of the second committee of five forensics experts. The second committee unanimously confirmed the findings of the first committee that all of the documents but one were authentic. In particular, it found that the signature of defendant Mizhir on the 1982 letter differed from his signature on the several documents the prosecutor had supplied the court for comparison. The second report also stated that the committee did not have access to specialized equipment to verify the age of the paper of the documents, as the defendants had requested.

Barzan then rose to repeat his objections about the authentication process. "I'm sure of the results, that it would be the same. Even if we form a committee of fifty experts, it would be the same, and its findings against us for political, unethical reasons. I ask the prosecutor, through you, Judge, from where did he get the documents?"

Ja'afar responded: "Barzan asked about the evidence, how we obtained the documents. One of the departments of the IHT is called the Evidence Unit. They are a group of technical and administrative staff. They have tons of evidence and documents, not just related to Dujail, but to all the cases. They catalog and store the evidence. The prosecutor makes a request for documents and then shows them to the court and gives a copy to the defense lawyers, and every document has a reference number. But as to where they got the document, I don't ask them this question."

Eric Blinderman laments that this brief exchange was the prosecutor's only explanation of evidentiary chain of custody throughout the trial. Blinderman told the authors that the RCLO had helped the IHT establish the Secure Evidence Unit. The SEU documented the manner of receipt of every document in its possession. "In fact," Blinderman explains, "each document in the SEU's possession is catalogued with a description of the date of seizure, person responsible for seizure, and transfer of custody of such documents from the point of collection to the SEU. Once a document arrives at the SEU, the chain of custody information is recorded, each document is meticulously analyzed by IHT investigators for relevancy to a particular case, the document is labeled with a unique identifying number, summarized, translated into English, and scanned into the IHT's computerized document management system so that judges and prosecutors are able to access the collection via the Internet and are able to have the document's full history before them. Privately retained defense attorneys are not provided full access to the IHT's document management system for security reasons, but they are able to conduct searches by submitting questions to the IHT defense office for relevant documents. This protocol was used, for example, to locate Awad al-Bandar's missing Revolutionary Court file."[26]

*Day 22 (May 15, 2006)*

For Western observers, May 15 was one of the more bizarre days of the trial, as it consisted of the presentation of the indictment (*tawjeeh al-tuhm*). In the United States, a charging instrument, which provides notice of the general factual allegations and laws that were allegedly violated, is presented before the trial. Consistent with the Iraqi civil law system, the IHT instead employed an "order for referral" specifying the offenses enumerated in the IHT statute that were allegedly committed and accompanied by the investigative case file, or dossier. The defense would have to review the lengthy case file to ascertain the facts relevant to the charges.

On May 15, the judges decided that the evidence presented in the dossier and reviewed in court was sufficient to warrant the issuance of the formal charging document, which Judge Ra'ouf read to the court. The formal charging documents for each defendant were far more detailed than a U.S. indictment, containing substantive charges, describing relevant facts, and setting forth modes of liability tailored for each defendant. For example, the charging document for Saddam stated that he was criminally liable for issuing direct orders; for knowingly participating in a joint criminal enterprise; and, as a commander, for failing to prevent or punish the crimes of his subordinates.

After reading each charging document, Judge Ra'ouf asked whether the defendant would plead guilty or not guilty. When it was Saddam's turn, Saddam said his response could not be summed up in only one or two words, adding, "You are sitting in front of Saddam Hussein, the president of Iraq. I do not recognize the collaborators who were brought as pawns to form a tribunal and to apply the law, which was prepared by Paul Bremer, with a retroactive effect against the president of the country, who is protected by the constitution and law. Therefore, I cannot respond to these charges with yes or no."

Immediately following the reading of the charging documents, the court began to hear the first witnesses for the defense. This procedure prompted human rights groups to complain that it was unfair to require the defendants to immediately present their defense following the issuance of the charging instrument. But the defendants actually had five months thereafter to synthesize their defense, since the court gave them until October 1, 2006, to submit closing briefs.

*Days 23–25 (May 16, 17, and 22, 2006)*

The first of the defense witnesses consisted of relatives of the defendants who testified about their good character. None presented an alibi or a conflicting eyewitness account of the defendants' role in the response to the Dujail incident.

It was ironic that after complaining so strenuously about the prosecution's presentation of witnesses who were juveniles at the time of the Dujail incident, the defense ended up presenting several witnesses who were as young as seven and fifteen at the time of the purported assassination attempt.

Also of note, when Taha Yassin Ramadan's lawyer said that the only witnesses for his client were "President Hussein and Mr. Barzan al-Tikriti," Judge Ra'ouf responded that "these defendants, according to the law, are not qualified to serve as witnesses since they are charged in the same case."

On May 22, witness Murshid Muhammad Jasim took the stand to testify on behalf of Awad al-Bandar. The witness said that he had worked for many years as Judge Awad al-Bandar's judicial clerk, but not in 1984 at the time of the Dujail case. Murshid told the court that defendants were always represented by counsel before the Revolutionary Court, and that the court was independent and the judges were honest. He added that the president never interfered in the course of trials.

Judge Ra'ouf then ended the session, saying that the other witnesses that the defense counsel called for that day had refused to testify. At the same time, Ra'ouf said that the court would not accept any new defense witnesses other than those identified on the first list.

*Day 26 (May 24, 2006)*

May 24, 2006, will likely be remembered as the high-water mark for the defense in the Saddam Hussein trial, for among the six witnesses who testified for the defense that day was Tariq Aziz, the foreign minister of Iraq during the Baathist regime. Even more than Saddam himself, Tariq Aziz was the Iraqi face most familiar to Westerners. Known for his white hair, glasses, expensive suits, and articulate statements in fluent English, Aziz had appeared frequently at the United Nations, in foreign capitals, and on the international media during the past two decades.

Many of the international advisers had expected that the seventy-year-old former diplomat, who had been in custody since 2003, would end up testifying against Saddam in a plea deal, and that he would provide the crucial insider's view that would nail the lid on the case against Saddam. Instead, Aziz testified passionately for his former boss. "I wanted to come and witness for President Saddam Hussein because I know he has not committed any crime in relation to Dujail," Aziz confidently told the IHT judges.

Building on a theme that defendant Barzan had spoken about earlier in the trial, Aziz asserted that the Iraqi government had reacted lawfully during what he described as a period of attacks by Iranian-allied terrorists and insurgents against Iraqi government officials, including an attempt on his own life at Mustansariya University a short time before the incident at Dujail in 1982. "No one is guilty of anything," Aziz opined. "The president of the state in any country, if faced with an assassination attempt during a time of war, is entitled to take procedures to capture and punish those who were involved." He added that there was nothing personal about the response to the Dujail assassination attempt.

Aziz compared the conflict in the 1980s to the current instability in Iraq, pointing out that the people in Dujail were treated no differently than the Americans were treating people in places like Fallujah. In concluding, Aziz contended that Saddam was being prosecuted selectively as the fallen leader of a country whose new rulers included members of the very group—the Dawa Party—that was responsible for the 1982 assassination attempt against Saddam. To highlight this point, as Aziz walked past the former Iraqi leader on the way out of the courtroom, he respectfully said, "Good-bye, Mr. President."

The problem for the prosecution was not just that the distinguished former diplomat made a compelling witness, but more importantly that the comparisons Aziz made between Baathist and American antiterrorism and anti-insurgency tactics were not all that far off the mark. In fact, at the very moment Aziz was testifying in the IHT courtroom in Baghdad, a thousand miles away in Kabul his point was being driven home when Afghan president Hamid Karzai announced an official inquiry into a U.S. military raid of a southern Afghan village suspected of hiding Taliban fighters, which reportedly ended up killing at least sixteen innocent civilians, including some at a religious school. And just a few days after Aziz had appeared before the IHT, the international press broke the story of the November 2005 massacre at the Iraqi town of Haditha, in which U.S. Marines reportedly went on a retaliatory killing spree, resulting in two dozen Iraqi civilian deaths a few hours after a makeshift bomb killed one of their comrades outside the town.

There are, however, several significant distinctions between the two situations. First, Saddam's disproportionate response to Dujail (destroying the houses, burning down the orchards, rounding up 600 people, including young children) suggests that his intent was to retaliate against the town and use it as an example to deter future acts of insurgency, rather than simply to root out the terrorists involved in the assassination plot. Second, rather than prosecute and punish his subordinates, documents and witness testimony indicated that Saddam issued medals of honor to the intelligence personnel who tortured and killed Dujail detainees during interrogation. Third, two years after the assassination attempt, when any threat they posed had long passed, Saddam ordered 148 of the Dujail detainees summarily tried en masse before the Revolutionary Court and executed at the end of a patently unfair proceeding, if indeed there was any actual trial.

### *Days 27–29 (May 29–31, 2006)*

A dozen witnesses testified for the defense over a three-day period at the end of May. Highlights included the testimony of an individual who had been a defendant in a case before the Revolutionary Court, who said that when he told Judge Awad Al-Bandar that he did not have a lawyer, the judge refrained from carrying on the trial until a lawyer was brought in to represent him. Another witness said he had been a member of the Popular Army at the time and stated that he and his colleagues had found huge quantities of various kinds of weapons, leaflets, printing machines, and communications devices in the orchard during the search after the assassination attempt. One of the witnesses testified that he had been governor of the province that included the city of Dujail in 1983, and that compensation was paid to the residents of Dujail for their property losses a year and a half after the assassination attempt. Another witness, who said that he had been Saddam's bodyguard on the day of the assassination attempt, gave a detailed account of the attack.

Things were going rather smoothly until three separate witnesses, supposedly from Dujail, testified that they had met prosecutor Ja'far at a July 8, 2004, memorial service for the victims of Dujail. The witnesses testified further that the prosecutor had offered them money to testify falsely against Saddam. The defense attorneys then sought to prove this allegation by playing a video of the memorial service, showing a man who, the defense claimed, was Ja'afar. In response, Ja'afar said he wasn't the man in the video and that he had never in his life been to Dujail.

The next day, Ja'afar called a man (Abd al-Aziz Muhammad Bandr) who looked fairly similar to him into the room, showed the video again, and asked the rebuttal witness whether he was the man on the video. The witness acknowledged that he was the man in the video and that he had organized the memorial service. According to Eric Blinderman, at this point, "the full trial chamber, prosecutors, and entire defense team acknowledged without doubt that the man on the tape was Abd al-Aziz Muhammad Bandr and not Prosecutor Ja'afar al-Moussawi."

The proceedings became increasingly bizarre when the next witness repeated the charge that Ja'afar had tried to bribe him, and testified that he personally knew that twenty-three of the people whom Awad al-Bandar had ordered executed were in fact still alive. When the witness was asked to identify these individuals, he began to read a list of names off a handwritten sheet of paper. Judge Ra'ouf confiscated the paper and asked the witness to write the names down on a separate sheet. The witness was able to provide only a few names, and the names he provided did not match any of the names on the sheet Ra'ouf had taken from him a moment earlier. According to Blinderman, "Even worse, the witness's handwriting was completely different than the handwriting on the confiscated list."

When Judge Ra'ouf asked the witness where he had gotten the list, the witness stated that the names were provided to him by an unknown source. In view of this admission and the behavior of the other three witnesses that day, the court ordered all four bound over for investigation into alleged perjury in violation of Iraq's penal code. The investigative session was held two days later. The witnesses were represented by an IHT-appointed defense attorney. They were questioned in videotaped sessions individually and together by one of the IHT judges, who asked them whether they had really seen Ja'afar at the 2004 memorial service and whether the prosecutor had offered them money to testify against Saddam. In response to these questions, the witnesses admitted that they were not from the town of Dujail, that they had not been at the memorial service, and that the prosecutor had not in fact attempted to bribe them. They admitted instead that they had been transported to Syria, where they were coached by defense counsel Khalil al-Dulaimi, who promised them jobs and houses in Damascus in return for their fabricated testimony.[27] According to Eric Blinderman, the matter was then referred to the Karkh criminal court for further investigation and prosecution. Each witness was photographed and examined for signs of mistreatment and released on bail.

The response of the defense team was to tell the press that the witnesses had been assaulted and detained incommunicado. Blinderman says that "this claim—like so many other unfounded claims of torture and abuse levied against the IHT throughout trial—was utterly false as the witnesses were detained in a location that permitted independent monitoring and videotape of the entirety of their incarceration." He adds, "More importantly, the investigative session against the four witnesses commenced only when, at the commencement of a perfunctory bail hearing that was supposed to take only minutes, one witness stated to IHT representatives that other witnesses were complicit in perjury and had threatened him upon release. Instead of torture, the chief prosecutor ordered a spaghetti dinner for the witnesses—since it quickly became apparent that the short bail hearing was transforming into a more lengthy affair—and simply told all present to treat each witness with respect. Upon release, each witness was again videotaped and asked whether they were mistreated. They all stated that they were treated fairly, and transported back to the secure witness camp inside the Green Zone, whereupon they left Iraq."[28]

*Day 30 (June 5, 2006)*

Several more witnesses testified for the defendants, but it was clear that the testimony was growing repetitive and focused more on character rather than eyewitness accounts. As the court's judgment explains, "Most of the defense witness statements [on those final days] were either general or irrelevant or based upon what they heard others say (hearsay) or focused on proving that there was an attempt to assassinate the former president [which was never in dispute]." So, after the fifty-sixth witness for the defense, Judge Ra'ouf announced that he would accept no more last-minute additions to the list of witnesses and that the prosecutor would make a closing argument on June 19, to be followed by defense closing arguments three weeks later.

## CLOSING ARGUMENTS

*Day 31 (June 19, 2006)*

"The prosecution asks for the harshest penalty against them, because they spread corruption on Earth, they showed no mercy even for the old, for women, or for children, and even the trees were not safe from their oppression," prosecutor Ja'afar said as he summed up the case against Saddam Hussein and the other defendants on June 19, 2006. There were three aspects of the prosecutor's closing argument in the Dujail trial that were particularly noteworthy.

First, it was very significant that the prosecutor asked the tribunal to drop charges against one of the lower-level codefendants (Mohammed Azawi Ali el-Marsoumi) and to be lenient on the other three lower-level codefendants. Ja'afar was obviously hoping that this move would show that the proceedings were fair, just as the three acquittals did for the 1946 Nuremberg trial.

Second, compared to other recent war crimes trials, this was a remarkably short prosecution closing argument. Closing arguments in other tribunals at The Hague, Arusha, and Freetown have been known to go on for days, not hours. The brevity here reflected the strength of the prosecutor's case. Like Nuremberg, the Dujail trial turned out to be based mostly on documents whose authenticity was confirmed by two panels of experts, rather than the testimony of witnesses whose credibility could be called into question. These documents established that Saddam ordered the assault on Dujail and the destruction of its buildings, palm groves, and water supply; that he ordered the rounding up of hundreds of Dujaili townspeople and their interrogation and detention at the Mukhabarat headquarters and Abu Ghraib; that he gave medals of honor to the security forces who tortured and killed the townspeople in the aftermath of the assassination attempt; that he ordered the Dujailis to be tried en masse before the Revolutionary Court; and that he signed the order of execution for 148 of the townspeople. Even Saddam confirmed during the trial that he was responsible for these acts.

In light of the strength of the documentary evidence, perhaps all the prosecutor really had to do in his closing argument was declare res ipsa loquitur—"the thing speaks for itself." The prosecutor did a competent job of summarizing the evidence and explaining the legal case for why the proven acts constituted crimes against humanity, defined as a systematic attack on a civilian population. However, the prosecutor did not do a particularly compelling job of rebutting the defense argument that the acts against the people of Dujail were justified and were no different than American actions taken to root out terrorists and insurgents in Afghanistan and Iraq in the context of its war on terrorism, for this may have been the most important legal question of the trial. On the other hand, the disproportionate cruelty of the regime against innocent civilians and their property was patently obvious from the evidence.

Third, the prosecution asked for the death penalty for Saddam Hussein and his half-brother, security chief Barzan al-Tikriti, even though this would mean that Saddam would not be around to stand trial for the more serious offenses, such as the killing of up to two hundred thousand Kurds in the Anfal campaign in 1988 or the killing of up to an estimated five hundred thousand southern Marsh Arabs in 1991. Saddam's regime destroyed thousands of Iraqi villages and filled mass graves across the nation with the corpses of Iraqi citizens. It was significant that the prosecutor also requested the death penalty for codefendant Awad al-Bandar; even the Nazi judge tried at Nuremberg had received only a life sentence.

During the recess, on June 21, 2006, a third member of the defense team, Khamees al-Obeydi, was gunned down in Baghdad. In response, the entire defense team notified the IHT that it would boycott the closing arguments. Rather than taking the occasion to state their legal case in public and on the record, the defense team chose to pack its portfolios and stay home. Judge Ra'ouf warned the defense attorneys on the record and in open court that he would not be bullied by obstructionist tactics and would instruct standby counsel to deliver closing arguments on the scheduled day if they chose to boycott. Given the obligation to represent their clients with vigor and legal precision, it was reasonable for tribunal officials to presume at the beginning of trial that the defense team would participate in good faith in the judicial process from start to finish. Instead, the defense team sought to pierce the decorum in open court in ways that were unprecedented even for a trial of this magnitude.

*Day 32 (July 10, 2006)*

Because of the boycott of the retained counsel, Judge Ra'ouf assigned the nine members of the IHT defense office to deliver the closing arguments for the defense. The nine Iraqi standby defense lawyers (whose names have never been made public for their protection) were assisted by an international adviser, a Canadian named Bill Wiley, who was recruited by the International Bar Association. Wiley came to Iraq with an impressive résumé, having graduated summa cum laude from Oxford with a law degree and a Ph.D. in international criminal law; and having worked previously for the Canadian Department of Justice, the Yugoslavia Tribunal, the Rwanda Tribunal, and the International Criminal Court in various capacities as a lawyer, investigator, and human rights officer. Wiley ghostwrote sample closing arguments, which the IHT standby defense lawyers translated into Arabic and delivered in court, adding their own thoughts and spin. There were a number of occasions when the Iraqi defense counsel ad-libbed their legal arguments or read short written statements before they would begin to deliver the lengthy prepared arguments.

In contrast to the process in an American court, where only the defense counsel presents the closing argument, the IHT followed the Iraqi tradition of allowing each of the defendants to speak following the arguments of his counsel. First up was the defense counsel for Ali Diyah Ali, whose theme was that his client was a very small fish caught up in a net intended for much larger prey. "My client did not commit the massacre of Rwanda," counsel said. "If he had I would ask for his execution myself." Ali's court-appointed lawyer proceeded to read a seventy-minute argument, refuting witnesses' testimonies against his client and stressing that some witnesses, especially those who were young at the time of the incidents, leveled accusations based on others' accounts of what took place. Quoting a study prepared by Arabic jurist Jamal Mustafa, the lawyer said the court should not accept hearsay as evidence.

During his closing, Ali Diyah Ali's lawyer stated that, if the allegations were proved true, at most Ali was guilty of mere complicity; "he had neither the purpose nor intent of perpetrating crimes against humanity. What he did was with good intent. His assistance was to the legitimate authorities at the time in accordance with the traditional role of the *mokhtar*." He explained that his client's father had been the *mokhtar*, or village leader, of Dujail. It is the job of the *mokhtar* to guide authorities to people's homes and make sure that they respect people's rights when making arrests or undertaking searches. Ali was simply "acting in a traditional capacity" as the son of the *mokhtar*, since his father was sick on the day of the Dujail incident. "All he did was accompany soldiers from house to house telling them where people lived," the lawyer said. "He couldn't protect the Dujailis from the repressive operations of the government, and the defendant could not see that the response of the government would be as large as it was. Did his report contribute to murder and torture and crimes against humanity? Should the judge find that the document was authentic, the response was unintentional and removed in time and space from the crimes."

The defendant repeated many of these arguments in a rambling twenty-minute speech, which concluded, "My family is a ship that doesn't have a captain anymore and the winds are blowing away this ship. I would like you to set me free and find me innocent."

Next, the standby lawyer representing Mohammed Azawi rose to present the closing argument for the man Ja'afar had urged should be acquitted of all charges during the prosecution's closing argument three weeks earlier. The attorney told the court that his client had given himself up to authorities because of his conviction that he was not guilty of anything. He then reminded the court that "no one has testified that Mohammed was with the perpetrators. The defendant himself was victimized by the regime. He was arrested and his orchards were taken. Here the defendant is again forced to suffer." The attorney then cited the precedent of the Yugoslavia Tribunal, saying that the prosecution had "failed to show participation in the crimes or intention to commit the crimes."

*Day 33 (July 11, 2006)*

The next closing argument was presented by the court-appointed counsel representing Abdallah Kasim Ruwayyid, who began by pointing out that his client was over eighty years old. Striking a recurring theme, the lawyer said that the crime connected with the assassination attempt occurred "when there was a state of war and the state can take certain exceptional measures." He also presented a letter signed by sixteen sheikhs from Dujail saying that the defendant was a good man who has done a lot of good work in Dujail. The defendant then briefly addressed the court, saying, "I am practically illiterate. I only graduated from elementary school. All my life I have been in the service of people. I am innocent."

Next, the court-appointed lawyer for Mizhir Abdallah Kasim Ruwayyid (Abdallah Kasim's son) delivered his closing. He began by noting, "My client and his family had forty farms bulldozed. And I am asking the court to add this point of information to the dossier." Next he once again contested the authenticity of the documents bearing the defendant's signatures and tying him to the liquidation of those implicated in the Dujail attack. Finally, he launched into a long discourse on Iraqi and international law, pointing out that crimes against humanity as defined by the IHT statute did not exist in the law of Iraq in 1982, and reminding the court of the general legal principle that someone cannot be tried for a crime that was not a crime at the time of commission. The lawyer acknowledged that Iraq had ratified the International Covenant on Civil and Political Rights, which states that the prohibition against ex post facto law is not applicable to international crimes under customary international law, but he pointed out that Iraq had never enacted implementing legislation, so the covenant was not applicable to this case.

Mizhir then addressed the court. He was wearing a white keffiyeh, and said, "Your Honor, I am innocent. My conscience is white, just like my scarf." He said that he was well liked among the Shia of Dujail, and added that his family was mixed—his wife was Shia, some of his sons had married Shia women, and some of his daughters had married Shia men.

*Day 34 (July 24, 2006)*

Throughout the trial, Barzan al-Tikriti had been by far the most combative of the defendants, and yet he often made the most important legal points. True to form, his closing argument was more significant than that of any of the other defendants, including Saddam Hussein.

The session began with Barzan telling the court that he refused to accept the court-appointed attorney. With three defense counsel assassinated during the trial, Barzan told the court, the "issue of security has exceeded endurance." He said that if he could not get his original attorney back, the court should delay the proceedings so that he could hire a new one of his choice. Trying to meet Barzan halfway, Judge Ra'ouf said, "We will listen to the court-appointed attorney today, but if you hire a new attorney, we will allow him to give a second closing argument or file a different closing brief at a later date."

In a peculiar start to a rambling argument, which took off on tangent after tangent, Barzan's court-appointed attorney spent the first ten minutes of his presentation singing the praises of the court, concluding "Iraq never witnessed such a court that worked in such an honest way." He then moved on to make the following points about the evidence: first, none of the testimony had directly tied Barzan to any of the alleged crimes; second, Barzan's mere presence at Dujail just after the assassination attempt did not establish that he played a role in the retaliatory actions; third, local security, not the Mukhabarat, which Barzan headed, carried out the retaliatory abuses at Dujail; fourth, the documents that implicated Barzan were forgeries; and fifth, the testimony of the witness who said Barzan beat her was not realistic in its details and all other testimony related to Barzan had been hearsay. Citing the precedents of the Yugoslavia and Rwanda tribunals, the appointed defense counsel argued that the mere fact that a superior holds a position of responsibility over officials who offend does not establish personal responsibility. Because there is no "presumption of knowledge" on the part of a superior, "the key question is, what did the accused know and when did he know it?" The lawyer closed his presentation by conceding that Barzan "is not a man that is likely to provoke sympathy," but went on to say that the judge could send the strongest message possible about the fairness of the tribunal by acquitting him.

Out to prove that he, Barzan, was the best lawyer in the courtroom, the defendant began his statement by arguing that "this trial is not legitimate because the invasion was illegal and whatever comes after the invasion is illegal as well." His next theme was that local security was in charge of the crackdown; he had only gone to Dujail to do a preliminary investigation, not to make arrests or take action against the townspeople. "If I had not gone to Dujail that day, the Dujailis would have suffered worse," he said, repeating the assertion that he had ordered not the arrest but the release of the detained residents. He maintained that many, if not all, of the documents were forgeries, citing as an example the document stating that he had asked to promote members of the Mukhabarat two weeks after the incident. "Why would I seek to promote people two weeks into a four-year-long complicated investigation?" He then said the witnesses gave hearsay evidence, many had been children at the time of the incident, and many were women, adding, "And you know very well what Islamic jurisprudence says about testimony of women—every two women equals one man's testimony." Turning to his final theme, Barzan reminded the court that the response to the Dujail assassination attempt had taken place in wartime, stating that "if the attempt had succeeded, Iran would have occupied Iraq and slaughtered thousands of Iraqis." There was, in fact, evidence that the orchards contained some weapons caches, but no evidence that any of the heavier weaponry buried in the orchards was used against Saddam. He added that the orchards of Dujail were shelters for bad people and members of the Dawa Party in league with Iran.

As Barzan wrapped up his statement, Judge Ra'ouf asked about his health. "Even my health is up to you," Barzan answered. "Why? It's in God's hands," Raouf replied. And then Barzan uttered the final words that he would ever say in public: "Yes, God's hands, but releasing me depends on you."

*Day 35 (July 26, 2006)*

On the day of his closing argument, Saddam Hussein strutted into the courtroom holding a Koran and dressed in his trademark dark suit and white shirt buttoned to the collar. He took his customary center chair in the front row, and immediately launched into a heated argument with Judge Ra'ouf. In a raspy voice, Saddam complained that he had been on a hunger strike since July 8, and that he had been taken directly from the hospital to the court. He said that he had been in the hospital for three days, where they force-fed him from a tube that fed nutrients from his nose to his stomach. "My lawyers are not here and I would like to remove myself from this courtroom," Saddam concluded.

In response, Judge Ra'ouf quoted from Article 145 of the Iraqi Criminal Code, which requires defendants to be present during trials, saying, "This provision was signed into law by you when you were president." Judge Ra'ouf then quoted from a medical report to the court dated July 26, pronouncing Saddam healthy enough to attend trial. He then blasted Saddam's absent defense team, saying, "They are in other countries giving political speeches, while their client is here." The defense team led by Khalil al-Dulaimi was literally sitting in another country, gathered in a hotel room with a BBC crew filming a documentary and watching the closing arguments on television. He concluded by telling Saddam that the court-appointed defense attorneys had been following the trial since its beginnings and would be giving the closing statement.

As the diminutive court-appointed lawyer approached the podium to begin his closing, Saddam stabbed a finger at him, warning, "If you present the argument, I will consider you my personal enemy and an enemy of the state"—words that inspired the title of this book. Despite these disquieting threats, the attorney took a drink of water and proceeded to present a cogent legal argument on behalf of Saddam. The defense arguments on Saddam's behalf were made by three separate attorneys and lasted several hours. The attorney who delivered the bulk of the argument was described as a "real hero" by an observer. Though other attorneys appeared in relief at one point, one knowledgeable participant described him as "the bravest and most principled man" associated with the trial. For their valor, the attorneys (along with the other court-appointed lawyers) were nominated for the prestigious Rule of Law Award given by the United Kingdom Bar Association.

Saddam's court-appointed attorney began by stating that the twenty-one witnesses who gave testimony in the case never explained how Saddam, specifically, was linked to the crimes. There was no evidence that Saddam was in the Dujail area during the roundups and arrests. He said that not one document introduced to the court had mentioned Saddam by name and added that his signature on various documents had never been properly authenticated. Referring to the Yugoslavia Tribunal, the attorney pointed out that in the Milosevic case witnesses were called to establish links in the chain of command to Milosevic, something that was missing in this case. The attorney pointed out that the file did not include a constitution to show what the president's powers were, and there was no testimony to prove that Saddam had control over the state organs. "Was the formal control also real control?" he asked.

This line of defense obviously hit a nerve with Saddam, who, according to a psychological profile prepared by Dr. Jerrold Post, prided himself on being a leader in absolute control like his hero Joseph Stalin.[29] Interrupting the lawyer, Saddam declared, "The Iraqi army is without a single Iraqi plane that could fly without my order."

Be that as it may, the court-appointed defense attorney pressed on, "the head of state has no power over the Revolutionary Court." He added that there was no evidence that the defendant had prior "knowledge of the response by state organs to the Dujail incident." He argued that the documents contained only brief reports. "Nothing was said to him about torture or mass arrests until long after they occurred." According to the attorney, the Yugoslavia and Rwanda tribunals had established that a defendant cannot be convicted of crimes against humanity unless "the defendant's actions were part of a systematic attack on civilians and were intended as part of a systematic attack on civilians."

Toward the end of his argument, the attorney mentioned that "the Baathist regime collapsed over a short period of time," provoking another outburst from Saddam: "This is the regime of the people. According to my orders, the Iraqi air force did not participate in the war. Yet Iraq and the Iraqi army stood up for twenty days. Is there a country in the world that could face for twenty days those who came to Iraq? And I'm sure that you hear the sounds of weapons just as we hear them, though we are in jail. This is the sound of the people. Let us see how the Americans will face the people."

To this, Judge Ra'ouf barked, "You are provoking the killing of people by car bombs." Saddam shot back, "I provoke against America and against the invaders. I urge to kill the aggressive invaders." And then Judge Ra'ouf uttered one of the most astonishing statements of the entire trial: "If you are urging to kill Americans, let your friends of the mujahideen attack the American camps and not blow themselves up in the streets and public places and cafés and markets. Let them blow up Americans." If anyone watching the trial had thought the IHT judges were American puppets, Judge Ra'ouf's words had bluntly dispelled that impression. At the same time, these words effectively reminded the millions of Iraqis who were following the proceedings that Saddam cared little about their welfare. He was not a man of the people, but rather the true enemy of the state.

*Day 36 (July 27, 2006)*

After the final fireworks between Saddam and Judge Ra'ouf, the last day of the trial, featuring the closing arguments of Taha Yassin Ramadan and Awad Hamad al-Bandar, was quite anticlimactic. The session began with Taha's court-appointed lawyer arguing that there was no crime in razing the orchards, since the owners had been compensated. His lawyer then argued that the Popular Army militia, which Taha had commanded, was just an unorganized militia, and if it killed some of the villagers in revenge, that was not something that Taha could control. Like Saddam, Taha could not stand to be seen as weak, even if it would exonerate him. So he followed his lawyer's closing with a brief speech, in which he insisted proudly that he had been the first and last leader of the Popular Army and said, "I was not known for any weakness. Weak people do not establish justice."

The last chapter of the trial was the closing argument of Awad al-Bandar. Up until a few minutes before the trial session began, Awad al-Bandar's son vacillated over whether to give the closing argument he had prepared on behalf of his father. Early that morning, he had met privately with Judge Ra'ouf to try to work out the issue. He was under intense pressure from Saddam's legal team to stand in unison with the boycotters, but it was his own father facing the death penalty. In the end, he caved and allowed the appointed lawyer to deliver the closing in open court, and only later submitted his prepared arguments in writing to the judges' chambers, which they accepted.

The former Revolutionary Court judge strutted into the courtroom wearing a white robe and a red-and-white kaffiyeh. Within seconds, he and Judge Ra'ouf were shouting at each other, with the defendant saying that he rejected the court and refused the court-appointed lawyer. "You think this court is a game. Be quiet, sit down," Judge Ra'ouf said, furiously.

After the guards gently pushed the defendant down into his seat, his court-appointed lawyer began his closing. During his speech, the lawyer defended Awad al-Bandar's record as a Revolutionary Court judge, who "had always worked on the principle that the defendant was innocent until proven guilty." When the lawyer was finished, Judge Ra'ouf gave the defendant the chance to speak, but he refused and the final session of the trial came to an abrupt end.

# 7

# JUDGMENT DAY

## TRIUMPH OF LAW OVER TYRANNY

Maintaining his façade of disdain when the trial chamber reconvened for its final act on November 5, 2006, Saddam Hussein entered the courtroom with an arrogant swagger and refused to stand until the guards made him do so to hear Judge Ra'ouf pronounce the court's judgment.[1] When Saddam interrupted the reading of the verdict, Judge Ra'ouf turned down the volume of Saddam's microphone and continued to speak over him without pause.

Speaking on behalf of the five-judge panel, Judge Ra'ouf announced the court's verdicts and sentences: one defendant, Mohammed Azawi Ali el-Marsoumi, was acquitted outright; three defendants—Mizhir Abdallah Kasim Ruwayyid, Ali Diyah Ali, and Abdallah Kasim Ruwayyid, the local Baath Party members in Dujail—were given fifteen-year sentences; Taha Yassin Ramadan, the former vice president of Iraq, was sentenced to life in prison; and Saddam Hussein, Awad Hamad al-Bandar, the former president of the Revolutionary Court, and Barzan Ibrahim al-Tikriti, the former head of the Mukhabarat, were sentenced to "death by hanging" for the crimes of unlawfully imprisoning, torturing, and willfully murdering Iraqi citizens from the town of Dujail. In response to the verdicts, Saddam railed, "God curse the enemies of the occupation." He demanded that the Arab people stand up, and proclaimed, "Death to the enemies of the nation!"

Initial international reaction to the verdict was positive as leaders from Iraq, the United States, the United Kingdom, and Kuwait competed for the most hyperbolic words to express the historic significance of the moment. Iraq's prime minister, Nouri al-Maliki, declared: "The verdict that the Iraqi High Tribunal issued today confirms the strength and independence of the Iraqi judiciary and its ability to try criminals and punish them. Justice is stronger than its enemies and the law eventually triumphs." His deputy prime minister, Barham Salih, said simply, "This vindicates the morality of liberation." U.S. President George Bush added, "Saddam Hussein's trial is a milestone in the Iraqi people's efforts to replace the rule of a tyrant with the rule of law. History will record today's judgment as an important achievement on the path to a free and just and unified society." Margaret Beckett, the foreign secretary of the United Kingdom, said, "I welcome that Saddam Hussein and the other defendants have faced justice and have been held to account for their crimes." And from the Kuwaiti government, "This is justice from heaven."

Despite the fact that the IHT rules of procedure obligate the trial chamber to produce a "reasoned opinion in writing" to support its judgment, surprisingly and without any explanation, no written opinion was issued at the time of the verdict. Some pundits speculated that the trial chamber had prematurely announced its verdict before the opinion was ready as a favor to President Bush in order to give his Republican Party a triumph with respect to its Iraq policy two days before scheduled U.S. congressional elections. However, the verdict, and the spike in violence that accompanied it, only served to focus American public attention on the coalition's failure to vanquish the insurgency and suppress the sectarian killings—after three years, the cost was more than seven thousand reported U.S. military killed and wounded, and $500 billion in taxpayer money. As a result, the Democrats virtually swept the board on election night, regaining a majority in both houses of Congress.

Insiders have told the authors that the real reason for the trial chamber's bifurcated approach was simply that the court had earlier publicly announced that its judgment would be issued on November 5. As a result, foreign dignitaries, human rights organizations, and international media representatives had spent substantial time, money, and effort to get to Baghdad for the event. Having grown increasingly sensitive to international criticism during the trial, Judge Ra'ouf and his four colleagues did not want to give the world yet another reason to disparage the tribunal. And yet, this was another judicial miscalculation, as it provided great fodder for conspiracy theorists.

Two weeks later, on November 22, 2006, the Arabic version of the Dujail trial opinion was finally completed and posted on the tribunal's Web site and provided to defense counsel and prosecutors in hard copy. An "unofficial" English translation was issued on December 3, 2006, and provided to the authors to post on their Grotian Moment: Saddam Trial Web site.[2] The English version of the opinion is 298 single-spaced pages, making it one of the longest opinions ever issued by a war crimes tribunal—though it was later dwarfed by the IHT's 900-plus-page Anfal campaign trial opinion, which was issued by Trial Chamber 2 seven months later.

## FINALLY RESPONDING TO THE PRETRIAL MOTIONS

On November 20, 2006, two days before the issuance of the Arabic version of the Dujail trial opinion, Human Rights Watch published a ninety-seven-page report concluding that the "proceedings in the Dujail trial were fundamentally unfair" and that "the soundness of the verdict is questionable." The timing of the issuance of the report was unfortunate, since the Dujail trial opinion provided credible answers to many of the Watch's most stinging criticisms.

The strongest Human Rights Watch complaint was that the trial chamber had not transparently resolved the defense's pretrial motions. The authors agree that it would have been far preferable if the judges had decided the motions in writing at the beginning rather than at the end of the trial, but the decision to follow the Iraqi tradition of addressing such issues in writing for the first time in the final opinion was not a violation of international law. At the same time, the authors observed during the trial that human rights groups and the media mostly ignored the frequent occasions when Judge Ra'ouf responded to defense allegations or motions orally and from the bench in public session.

The first fifty-four pages of the Dujail trial opinion are devoted to providing detailed responses to the defense pretrial and trial motions and other challenges. These include:

1. The issue of the legality of imposing the death penalty in light of the fact that the Coalition Provisional Authority had suspended it in 2003
2. The challenge to the legitimacy of the tribunal in light of the fact that it had initially been established during the period in which Iraq was subject to the authority of an occupying power
3. The defense claim that it did not receive the case dossier and other evidence in a timely manner
4. The defense claim that the security conditions and the murder of three defense counsel during the trial rendered the climate inherently unfair
5. The request for the removal of the presiding judge, Ra'ouf Rasheed Abdel Rahman, for bias
6. The argument that Saddam Hussein had head of state immunity
7. The argument that the tribunal's statute constituted ex post facto law since crimes against humanity were never before recognized in Iraqi law

The authority to impose criminal liability for crimes against humanity for acts committed in 1982 was clearly established as a matter of international law, even though Iraqi law did not specifically list the international offenses until the 2003 statute. The text of the opinion provides extensive factual and legal reasons why each of the major issues raised by the defense did not prevent the court from reaching a verdict in the Dujail case.

In discussing these matters, the text of the Dujail trial opinion discloses some intriguing information that had not been publicly revealed during the trial. For example, early in the trial, the defense had filed a motion to remove Judge Ra'ouf on the grounds that he was biased against the defendant because Judge Ra'ouf had allegedly been sentenced to death by Saddam Hussein and had been the leader of an anti-Baathist organization. Judge Ra'ouf never publicly rebutted this claim during the trial, leaving the impression that these allegations were not unfounded. The Dujail trial opinion, however, revealed that Judge Ra'ouf had been arrested and sentenced under the Abdul Salam Aref regime in 1963, which had also arrested and sentenced Saddam Hussein and other members of the Baath Party at the same time. According to the opinion, Judge Ra'ouf was released before Saddam came to power, and he practiced law in Baghdad without incident during Saddam's reign. And the so-called anti-Baathist organization Judge Ra'ouf established in 1992 was actually a human rights organization in Kurdistan, which was then an autonomous region outside the control of the central government and protected by an American no-fly zone. The opinion acknowledges that statistically nearly all Iraqi civilians had relatives and friends who suffered during the rule of Saddam Hussein and that the defendants' tactics sometimes provoked the judges' ire during the trial. But the opinion reminds us that the IHT judges had taken an oath to decide the case impartially—a point that other war crimes tribunals have also stressed in explaining why presiding judges should be deemed capable of fairly deciding a case in the absence of specific evidence of bias.

Human Rights Watch also criticized the trial chamber for failing to disclose evidence to the defense on a timely basis, cutting off the defense presentation midstream, and proceeding at times without Saddam Hussein's retained counsel, which included former U.S. attorney general Ramsey Clark. Contrary to the public claims of the defense, the trial chamber opinion reaffirms that the defense counsel were provided the entire 1,120-page "referral file" compiled by the investigative judge forty-five days before the trial commenced, as required by the statute. In terms of "equality of arms," the opinion states that the trial days were evenly split between prosecution and defense witnesses, with about twenty trial days allotted to each. Ultimately, nearly three times as many defense witnesses testified as prosecution witnesses, and the opinion explains that the trial chamber only cut off the defense presentation when the defense witness testimony became cumulative and focused on the character of the defendants rather than on proving or disproving material facts.

The opinion also explains the appointment of standby defense counsel at the beginning of the trial; they were called on to step in when, despite warnings from the bench, the retained counsel frequently boycotted the proceedings. The opinion catalogs the many instances of misconduct of the foreign and Iraqi retained defense counsel, describing their actions as "anarchist" and an "organized offensive course" intended to provoke the court.[3] The judgment notes that such misconduct would have resulted in disciplinary proceedings in an ordinary case before the courts of any country. Despite the frequency of outbursts and disruptive conduct, the trial chamber stressed in its opinion that it strove to demonstrate "magnanimity" and "tolerance . . . for the purpose of serving . . . justice," and hence "disregarded all these fabrications and violations" by basing its decision solely on the evidentiary record.[4]

Perhaps most important of all is the section of the opinion addressing the motions on the legality of the tribunal. Responding to the defense challenges to the tribunal's legitimacy, the Dujail trial chamber opinion strikes something of an indignant tone. The judges were apparently offended by the constant defense insinuation that they were "propelled by others" as a result of the occupation and wrote that the defense allegations constituted "degrading statements" that amounted to an "indecent attack" on their character.[5] Citing the series of UN Security Council resolutions, beginning with Resolution 1483, the trial chamber flatly rejected the defense argument based on the "self-evident" truth that the Iraqi government retained the right to prosecute Baathist officials for "the crimes determined and adopted in international criminal law."[6]

In Resolution 1483, adopted during the temporary reign of the Coalition Provisional Authority, the Security Council had implicitly endorsed the establishment of the Iraqi High Tribunal by highlighting the need for an accountability mechanism "for crimes and atrocities committed by the previous Iraqi regime."[7] The trial chamber also supported its conclusion by citing the text of Security Council Resolution 1511, which reaffirmed "the sovereignty and territorial integrity of Iraq."[8] In the operative paragraph of that resolution, the Security Council determined "that the Governing Council and its ministers are the principal bodies of the Iraqi interim administration, which, without prejudice to its further evolution, embodies the sovereignty of the State of Iraq during the transitional period until an internationally recognized, representative government is established and assumes the responsibilities of the Authority."[9]

Thus, buttressed by the Chapter 7 power of the Security Council at the time of its creation,[10] the Iraqi High Tribunal rested not only on the authority of the occupation officials, but directly on the legal power of the Interim Governing Council responsible for drafting and adopting the original statute of the tribunal. Apart from the authority of occupation law that had been conveyed to the succession of interim Iraqi governments, the opinion notes that 78 percent of the Iraqi people had elected the sovereign Iraqi government that amended and repromulgated the tribunal's statute in October 2005.[11] The opinion also cites the principle embedded in the International Criminal Court that sovereign states have the primacy for enforcing international norms.[12]

The legality portion of the Dujail judgment is an important example of modern state practice that will guide future postconflict occupations. It reinforces the premise that the law of occupation should not be interpreted to doggedly elevate the provisions of prior-existing domestic law and the structure of domestic institutions above the pursuit of justice. Rather, international law allows reasonable latitude for an occupying power to modify, suspend, or replace the existing penal structure in the interests of ensuring justice and the restoration of the rule of law. The Dujail judgment thus builds on the state practice in the post–World War II context that permitted the Allies to set the feet of the defeated Axis powers "on a more wholesome path,"[13] rather than blindly enforcing the institutional and legal constraints that had been the main bulwarks of tyranny.[14]

## FINDINGS OF FACT AND CONCLUSIONS OF LAW

After its lengthy analysis of the defense motions and challenges, the opinion turns to the question of each defendant's guilt, which it considers in six stages: First, the trial chamber recites the type of charges brought against each defendant and the required elements of each of the charged crimes. Second, the court summarizes the statements of the complainants and witnesses who testified against the defendant during the investigation and trial, and details the documentary evidence admitted into evidence. Third, it summarizes the pleas and arguments by the defendant during the investigation and trial. Fourth, the trial chamber summarizes the statements of the witnesses who testified for the defendant. Fifth, it weighs the prosecution and defense evidence, including considering questions of credibility and authentication, as well as discussing possible exculpatory grounds or inferences drawn from the available evidence. Finally, the trial chamber applies the law to the facts, including theories of liability, in determining whether the specific charges were proven "beyond a reasonable doubt."

In this uniquely Iraqi format, the opinion consists of a thorough and organized catalog of the factual record of evidence from the trial and the investigative file given to the defense and to the trial chamber. The trial chamber opinion carefully assesses the elements of each charged offense along with the relevant mens rea (intent or knowledge required for conviction) as shown by the available evidence, and applies the relevant domestic and international law to each and every charge against each of the eight defendants in detail.

Following the lead of the modern international criminal tribunals, the trial chamber examined three modes of liability for each defendant:

1. direct liability for giving orders, aiding and abetting, or personally committing criminal acts
2. indirect liability for the acts of others stemming from participation in a joint criminal enterprise
3. indirect liability for the acts of subordinates under the doctrine of command responsibility

Joint criminal enterprise liability requires a finding that the defendant participated in a common criminal plan or purpose with one or more other persons and that the defendant knew of the common plan or purpose.[15] The common plan need not be express; an unspoken understanding among the members of the group can suffice.[16]

Each of the defendants played his direct part in the suffering of the people of Dujail. But they were also found liable under the theory of joint criminal enterprise, rendering each responsible for the crimes of the others. Human Rights Watch has asserted that the convictions on this basis were unsupportable because there was no evidence of the habitual practice of the security agencies, the Revolutionary Court, or Baath Party institutions.[17] Human Rights Watch would have a valid point if the tragedy of Dujail (including the rounding up, imprisonment, and torture of its citizens, the use of the Revolutionary Court as an instrument of murder, and the destruction of the town and its palm groves, orchards, farms, and vineyards) had been portrayed during the trial as an isolated incident. But as both the evidence presented and the court's findings attest, this was not an exceptional case. Nor did the Baath Party endeavor to keep such incidents of repression secret. Indeed, the trial chamber explained that it had decided to acquit all the defendants of the charge of committing the crime against humanity of "enforced disappearance" because the perpetrators made no attempt to hide the fate of the victims, but rather publicly documented their deaths as a warning to others who would oppose the Baathist regime.

Thus, the trial chamber found that as local Baath Party officials the three lesser defendants knew full well what fate awaited the neighbors they informed on and helped arrest. As officials occupying the highest levels of power in the Baathist regime, Barzan (head of the intelligence and security agency), Taha (head of the Popular Army), and Awad al-Bandar (president of the Revolutionary Court) were fully aware of the role they were playing in the larger picture of Baathist repression. And Saddam himself made it abundantly clear during his "I'm responsible" speech to the court on March 1, 2006, that he was a hands-on leader, fully informed and in control of even the most minute operation of his subordinates.

## NOTEWORTHY PRECEDENTS

Throughout the Dujail trial opinion, the trial chamber included numerous citations to international tribunal precedent. From the point of view of establishing a notable legal precedent of its own, three points stand out. First, Saddam's main defense was that as a leader, he was entitled to take action against a town that had tried to assassinate him and was populated by insurgents and terrorists allied with Iran at a time when Iraq and Iran were at war. The opinion details why the actions taken against the town of Dujail and its inhabitants were "not necessary to stop an immediate and imminent danger" and how the actions were disproportionate to the actual threat.

This precedent is particularly relevant to the United States. On the eve of the Dujail trial, U.S. government officials had opined that the Geneva Conventions were "quaint" and "obsolete" and did not apply to a "new kind of warfare." They took the position that "unlawful enemy combatants" (i.e., terrorists) are within the full scope of executive authority outside normal extradition rules and could be subject to "targeted killing," "rendition," and even "waterboarding" (a technique in which the subject is repeatedly drenched with water and made to believe that drowning is imminent, then revived, until he provides the information sought).[18] The Dujail opinion stands for the proposition that there is a line to be drawn in a country's fight against terrorism, and that Saddam and the other defendants crossed that line. It is a proposition that is pertinent to the United States as its lawmakers and judges continue to struggle with where to draw that line in the fight against terrorism within the bounds of the law.

The second significant aspect of the Dujail precedent concerns the concept of "crimes against humanity"—the crime of which seven of the defendants were convicted. According to Article 12 of the IHT statute, which was modeled upon the provisions of the Yugoslavia and Rwanda tribunal statutes, to be convicted of crimes against humanity, the defendant had to commit willful murder, extermination, deportation, torture, enforced disappearances, or other inhumane acts of a similar character. In addition, the act had to be part of a widespread or systematic attack against a civilian population. Finally, the defendant had to have knowledge of the widespread attack.

Similar to the European Court of Human Rights approach in *Kolk and Kislyiy v. Estonia*,[19] the trial chamber engaged in an extensive analysis to determine whether the Iraqi High Tribunal could lawfully impose punishment for crimes against humanity committed in 1982, since they were not specifically criminalized in Iraqi domestic law until the enactment of the December 2003 Iraqi Special Tribunal statute and the October 2005 amended IHT statute. The trial chamber's discussion is a sophisticated discourse on the interface between international and domestic law as well as between treaties and international custom as authoritative sources of law.[20] Like every international tribunal going back to Nuremberg,[21] the trial chamber concluded that "the actions attributed to the accused in the Dujail case are considered international and internal crimes simultaneously, and the committing of such crimes is considered a violation of international criminal law, and at the same time a violation of Iraqi law."[22] Because abduction, torture, murder, and despoliation of property were criminal offenses in Iraq in 1982, those crimes committed on a mass scale (amounting to crimes against humanity) were also offenses under Iraqi law. In addition, the trial chamber cited Article 15 of the International

Covenant on Civil and Political Rights, which reaffirms that the international prohibition against ex post facto application of criminal law shall not apply to acts that constitute a crime under international law. Consequently, the trial chamber concluded, the procedural and due process principle of nonretroactivity cannot be perverted to provide impunity for those who committed crimes against humanity during the Baathist era.[23]

It is also significant that the tribunal convicted Taha Yassin Ramadan of the crime against humanity of "other inhumane acts" in relation to the destruction of the palm groves, orchards, and vineyards of Dujail. According to the case law of the Yugoslavia Tribunal, the crime of other inhumane acts was "designed as a residual category, as it was felt undesirable for this category to be exhaustively enumerated. An exhaustive categorization would merely create opportunities for evasion of the letter of the prohibition"[24]

The judges found that Taha had been the one to propose that the regime destroy the orchards and fields around Dujail, and under his personal direction three months after the assassination attempt the fields and orchards of Dujail were razed and all of the fruit trees carted off and destroyed. The trial chamber determined that "he was aware that this destructive act was part of a planned and organized extensive attack against the people of Dujail as a horrible revenge due to the shooting at Saddam Hussein's convoy."

The defense had argued that the government had a right to take such action, provided compensation was paid to the landowners for their loss. The trial chamber responded that "the operation was harsh and backward in a way that puzzles the mind. How could an authority or government be capable of destroying the living life of a city just because shooting originated from one of those fields?" As international humanitarian law is applied more frequently, the trial chamber decision to convict Taha Yassin Ramadan for the crime of inhumane acts may become the very embodiment of that catchall crime. After all, destroying the sustenance and prosperity of an entire village is the epitome of acts "intentionally causing great suffering, or serious injury to the body or to the mental or physical health."[25]

Finally, we turn to the conviction of Judge Awad Hamad al-Bandar for the crime against humanity of willful murder, which is perhaps the most significant aspect of the entire opinion. This marks the first time since World War II that a jurist has been convicted of crimes against humanity for perverting the power of the law into the tool of political power. A U.S.

military court at Nuremberg convicted ten Nazi-era judges in the famous *Alstoetter* case.[26] Awad al-Bandar served as the president of Saddam's Revolutionary Court. As detailed in the trial chamber opinion, the Baathist regime could never completely destroy the Iraqi judiciary, and Saddam therefore created the Revolutionary Court as a convenient mechanism for imposing his personal will in the guise of justice. The Revolutionary Court had jurisdiction over any cases directed by Saddam, in particular cases involving national security matters.[27] Defendants could expect little or no due process and their verdicts could not be appealed, although Saddam had to personally approve death sentences.[28]

On May 27, 1984, Saddam referred 148 men and boys of Dujail to the Revolutionary Court for "trial," whereupon Awad al-Bandar dutifully sentenced them to death for their involvement in the 1982 assassination attempt. The trial chamber noted that Judge Awad al-Bandar characterized the civilians as "ravaging traitors" in the papers for the case,[29] and the court supported its findings regarding the criminal use of an ostensibly legal process by observing that the systematic "attack directed against the civilian population" required to constitute a crime against humanity need not be a purely military attack.[30]

The opinion describes the great weight of evidence leading it to "form a solid conviction without any reasonable doubt" that the 148 civilians, including 39 minors, were sentenced to death by Judge Awad al-Bandar without any trial at all.[31] The trial chamber stressed that at the request of the defense, the missing 361-page Revolutionary Court case file had been located and provided to Awad al-Bandar's lawyer on June 19, 2006, and that rather than exculpate the judge, the file further proved that the 1982 trial was a complete sham. Just as the Nuremberg *Alstoetter* judgment concluded that "the dagger of the assassin was concealed beneath the robe of the jurist," the IHT trial chamber determined that the Revolutionary Court's sentence in the case of the 148 Dujailis was "in fact an order of murder and not a judgment issued by virtue of the law and in conformity with it." Further echoing the *Alstoetter* judgment, the IHT trial chamber rejected Awad al-Bandar's defense that he "was obliged to do this," pointing out that he was no "ordinary administrative employee," but "a judge and president of the tribunal." His crime was one of enthusiastically "following the whims and moods of those that outranked him in power."[32]

In many ways, the Nazi judges were more culpable than Judge Awad al-Bandar, as they were found to have presided over numerous sham trials involving thousands of victims, while Awad al-Bandar was accused only in relation to a single case; the Nazi judges applied a racial purity law that was on its face illegitimate, while there is nothing inherently wrong with trying persons accused of attempted assassination; and the Nazi judges were found to have received enormous sums from Hitler in bribes, while there was no evidence that Awad al-Bandar ever received illegal compensation.[33] Although the tribunal at Nuremberg had sentenced others to death, the Nazi judges received relatively light sentences—all were released from prison within ten years.[34] This raises the question of whether a death sentence was appropriate in the case of Judge Awad al-Bandar. Yet this was far from the only controversial aspect of the death sentence, as will be discussed in the next chapter.

In his opening statement in the *Alstoetter* case, the U.S. prosecutor, Telford Taylor, argued that the German judges had "defiled the German temple of justice, and delivered Germany into the dictatorship of the Third Reich, with all its methods of terror, and its cynical and open denial of the rule of law. The temple of German justice must be reconsecrated."[35] By ruling that a judge could be criminally liable for perverting the system of justice and using it as a vengeful weapon, the IHT trial chamber's conviction of Judge Awad al-Bandar helped begin the reconsecration of the Iraqi justice system. And by reaffirming the continuing vitality of the *Alstoetter* precedent, the conviction of Judge Awad al-Bandar sent an important message not just to those in the new Iraqi government, but also to those in governments around the world (including the United States) who might be tempted to argue that in time of war the law must be silent.

Unfortunately, this message has been obscured, as human rights organizations have labeled the IHT guilty of essentially the same crime for which it convicted Judge Awad al-Bandar.[36] There was even an attempt to bring a criminal indictment against Judge Ra'ouf while he was visiting the United Kingdom a month after the trial.[37] If nothing else, we hope the detailed description of the Dujail trial that is contained in this book will convince the reader just how extraordinarily different the IHT was from both Hitler's People's Court and Saddam's Revolutionary Court.

# 8

## APPEAL AND EXECUTION

**The short-term significance** of the Dujail trial as an icon of a new Iraqi justice system died along with Saddam Hussein on December 30, 2006. Mark Ellis, executive director of the International Bar Association, believes that the shortcomings of the Dujail trial "actually had very little to do with what occurred inside the courtroom. The most fundamental component of a fair, independent, and impartial trial is the absence of government interference."[1] For observers around the world, the timing of the execution smacked of sectarian revenge. Saddam's execution was carried out on the first day of the Sunni religious holiday Eid al-Adha[2] despite a provision of Iraqi law that a death sentence "cannot be carried out on official holidays and special festivals connected with the religion of the condemned person."[3] The Shiite-dominated government pushed through the execution only days after the denial of Saddam's appeal. The executioner's rope tightened around his neck and interrupted him as he prayed the most sacred Islamic prayer, the Shahadah: "There is no God but Allah . . ." By some reports, Saddam's last word was "Muhammad" as he began the second verse.[4]

The execution was captured on a digital file filmed on a cell phone smuggled into the execution chamber by an Iraqi official who worked for the Parliamentary Legal Committee. Though the official camera had no sound, the grainy and poorly lit cell phone images captured guards taunting Saddam and reveling in his death. The atmosphere was celebratory and crude. The disrespectful and demeaning end to the dictator's life that flashed around the world for all to see was an affront to the victims who had suffered so much for so many years at the hands of the regime. The Iraqi people deserved better. They had every right to expect that a government representing their interests would be professional in accomplishing perhaps its most significant official act since the return of full sovereignty. The botched execution fell far short of the aspirations of the IHT, and the powerful images created a lasting impression of illegitimacy and incompetence in the minds of many who knew nothing else about the tribunal's processes.

The great irony of the execution and its sectarian overtones is that it accomplished in two minutes and thirty-six seconds the very thing that the defense had sought to achieve throughout the months of trial. Though the defense strategy was driven by Saddam's decision to inject a political defense based on emotive appeals to Iraqi nationalism, Judge Ra'ouf strove to maintain an orderly process at the trial level. The subtext of his clashes with the defendants and their lawyers was his determination to preside over a transparent process that provided proof that it was not a political spectacle or a show trial to reach prearranged political objectives. Iraqi law provides that the trial chamber "is not permitted, in its ruling, to rely upon a piece of evidence which has not been brought up for discussion or referred to during the hearing, nor is it permitted to rely on a piece of paper given to it by a litigant without the rest of the litigants seeing it."[5] After all, a fair trial is one that is grounded in law and evidence that is accessible to the defendants, and in which the findings and punishment are based on judicial deliberation rather than emotion and external manipulation.

Thus, Judge Ra'ouf warned the defense in open court: "From the beginning, we have said that this court is a transparent one and the defense team and defendants are allowed to express their attitude in a democratic way. No one is allowed, whoever he is and under any name, to attack the court, its employees, and the Iraqi people." In its judgment, the Trial Chamber 1 describes the conduct of the defendants and their lawyers as "anarchist" and an "organized offensive course" intended to provoke the court.[6] Despite the frequency of outbursts and disruptive conduct, the trial chamber expressly noted that it endeavored to demonstrate "magnanimity" and "tolerance . . . for the purpose of serving . . . justice," and hence "disregarded all these fabrications and violations" by basing its decision on the evidentiary record.[7]

## A MATTER OF TIMING

Trial Chamber 1 announced its verdicts on November 5, 2006, which meant that the defendants had until December 5 to raise matters to the appeals chamber. This handicapped the defense attorneys somewhat because the full text of the trial judgment was not published until November 17, 2006. Even at that, some members of the defense teams never picked up their copy of the judgment from the clerk of the IHT. Lawyers for the seven persons convicted by Trial Chamber 1 filed lengthy submissions to the appeals chamber on December 3, just before the deadline. The prosecution declined to appeal the one acquittal from the trial chamber, which could have been done under Iraqi law. At the other extreme, the sentence of Taha Yassin Ramadan to life imprisonment was challenged and the prosecution reiterated its position from the closing arguments in asking for the appeals chamber to sentence him to death.

Iraqi law requires the appeals chamber to review the referral file compiled by the investigative judge as well as the evidence presented at trial by the prosecution and defense. These materials are to be reviewed in light of the arguments made by the defense attorneys in the appeals submissions. The Dujail case also represented another milestone for the Iraqi legal system in that the RCLO supplemented the documentary record with an actual transcript of the trial proceedings, which to our knowledge had never previously been done for an Iraqi appellate court. The documents filled more than twenty binders, several thousand pages in all.

Before the defendants even had the opportunity to file their briefs to the appeals chamber, Prime Minister Nouri al-Maliki told the BBC in a televised interview, "We are waiting for the decision of the appeals court, and if it confirms the sentence, it will be the government's responsibility to carry it out."[8] He went on to add, "We would like the whole world to respect Iraq's judicial will. I expect the execution to happen before the end of this year." IHT officials responded publicly that the prime minister's prediction was unrealistic because the deliberations of the nine members of the appeals chamber could not formally begin until the December 5 deadline for defense submissions and because of the sheer volume of evidence the appellate judges would have to review. IHT officials predicted that if there was to be an execution, it was far more likely that the hanging would not take place until January at the earliest, and probably later.[9]

Prime Minister Maliki's public prediction could be cast as a reflection of personal impatience to see the leader responsible for the persecution of his own Dawa Party brought to justice. Taken at face value, the prime minister's statement seems innocuous. He merely affirmed that the matter remained in judicial hands, and that he was determined to move expeditiously to implement the legally adjudged sentences of the IHT once the judges had decided the case as a matter of legal process and its implementation shifted to the political branches of the Iraqi government. In fact, Prime Minister Maliki expressly said in the same interview, "I think the court is determined to pursue this case that they are looking at, but we will not interfere."[10]

However, the prime minister's comments cannot be viewed in isolation. During the Dujail trial, the Iraqi De-Baathification Commission had used its political muscle to sideline Judge Sa'eed al-Hammashi following the resignation of Judge Rizgar. Other judges described Judge Sa'eed's plight as "being frozen." Rumors swirled that Iraqi political officials had used the threat of de-Baathification to engineer the replacement of one of the judges from Trial Chamber 1 during the actual deliberations in the Dujail trial in order to achieve a more severe sentence for the defendants. Observers reported that when the life sentence against Taha Yassin Ramadan was announced in open court during the November 5 hearing, one Iraqi official with close connections to the prime minister had expressed surprise and was reportedly heard to mutter something to the effect of "we will remedy that." The rising tide of politicization created the perception among close observers that all of the procedural and practical progress that had been demonstrated in open court would be corroded by a hastily organized execution that would be little more than a symbol of personal revenge and sectarian division. None of this could have been lost on the appeals chamber as it began its deliberations.

With particular respect to the execution of Saddam, the moral imperative was clear, and this in turn generated a strong political dynamic. Shortly after Saddam's capture in December 2003, Mowaffak al-Rubaie, who was serving at the time as a member of the Interim Governing Council and would later become the new government's national security adviser, publicly expressed the desire of the council to move swiftly. "We can't delay this. It's an integral part of national reconciliation. We can't begin the process of reconciliation until we show the people that the man at the top, who was responsible for unspeakable terror, is brought to justice."[11] He admitted that the IGC hoped that Saddam would be tried before anyone else and prophesied that "he must be tried first—and executed first."[12] Jalal Talabani, the Kurdish leader who has spent more than fifty years of his life fighting for human rights and was reportedly the target of many unsuccessful attempted assassinations by Saddam, personally opposes the death penalty on moral grounds. Nevertheless, Talabani, who was elected to succeed Saddam as president of Iraq and occupied that office as the Dujail appeals chamber began its deliberations, said publicly before the trial began, "Saddam Hussein is a war criminal and he deserves to be executed twenty times a day for his crimes against humanity."[13]

Despite his personal opposition to the death penalty, Talabani delegated authority for signing death warrants to his Shiite vice president, Adel Abdul-Mahdi, in the fall of 2005. In describing this ministerial policy prior to the start of the Dujail trial, Talabani stressed that political pressure would have no part in the judges' decisions and expressly said that his previous political support for an international ban on death sentences "does not mean that I will block the decision of the court."[14] The new government's decision to consider the approval of death sentences as a ministerial act that could be delegated by Talabani began before the Dujail trial even started. This approach permitted the substitution of Talabani's signature despite the argument that the president's personal approval is a constitutional function that cannot be avoided. The Central Criminal Court of Iraq handed down three death sentences in September 2005, which were implemented using exactly the same ministerial sleight of hand that would later support Saddam's execution.

Thus, the processes for approving death sentences, while respecting

Talabani's personal moral opposition, cannot be correctly described as a matter of political expediency that was hastily adopted in the wake of Saddam's conviction. This distinction is important in considering the allegations of political bias that later shadowed the execution. The executive signature on Saddam's death warrant was not obtained using a rigged work-around, but rather using an established procedure in place before his trial began in October 2005.

## THE DEATH PENALTY CONTROVERSY

The death penalty has been both permitted and utilized within Iraqi criminal courts throughout the modern era and dates back to the Code of Hammurabi. The Iraqi Penal Code of 1969 listed the death penalty among the range of permitted penalties for criminal offenses.[15] Regardless of the procedural forms adopted, international law is clear that no accused should face punishment unless convicted pursuant to a fair trial affording all of the essential guarantees embodied in widespread state practice.[16] International human rights law permits the imposition of capital sentences in nations that have not banned its practice, provided that the trial and appeals process meet the highest standards of due process and fundamental fairness. The modern trend among nations is to eliminate capital sentences on moral grounds. As of 2006, 135 countries, including all the European countries, had abolished the death penalty or allowed it to fall into disuse, according to Amnesty International. On the other hand, at the time of this writing, nearly 60 nations support retention of the death penalty, based in part on "the rights of the victims and the right of the community to live in peace and security."[17]

In order to prevent the coalition from shattering over legal objections once the occupation began, Ambassador Bremer promulgated Coalition Provisional Authority Order No. 7 in June 2003 seeking to align Iraqi practice with human rights norms. Section 3, paragraph 1, of CPA Order No. 7 was the most controversial provision within Iraq because it provided that "capital punishment is suspended. In each case where the death penalty is the only available penalty prescribed for an offense, the court may substitute the lesser penalty of life imprisonment, or such other lesser penalty as provided for in the Penal Code."[18] Iraqis were incensed that the occupation authorities would take away the possibility of capital sentences, despite the gross abuses suffered under what they termed "the entombed regime" and its Revolutionary Court.

The insistence of the Iraqis on retaining the possibility of capital sentences in the IHT statute provided a polarizing dimension from the very beginning of the IHT that prevented European countries from assisting with the work of the tribunal. Despite the promulgation of CPA Order No. 7 and its temporary abolition of capital sentences, the original tribunal statute adopted by the Interim Governing Council in December 2003 permitted the range of punishments "prescribed by the Penal Code of 1969," and this language was retained in each of the subsequent legislative enactments following the restoration of full sovereignty.[19] Shortly thereafter, British government lawyers decided to withdraw formal support from the court because its text could permit the possibility of death sentences. When Charles Garroway's assignment ended, he was withdrawn and no other official British representatives were ever sent to assist the court. U.S. and Iraqi diplomats traveled across Europe seeking judicial and legal assistance in setting up the court, but none was proffered due to opposition to the death penalty. Despite the provisions allowing for international judges to be appointed to the tribunal, no other government allowed its judges to participate. Of course, if American jurists had served alongside Iraqi jurists, there would have been howls of illegitimacy and "victor's justice" from the very countries that had refused to dispatch any of their judges to respond to the Iraqi requests.

Even more troubling, when the Iraqis asked for advice from the experienced lawyers and practitioners from the International Criminal Tribunal for the Former Yugoslavia, the secretary-general of the United Nations specifically forbade such assistance. The pool of experienced jurists around the world capable of handling such complex and highly charged cases is small indeed. The Iraqis sought to augment the legal substance that they were learning from international legal experts (including the authors) with the practical, hands-on details that international judges could provide about how to run a courtroom and write opinions that would be embraced as legitimate by the international legal community. The interim Iraqi prime minister, Dr. Ayad Allawi, personally asked Secretary-

General Kofi Annan to support the efforts to bring the Baath Party officials to justice in accordance with international standards.

Although the IHT judges had already met informally with judges and prosecutors of the international tribunals during a visit to The Hague, in a rank demonstration of personal pique and political vendetta, Annan forbade the experienced judges from traveling to London in October 2004 to share their experience and perspectives with the judges of the IHT. He wrote a letter to the Yugoslavia Tribunal prosecutor, Carla del Ponte, opining that "UN officials should not be directly involved in lending assistance to any court or tribunal that is empowered to impose the death penalty."[20] At the same time as he was expressing "serious doubts" that the Iraqi High Tribunal jurists would meet "relevant international standards," Annan actively opposed them in their efforts to do just that. Much of the international community was similarly willing to demand that the Iraqis ignore their centuries-old legal traditions in favor of simply deferring to European standards of punishment.

The prohibition of assistance by the secretary-general came about partly due to basic misunderstandings about the operation of the Iraqi judicial system, but primarily as a protest against the invasion and occupation. Annan's letter also directly contradicted the letter and spirit of the resolution passed unanimously by the UN Security Council that affirmed "the need for accountability for crimes and atrocities committed by the previous Iraqi regime." Resolution 1483, adopted in May 2003, had also specifically tasked Annan to appoint a Special Representative to coordinate a wide range of tasks, one of which was "encouraging international efforts to promote legal and judicial reform."[21]

Retired judge Gabrielle Kirk McDonald, who had served as both judge and president of the Yugoslavia Tribunal until 1999, went to London to share her expertise with the Iraqis because she felt a duty to help.

Judge McDonald knew what it was like for a domestic judge to suddenly be faced with the leap into the application and explication of the dense body of international law that was embedded in the IHT statute because she had made precisely the same leap from a federal bench in Texas to the International Tribunal in The Hague. She termed the secretary-general's order "a travesty" and explained that "this is about judges helping judges. This is not about politics."[22] One of the Iraqis who were with the authors in the secret London training session explained that he would like international judges to sit alongside Iraqis, partly because it would help relieve the pressure of being caught between Iraqi public opinion and that of other nations, and partly because "it would stop the impression that the whole thing is run by Americans."

It was not until the Dujail appeals decision that the consequences flowing from these decisions were fully felt. Unlike the trial chamber, which had been assisted by a British judge recruited by the International Bar Association, the appeals judges had no permanent international legal advisers to aid them. And since there were no international judges present because of their moral opposition to the death sentence, the process was completely hidden from any international oversight or assistance. The paradox is that the fear of Western nations that the IHT could be used for political purposes to impose death sentences was precisely the factor that created the conditions that made such a thing possible. No one will ever know with certainty the depth of legal thinking that went into the appeals decision upholding the death sentences. The authors' discussions with those judges found them to be extremely knowledgeable of the nuances of Iraqi law. The intellectual leap to the sophisticated structure of mens rea requirements and the substantive body of international law was one that they worked hard to make, and they took the legal debates seriously.

No one from the outside can know with certainty whether personal fears or political pressures overrode the appeals judges' legal instincts to shape their written opinion. The presence of international judges would have been the only real way to avert the outside perception that the appeals chamber was solely motivated by internal Iraqi politics or by Prime Minister Maliki's publicly stated desire to see any death sentence implemented before the end of 2006. Human Rights Watch simply assumed that "the speed of the decision, the brevity of the opinion (17 pages) and the cursory nature of the reasoning make it difficult to conclude that the Appeals Chamber conducted a genuine review as required by international fair trial principles."[23] Though that may not be an unreasonable assumption, it is wholly based on perception and appearance. In fact, appeals opinions around the world frequently uphold large swaths of legal reasoning from the lower court with the simple acknowledgement that the defense claims have been considered and rejected, so the brevity itself does not provide conclusive evidence that the judges were driven by politics in their deliberations.

As the final judicial body standing between the Dujail defendants and the popular urge for revenge, the appeals chamber bore grave responsibility for careful analysis of the trial itself in light of fundamental rights of the defendants and the legal issues they raised on appeal as they sought to preserve their lives. The judges of the appeals chamber were reportedly dismayed when non-Iraqi advisers later read them the Human Rights Watch critique of their Dujail decision. Though it is brief, the decision is constructed in a logical sequence that does address the most significant residual issues from the trial chamber judgment. Its first six pages address the procedural aspects of the case and highlight the core legal arguments raised by each of the defendants.

Rejecting the argument that the IHT was illegitimate because it had been formed during the coalition occupation, the judges found that the IHT had authority to decide the Dujail case because the interim Iraqi governments "continued to fund the court until a permanent Iraqi government assumed power on May 20, 2006. A new law for the court was then issued. It is law number (10) for the year 2005. It was named the Iraqi High Tribunal. The law was issued by an Iraqi government elected by 78% of the Iraqi people in a national referendum. Therefore, for all the reasons above stated the Iraqi High Tribunal is a legitimate court, and accordingly, the appeals on that basis are rejected."[24] This predicate finding provided the jurisdictional authority for the appeals chamber to consider and resolve the other legal issues raised on appeal.

## THE APPEALS DECISION

The appeals chamber began its review of the trial record and its internal discussions even before the defense submissions were filed with the clerk of the IHT. (On this score the Human Rights Watch assumption that deliberations began as late as December 12 is factually inaccurate, based on the firsthand knowledge of the authors.) The decision was issued with shocking swiftness on December 26, 2006. The U.S. ambassador and a host of other Western officials had returned home to be with their families after missing many holidays, birthdays, and other family events. Had there even been an inkling that the decision would be issued during the holiday season, many of them would likely have put the demands of duty above their personal desire to be home for the holidays. The speed of the decision caught Western policy makers completely off guard. The length of the decision (eighteen pages in Arabic) might have been a product of a desire to reach a speedy outcome, or it might merely have reflected the swift agreement of the judges on the legal issues that they confronted.

In Iraqi practice, decisions are normally verbal and very brief. For experienced Iraqi jurists, the prevailing practice of the appeals chambers of international tribunals is literally and figuratively foreign. In the UN-established war crimes tribunals, appellate decisions are often monuments to convoluted reasoning and frequently take many months and hundreds of pages to address each and every nuanced issue with exhaustive (and often repetitive) detail and cross-citation. The authors do know that the appeals chamber judges were very conscious of their role on behalf of the Iraqi judiciary as the arbiters of the law and not the actors in a political farce. It is also true that the judges genuinely cared about the historical record of the Dujail trial and the credibility of the process both in the eyes of the Iraqi people and among international experts.

With the exception of Judge Muneer Haddad, who had been promoted to the appeals chamber just before the Dujail deliberations began, the judges were all very experienced jurists. Of course, their names and backgrounds cannot be provided at the time of this writing for security reasons. One thing that is certain is that they had access to a range of international expertise to facilitate analysis of the international jurisprudence relevant to the complex legal issues that they knew would be at the heart of their appeals decision. However, one of the great weaknesses of the decision is that it completely omits citation to the many relevant international cases that would have lent support to its legal conclusions, even though the judges knew of their relevance.

Each of the legal conclusions of the appeals chamber is in accordance with jurisprudence from around the world. If the world would not stand with the Iraqis, then at least they could have used the international jurisprudence to make it clear that their conclusions stood with the weight of legal opinion across the world. It is also true that the drafting of the actual appeals judgment was an internal deliberative process that was opaque to outsiders. In fact, during that time frame, Judge Muneer reportedly left Baghdad on hajj.

Nevertheless, the December 26 decision addressed each major area raised by the defense allegations. The vast majority of the defendants' submissions were dedicated to very particularized allegations regarding factual gaps and alleged inaccuracies in the evidentiary record at trial. There are dozens of inconsistencies and mistakes alleged regarding the documents and testimony supporting the trial chamber findings. Many misstatements were described along with mismatches between the referral file and the live testimony of complainants. In total, the defense argued that the amalgamation of these many alleged small mistakes ostensibly operated to deny the defendants the full and fair right to present their defense. The legal term of art is "equality of arms," meaning that the defense and prosecution must have the same opportunity to investigate the facts and present their case.

Of course, faced with exactly the same factual questions, the trial chamber had drawn other inferences or found other evidence disproving each alleged mistake. Across the globe, appeals courts ordinarily accord great deference to the factual findings of trial courts, and usually focus on errors of law. Consistent with international practice, the appeals chamber responded to these fact-based issues with a cursory and sweeping dismissal.

> As for the other defenses, the defendants were given enough guarantees to have fair trials. Each suspect was informed of the kind of accusations filed against him. He was given ample chance to defend himself and to choose his legal advisors and attorneys in person with the assistance of legal counselors. He was given the chance to interview the defense witnesses. He used his rights to fully defend himself. He was not forced to say what he did not want to say. Then the defense he is using in this regard is rejected too.[25]

Next the appeals chamber turned to the trial chamber's legal conclusions regarding the defendants' claims of immunity. The IHT statute revoked any presumption of official immunity that would otherwise have attached to Iraqi officials working on behalf of the sovereign state. The principle of individual responsibility is the single most powerful and important principle to have emerged since Nuremberg. At Nuremberg, Robert Jackson famously said that "crimes are committed by men, not abstract entities." Criminals cannot hide behind the shield of state sovereignty or official status to escape punishment. The appeals chamber recognized that immunity belongs to the sovereign state rather than the official, and is conveyed for a limited time in order to serve "the welfare of society." While immunity has been stripped from officials of other states by the power of the UN Security Council, the judges quite logically concluded that the domestic country in which the crimes were committed has a stronger legal and moral right to revoke it because the immunity only arose based on the official status of the defendant on behalf of the state. In other words, the immunity from prosecution is not the personal property of the public official, but rather a revocable right granted by the nation. Based on the principle of personal responsibility that is embedded in every extant international tribunal, the Iraqi judges concluded that "the law allows the trial of any person accused of committing a crime, regardless of his official capacity, even if he was a president or a member of government or of its council, as his capacity does not excuse him from penalty and does not constitute extenuating circumstances."

The principle of individual responsibility means that any personal immunity flowing from the official position of an accused is property of the state and cannot be perverted into an irrevocable license to commit the most serious crimes known to humanity. Judge Awad al-Bandar could therefore be held accountable for ordering the murder of innocent civilians, despite the trappings of his office. The lower-level Baathist officials could be punished based on the evidence against them. And, of course, the president of the country cannot take the law into his own hands to commit crimes against his own citizenry. Not only does a sovereign state have the right to revoke immunity flowing from constitution or statute, the judges extended the principle to postulate that "it is the *duty of the state to exercise its criminal jurisdiction against those responsible for committing international crimes* since the crimes of which the defendants are accused of in the Dujail case form both international and domestic crimes and committing them constitutes a violation of the International Penal Code and the Law of Human Rights while at the same time violating Iraqi laws" (emphasis added).[26]

In what is perhaps the clearest articulation in world history related to the rejection of head of state immunity for crimes against humanity or genocide, the judges concluded that atrocity crimes committed while a person is in an immunity status should be subject to more severe punishment. The Iraqi jurists had no precedent for this proposition, but their analysis would easily be replicated in other tribunal decisions. In their words, the cloak of official immunity is a factor for aggravating (making more severe punishment appropriate) the sentence.

> A person who enjoys it [official immunity] usually exercises power which enables him to affect a large number of people, which intensifies the damages and losses resulting from commitment of crimes. The president of the state has international responsibility for the crimes he commits against the international community, since it is not logical and just to punish subordinates who execute illegal orders issued by the president and his aides, and to excuse the president who ordered and schemed for commitment of those crimes. Therefore, he is considered the leader of a gang and not the president of a state which respects the law, and therefore, the head chief is responsible for crimes committed by his subordinates, not only because he is aware of those crimes, but also for his failure to gain that awareness.[27]

This concept may represent the single most important legal precedent to come out of the Dujail verdicts, and, in the authors' view, is worthy of emulation.

None of these principles would matter if the law under which the defendant was being prosecuted was illegal on its face. The defense submissions argued that none of the convictions could be upheld because they were based on law that had been created after the fact, which was then applied retroactively. This protection is familiar to Americans as the constitutional principal that they cannot be punished on the basis of ex post facto laws. The International Covenant on Civil and Political Rights, which Iraq ratified in 1971, states that same principle, as follows: "No one shall be held guilty of any criminal offence on account of any act or omission which did not constitute a criminal offence, under national or international law, at the time when it was committed."[28] The principle that crimes against humanity can be punished despite the fact that, other than genocide, they have not been made offenses by an international treaty goes back to Nuremberg. The London Charter of 1945 introduced the phrase "crimes against humanity" into the legal landscape for the first time. Courts have applied and expanded this body of law ever since.

Human rights chambers have concluded that punishment for crimes against humanity is lawful, even where the sovereign nation enacted legislation criminalizing those offenses decades after the commission of the crimes. The Iraqi judges observed that crimes against humanity are "international norms presumed to be international crimes" and that states around the world have accepted their prosecution in both domestic and international courts.[29] Because Iraq is part of the international community, the appeals chamber concluded that

> if a provision is stated in an international treaty or agreement for a specific incriminating act, the application of this provision on acts perpetrated before its issuance does not mean that the provision was applied retroactively. This provision was preceded by international norms which entail non-legitimacy of the act. The provisions did no more than record and clarify the substance of previous norms and traditions for the perpetrator of the act and his presence. Therefore, the principle of legitimizing crimes and criminal penalties is consistent with justice principles since it is a fundamental principle in all laws, including international criminal law. Therefore, the appeal to reject the law's retroactivity is also rejected.[30]

Finally, sweeping aside objections to the imposition of the death sentences ordered by the trial chamber, the appeals judges affirmed the holding from the judgment on the issue of "lesser punishments," or lex mitior. Enshrined in Article 15 of the International Covenant on Civil and Political Rights, the lex mitior principle requires that, when the applicable law is changed so as to allow for a lighter penalty after the commission of a crime, the offender shall benefit from the change.[31] The Iraqi Penal Code of 1969 expressly adopts this principle in subsection 1.

> (1) The occurrence and consequences of an offence are determined in accordance with the law in force at the time of its commission and the time of commission is determined by reference to the time at which the criminal act occurs and not by reference to the time when the consequence of the offence is realised.

> (2) However, if one or more laws are enacted after an offence has been committed and before final judgment is given, then the law that is most favourable to the convicted person is applied.[32]

Lex mitior is meant to give the accused the benefits of a change in the value judgments of society at large. Laws imposing new and lighter penalties are often the concrete expression of some change in the attitude of the community toward the offense in question.[33] As a result, the principle of lex mitior "applies only to cases in which the commission of the criminal offence and the subsequent imposition of a penalty took place within one and the same jurisdiction."[34]

The trial chamber addressed this issue as the first substantive issue in its judgment. One of the central pillars of the law of occupation is that the occupying power does not acquire sovereignty over the territory. Because an occupying power is merely a temporary custodian of the status quo in the territory it controls,[35] an assertion of de jure authority through annexation is fundamentally at odds with the temporary nature of occupation.[36] During the fourteen months of occupation, the CPA effected a displacement, rather than a replacement, of Iraqi sovereignty. Trial Chamber 1 specifically highlighted its unanimous opinion that "the Temporary Coalition Government is considered a transitional authority in Iraq until achieving full sovereignty according to article (43) of The Hague Laws of 1907—the orientation of the occupier is to respect the language, norms and traditions of the occupied country."[37] The judgment implicitly concluded that a "procedure made by law" (to borrow the phrase from the International Covenant on Civil and Political Rights) is one that has been enacted in accordance with Iraqi legislative procedure. Hence, the CPA's purpose was to protect the people of Iraq, not to speak for them.[38]

The appeals chamber addressed this issue squarely and upheld the assessment of the trial chamber that lex mitior was inapplicable due to the ephemeral nature of CPA authority. It decided that CPA Order No. 7

> did not stem from the Legislative Authority in Iraq, nor did it include any standards of the public opinion, and it merely reflected the necessity that the Coalition was supposed to act according to the authority entrusted in it in accordance with the occupation law being the interim sponsor during that present period in Iraq; and because that

> Authority had no legal sovereignty over the occupied region, and consequently, the Coalition Authority was kind of a separate legal jurisdiction; and according to well-established international laws, the Iraqi High Tribunal was not obliged to implement its rulings or its laws. The order of the Interim Coalition Authority, which suspended execution of capital punishment, was merely a temporary procedure imposed by an interim authority, and therefore, this law could not have been considered a law issued before the sentencing and consequently would have the power to make the law of capital punishment null and void and a law that would be an applicable legal choice of the legal judgment.[39]

In other words, the phrase from the Iraqi Penal Code "one or more laws" implies that a law decreasing the punishment for criminal acts must be enacted within the formal process of the domestic state. The CPA order that suspended the death penalty in Iraq contained no measure of public opinion, but only represented the political imperative of the CPA acting in light of its powers under occupation law. The imposition of the capital sentences was therefore lawful because the previous suspension of death sentences in Iraq had not been achieved through the legislative process on behalf of the Iraqi people.

## THE RUSH TO THE GALLOWS

The speed with which the death sentences were implemented pitted the professional ethos of the Iraqi politicians against powerful political crosscurrents and the expectations of the Iraqi people. The judicial process was over. Any barriers to the direct political will of Iraqi politicians inside the workings of the IHT were gone. Unlike criminal trials held under the normal Iraqi rules of criminal procedure, the decision of the appeals chamber was final and could not be appealed again. The implementation of lawful sentences is the quintessential task for the executive branch of government. The Iraqi people should have had a right to expect a deliberate and careful process befitting such a momentous and solemn occasion. No one had forgotten the prime minister's declaration that sentences should be carried out before the end of 2006. At the same time, no one expected that the appeals chamber would issue its opinion before mid-January at the very earliest. In any event, when the decision affirming Saddam's death sentence came out on December 26, it created a tidal wave of confusion and backroom politicking, both for Iraqis and for the American officials who still held Saddam and the other defendants safely at Camp Cropper. The physical custody of Saddam represented a sort of trump card by which American politicians could have controlled both the timing of the execution and its tone.

As the rush to the gallows gained its own peculiar momentum in the days before Saddam's execution, Western politicians were bound by the exquisite irony of their own consistent position vis-à-vis the IHT. As a pragmatic and public relations matter, the politicized rush to the gallows clouded reason and threatened to forestall adequate planning and coordination. Demanding that the Iraqis follow the precise wishes of Washington would have been a complete reversal of the underlying policy toward the IHT. Even during the invasion, Pierre-Richard Prosper, the U.S. Ambassador-at-Large for War Crimes, told the *Daily Telegraph* that "the Iraqis themselves should take the lead" with respect to punishing Saddam's crimes. "We really need to allow the Iraqis the opportunity to do this," he said. "They are the victims. It is their country that was oppressed and abused. We want them to have a leadership role, and we're there to be supportive."[40] The British foreign secretary echoed this position. In April 2003, Jack Straw said: "We want the Iraqi people, in the main, to take responsibility for ensuring justice in respect of former members of the regime."[41] The Americans on the ground had consistently worked to support the fledgling Iraqi institutions. In the context of the IHT, this relegated the Americans to the position of coaxing, cajoling, and counseling. The American advisers and diplomats began to stake out strong advice on the wisdom of hastily implementing the appeals decision. But they were arguing in vain.

The urgency with which the Iraqis negotiated to obtain physical custody of Saddam and to carry out the execution has largely been attributed to the desire of the Shiite-led government to exact revenge on the "enemy of the state." The IHT statute mandated that sentences would be implemented within thirty days, but the government began to push for Saddam's transfer almost immediately. In training sessions during 2004 and 2005, the authors repeatedly discussed death penalty procedures with

IHT officials. Sentences in Iraq are normally implemented shortly after the conclusion of the trial. Experienced Iraqi judges were appalled when told of the American practice of holding condemned prisoners on death row for a decade or more; they believed that such a prolonged wait on death row would in itself represent a cruel process.

As a cultural matter, swift execution was the norm. However, there were far more complex factors at work that have received no public recognition. The first and most essential function of government is to protect its citizens. The Maliki government had been rightfully criticized for its abysmal failure in eliminating the sectarian death squads that slaughtered Iraqis daily. Having watched thousands of Iraqis die in the streets, the government sought to do everything in its power to decouple Saddam from the insurgency. Saddam continued to exert a powerful hold on the Iraqi psyche. Khalil al-Dulaimi, for example, came out of one of his last meetings with Saddam in tears after the convicted tyrant told him, "I don't care what they do to me."

From the perspective of a government whose citizens were slaughtered daily by insurgents and terrorists in their midst, a lackadaisical approach would inevitably mean more fatalities. During the Dujail trial, Saddam had a perfect forum to foment unrest and sustain the insurgent operations. Even as he approached death, he wrote a letter to the Iraqi people from his cell signed "President and commander in chief of the holy warrior armed forces." He urged them to fight because "the hour of liberation is at hand, God willing. But remember that your near-term goal is confined to freeing your country from the forces of occupation and their followers, and not to be preoccupied in settling scores."[42] Prime Minister Maliki had a strong, and eminently reasonable, belief that Saddam's death would strike at the heart of the insurgency and thereby save some citizens' lives.

Rumors were also rampant in Baghdad that as soon as the government announced an execution date, insurgents would round up Iraqi civilians off the streets and kill fifty per day until Saddam was released or the sentence was commuted to life in prison. Doing the math, an announcement followed by a carefully planned execution a month later could have triggered the murder of as many as two thousand Iraqi civilians. Maliki wanted to speed the execution to prevent such violence. Moreover, the lingering concern that Saddam would somehow return to power was still enough to strike fear into Iraqi hearts. There were wild rumors that Saddam's daughter had bribed American officials with $1 billion to send him into exile. Other Iraqis believed that American and Iraqi officials had agreed to a behind-the-scenes settlement in which one of Saddam's body doubles would be executed in his stead, in return for which the American government would receive information about Saddam's secret bank accounts. This background at least provides a rational reason why an Iraqi government official would have dared to smuggle in a cell phone and tape the images of Saddam's last moments as a way of proving the dictator was gone once and for all.

## THE EXECUTION

Despite their discomfort, American officials in Baghdad were ordered by their superiors to support the Iraqi desire for a swift execution. The pace of events quickened with building momentum. "The Americans said that we have no issue in handing him over, but we need everything to be in accordance with the law," relayed an Iraqi official. "We do not want to break the law."[43] Judge Muneer Haddad and deputy prosecutor Munqith Takleef Mibdir al-Firaoon received telephone calls alerting them to be prepared to attend the execution within twenty-four hours. Prosecutor Munqith is a decent man who would later deliver very powerful opening and closing statements in the Anfal genocide trial. Barely seventy-two hours after the appeals chamber issued its decision, Iraqi officials presented the Americans with the two important documents. First, they delivered a letter signed by President Talabani stipulating that he had no objections to an execution proceeding without his signature. This ministerial function was identical to the procedure he had previously followed with regard to convictions from the Central Criminal Court of Iraq. Second, in order to overcome the legal restriction on executions during religious holidays, the prime minister sought an opinion from the supreme religious body of Iraqi Shiism. The ayatollahs in Najaf approved, and Maliki signed a letter to the justice minister ordering him to "carry out the hanging until death" only a few minutes before midnight on Friday, December 29.

The Iraqi vice president, Adel Abdul-Mahdi, had privately suggested that Saddam be executed by a firing squad in order to ensure that the execution was swiftly and professionally accomplished. He was overruled, in no small measure because Saddam himself had demanded to be shot in accordance with the Iraqi law applicable to military officers. In hindsight, the appearance of yielding to Saddam's wishes might have been far preferable to the appearance of sectarian hatred and personal revenge portrayed by the actual execution. Saddam was turned over to Iraqi custody at around 5:30 A.M. after a short flight from Camp Cropper through the bone-chilling predawn air of the Iraqi winter.

Some officials had planned for an execution under the colossal Hands of Victory monument in the International Zone, which can be seen from all over Baghdad. To celebrate his "victory" over Iran, Saddam had built the 140-foot-high monument of two twenty-four-ton crossed swords made from the guns of dead Iraqi soldiers. The hands and forearms holding the titanic rapiers were supposedly based on castings from Saddam's own body. His execution under that monument would have been hugely symbolic to the Iraqi people who had lost so many children to Saddam's wars of aggression. But Iraqi officials did not fully trust that the Americans would not change their minds at the last moment. They therefore did not want to conduct the execution in the International Zone, where the Americans could have intervened on very short notice. After he was delivered to Iraqi custody, Saddam was immediately driven out of the Green Zone to the old Istikhbarat (military intelligence) headquarters in the northern Baghdad suburb of Khadimiya. One of the ironies of Saddam's death was that he was executed less than a quarter mile from the converted prison unit that housed the Secure Evidence Unit of the IHT. He literally died almost on top of the evidence that had helped to convict him.

The small room housing the gallows was unpleasantly cold in the early morning and had a foul smell. The lighting was bad and the room was cramped. There were a dozen people in all: Iraqi guards, the official witnesses, and a video crew. Saddam stood quietly as the verdict was read aloud in accordance with Iraqi procedural law. The mood was melancholy. According to some accounts, Saddam interrupted the reading of the verdict to shout, "Long live the nation. Long live the Palestinians."[44] One of the guards shouted at Saddam, "You have destroyed us. You have killed us. You have starved us." Deluded to the last, Saddam replied, "I have saved you from destitution and misery and destroyed your enemies, the Persians and the Americans."

After this exchange, Saddam's hands were tied behind his back and he was led up a flight of stairs to the small room dominated by the gallows. As he shuffled along, he recited, "God is great!" He said, "Down with the Americans!" and added, "We're going to heaven and our enemies will rot in hell!" Saddam refused to wear a hood. The room got quiet as everyone began to pray, including the convicted tyrant.

From that point onward, the illicit video records an almost surreal scene of ghoulish glee. Several voices can be heard at once praising Mohammed Bakr al-Sadr, the founder of the Dawa Party and an uncle of Moqtada al-Sadr, whose sectarian militia had terrorized Baghdad. "God damn you," one guard said.

Saddam snapped back, "God damn you." Guards could be heard excitedly saying, "Moqtada, Moqtada." It is the accepted wisdom in Iraq that Saddam ordered the murder of the revered Shiite cleric Mohammed Sadiq al-Sadr, the father of Moqtada al-Sadr. Prosecutor Munqith, whose brother had been murdered during the Dujail trial by unknown assailants, interjected, "I will not accept any offense directed at him." Munqith's voice can be heard on the cell phone video pleading for some dignity in the unruly proceedings: "Please no . . . this man is about to die." Looking back on those moments, Munqith shakes his head sadly in disgust at what he calls "those guards."

Saddam managed a wan smile. He looked down, with the noose around his neck, and asked, "Moqtada? Is this how real men behave?" The taunting made Saddam appear somewhat stoic and dignified as his evil life drew to an end.

At 6:10 A.M., Saddam dropped through the trapdoor and was instantly dead. The smuggled cell phone image shows his face from a distance of no more than three feet away. The voices are excited and celebratory at the sight of the dictator's demise. When news of the execution was made public, Iraq erupted in a sea of celebration. AK-47 fire lasted through the day, and officials declared that there would be no curfew that night.

Baghdad was full of rumors that Moqtada al-Sadr personally attended the execution in retribution for his father's murder. After the video surfaced and caused outrage across the world, Munqith later went on record to declare, "For reality and the sake of history, I say none of the militias attended the execution—only guards from the Ministry of Justice. I believe that there wasn't any legal abuse, only moral violations." Bassam al-Husseini, one of Prime Minister Maliki's closest aides, described Saddam's hanging as "an Eid gift to the Iraqi people."

The outrage over the undignified execution caused some American officials to argue that the body should not be entrusted to the Iraqis. There was also concern that his final resting place would become a shrine and gathering place for those opposed to the new government and continuing American military presence. But Iraqi law requires that the body of an executed defendant be returned to the family so that it can be buried within one day, as required by Islamic practice. Sheikh Ali al-Nida, the leader of Saddam's Abu Nasir tribe, told Al Jazeera that Saddam was buried in a family plot in Awja village, near Tikrit. In fact, the burial place had been prepared during Saddam's reign.

Iraq collectively shrugged amid the speculation that the execution would make Saddam a martyr. Once the celebrations ended, Saddam was gone. On the one-year anniversary of his death, there were no large-scale memorial celebrations, no mass protests, not even a spike in violence. As far as Saddam was concerned, the country had simply moved on.

# 9

# ECHOES OF NUREMBERG: THE DUJAIL TRIAL IN HISTORIC PERSPECTIVE

## THE OBJECTIVES OF A WAR CRIMES TRIAL

Considering all that went wrong during Saddam's trial, there are those who believe it was a mistake to have ever taken the former leader into custody. Things certainly would have been much easier had Saddam simply been killed during the encounter on December 13, 2003, instead of being brought to trial before the Iraqi High Tribunal. But it would not have been the right thing to do.

This was not the first time in history that the United States faced such a quandary. At the end of World War II, as Allied forces pressed into Germany and an end to the fighting in Europe came into sight, the Allied powers faced the similar challenge of deciding what to do with the surviving Nazi leaders who were responsible for terrible atrocities. British prime minister Winston Churchill proposed the summary execution of the Nazi leaders. He opposed the idea of trying them in a court of law because their "guilt was so black" that it was "beyond the scope of judicial process." Soviet leader Joseph Stalin agreed, and said that the Soviet Union "had concocted a list of 50,000 names for execution." At Potsdam, President Franklin Roosevelt indicated tentative willingness to accede to Churchill's proposal, but upon his death in April 1945, President Harry Truman made it clear that he would not stand for summary execution. At the urging of the U.S. secretary of war, Henry Stimson, Truman pushed for the establishment of an international tribunal to try the Nazi leaders.[1] Like the IHT, the International Military Tribunal at Nuremberg was intended to be far more than the type of show trial summary justice common under Stalin's repression.

Truman's case for a war crimes trial was based on two propositions. First, he believed that judicial proceedings would avert future hostilities that would likely result from the execution, absent a trial, of German leaders. A trial would permit the Allies, and the world, to exact a penalty from the Nazi leadership rather than from Germany's civilian population. Truman reminded his counterparts that collective responsibility, in the form of harsh reparations imposed on Germany after World War I, had led to the rise of Hitler in the first place. Discrediting the Nazi leaders through a trial, he felt, was the key to reforming Germany.

Second, Truman argued that legal proceedings would bring the horrors of the Nazi atrocities to the attention of the entire world, thereby legitimizing Allied conduct during the war. This was especially important to the United States and Britain, which had been criticized for firebombing the historic German city of Dresden—a sad chapter that would likely have lapsed from the popular consciousness if it had not later been the subject of Kurt Vonnegut's classic 1969 novel *Slaughterhouse-Five*.

These points quickly won over Joseph Stalin, who saw merit in trying the Nazi leaders in show trials followed by a quick execution, in the same manner that he had dealt with dissidents in his own country during the purges of the 1930s. But Truman and Churchill countered that if there were going to be trials, they would have to be real trials. Thus, from October 1945 through August 1946, twenty-two Nazi leaders were tried together before history's first international war crimes tribunal at Nuremberg, a court presided over by judges from each of the four victorious powers. The defendants were charged with war crimes, crimes against humanity, and crimes against peace. Nineteen were found guilty, and twelve were sentenced to death by hanging.

Contemporary American leaders had these same two objectives in mind when they decided that Saddam Hussein should be brought to justice before a war crimes tribunal. First, they hoped the trial would have a cathartic effect on the Iraqi population. If Shiites and Kurds who had been victimized by the Baathist regime could confront Saddam in the courtroom, they might not be compelled to resort to vigilante justice against Sunnis in the streets of Baghdad. Second, they believed a trial that highlighted the terrible things Saddam had done would help legitimize the controversial 2003 invasion, especially since no weapons of mass destruction had been discovered in the months since.

While an international tribunal like Nuremberg might have been preferable, that option was not on the table in 2003 for a variety of reasons. The newly established International Criminal Court, headquartered in The Hague, was not available for the trial of Saddam Hussein because of the "nonretroactivity" clause in its statute, prohibiting the court from trying cases that arose before July 1, 2002. There had been some interest among the members of the UN Security Council immediately following the 1991 Gulf War in creating an international tribunal to try Saddam Hussein. But after the March 2003 invasion, France, Russia, and China let it be known that they would veto any effort to create such a court because they felt the invasion was unlawful. Turning Saddam over to the ordinary Iraqi courts, on the other hand, was not seen as a viable option either, since the Iraqi judiciary had been left in shambles after three decades of Baath Party rule. In any event, ordinary domestic judges around the world are rarely required to apply the complex principles of international criminal law as it has evolved in the modern era.

Thus, the decision was made to create an "internationalized domestic court"—so called because the Iraqi High Tribunal's statute and rules of procedure were modeled on the UN war crimes tribunals. Its statute requires the tribunal to refer to the precedent of the UN tribunals; its judges and prosecutors are to be assisted by international experts; foreign lawyers are permitted to serve as defense counsel; and the tribunal is to be completely independent from the ordinary Iraqi court system. The substance of the prohibitions against genocide, crimes against humanity, and war crimes derives from international law, as does the authority to punish those offenses in domestic courts. But in keeping with strong Iraqi public opinion, the tribunal is not fully international, since its seat is in Baghdad, its prosecutor is Iraqi, and its bench is composed exclusively of Iraqi judges.

## THE MYTH OF NUREMBERG

The American advocates of the Iraqi High Tribunal were clearly influenced by the myth of Nuremberg. They would have perhaps been better served if they had studied the history a bit more closely. For despite Truman's hopes (and chief prosecutor Robert Jackson's boast that he had proved "incredible events with credible evidence"), the Nuremberg trials did not in fact discredit the Nazi leaders. Indeed, recently declassified opinion polls that were conducted by the U.S. Department of State from 1946 through 1958 indicated that over 80 percent of the West German people did not believe the findings of the Nuremberg Tribunal and considered the Nuremberg proceedings to be nothing but "acts of political retribution without firm legal basis." By 1953, the State Department had concluded that the Nuremberg trials had completely failed to "reeducate" West Germans.[2]

Yet the proponents of the Iraqi High Tribunal were not alone in overestimating the benefits of war crimes prosecutions. In 1993, the UN Security Council established an international war crimes tribunal to prosecute Slobodan Milosevic and other leaders responsible for atrocities in the former Yugoslavia. Security Council Resolution 827, which established the Yugoslavia Tribunal, stated that war crimes prosecutions would contribute to the restoration of peace in the region by discrediting the former Serb leader. However, during the four-year Milosevic trial (2002 through 2005), the defendant's popularity soared. Polls conducted during the trial indicated that 75 percent of Serbs felt that Milosevic was not receiving a fair trial, and 66 percent did not believe that he was actually responsible for war crimes. And halfway through the trial, Milosevic, campaigning from the courtroom in The Hague, won a seat in the Serb parliament in a landslide.[3]

The true lesson from the Nuremberg and Yugoslavia tribunals is that war crimes trials have always been, and are likely always to be, divisive, at least in the short term. No matter the strength of the evidence that is presented in the courtroom, and no matter how many people watch the proceedings, those who support the defendants will continue to support them and perceive the proceedings as unfair.

Two generations after the Nuremberg trials, the German people largely speak of the Nuremberg Tribunal with respect, Holocaust denial is shunned, and the Nazis are remembered with utter contempt. Some believe that this indicates that it just takes a few decades for the positive effects of a war crimes trial to take hold, but take hold they will—largely through the accretion of a definitive historic record that is widely accessible to the target population. But even that is a gross oversimplification. Rather, changing German attitudes must be viewed in light of the aggressive "reorientation" program that the United States imposed on Germany in the decade after the end of World War II. Holocaust denial was made a crime. Elementary and high school history textbooks were written to glorify Nuremberg and demonize the Nazis. And *War and Remembrance*, an American-made miniseries about the Holocaust starring Jane Seymour and John Gielgud, became the most highly watched television broadcast in the history of Germany. What many Germans know (or think they know) about the Holocaust came not from the pages of the Nuremberg judgment, but from the imagination of Hollywood screenwriters. Some scholars trace the sea change in German popular attitudes to the period in which German judges began to try German concentration camp commanders under German law for crimes committed during the war.

Consequently, a realistic assessment of Nuremberg should have led the advocates of the Iraqi High Tribunal to downplay expectations that the trial of Saddam Hussein would positively contribute to peace in Iraq in the near term. Such an assessment would also have better prepared them for the onslaught of criticism the Iraqi High Tribunal would ultimately engender. War crimes trials are inherently messy. To date, not one has been praised as a model of fairness, efficiency, or decorum. Indeed, at the conclusion of the Nuremberg trials, two U.S. Supreme Court justices publicly castigated the proceedings as "a high-grade lynching party" and "a retroactive jurisprudence that would surely be unconstitutional in an American court." Echoing the sentiment of many in Congress, Senator Robert Taft of Ohio gave a speech in 1946 criticizing every aspect of the trials—remarks that were immortalized when John F. Kennedy reproduced the speech in his Pulitzer Prize–winning 1956 book, *Profiles in Courage*.

Sixty years after Nuremberg, most Americans forget these criticisms. Today, Nuremberg is venerated. But the authors' colleague Henry King, who was the youngest prosecutor at Nuremberg, starkly remembers the negative reception he encountered upon his return to the United States in 1948. "It was like the soldiers returning from Vietnam in the 1970s. The tribunal was a tarnished institution, and no one respected what we had done," the eighty-seven-year-old law professor told the authors in a recent interview. A graduate of Yale Law School, Henry King would go on to become director of the Agency for International Development, and later chief international counsel for TRW and professor of law at Case Western Reserve University, but upon his return from Germany in 1946, doors were slammed shut when he sought a job. Sixty years later, Professor King has attained the academic equivalent of rock-star status, speaking at dozens of conferences around the globe, celebrating the Nuremberg legacy.

## APPLYING THE LESSONS OF NUREMBERG TO THE DUJAIL TRIAL

The trial of Saddam Hussein will always be remembered for the defendant's outbursts and provocative speeches. But if the judges of the Iraqi High Tribunal had been students of Nuremberg, they might have avoided much of the chaos that permeated their courtroom. The Saddam Hussein of Nuremberg was Hitler's deputy, Hermann Göring, the highest-ranking Nazi to be tried. Robert Jackson, the U.S. chief prosecutor at Nuremberg, savored the chance to get Göring on the stand. "He was arrogant and conceited—why not turn his weakness against him?" Jackson told his staff. But once the cross-examination began, Göring turned the tables on Jackson. With the indulgence of the judges, who refused to require the defendant to reply with simple yes or no answers, Göring spent hours rehashing many of the Nazis' most egregious propaganda arguments. Throughout the cross-examination, Göring appeared the intellectual superior to Jackson, who was himself a former U.S. solicitor general and Supreme Court justice.[4]

Fifty years after Nuremberg, Slobodan Milosevic actually topped Hermann Göring's courtroom performance. Using his right of self-representation, the Serb leader hijacked the proceedings in The Hague on a daily basis. He transformed cross-examinations into hour-long speeches rationalizing his ultranationalist policies and railing against the 1999 NATO bombing campaign, which destroyed much of Serbia. Short of expelling the defendant from the courtroom, there was little the judges could do to rein him in.

The authors were determined to help the Iraqi High Tribunal better maintain control of their proceedings. Like Milosevic, Saddam Hussein also had a law degree, and the specter of him representing himself before the Iraqi High Tribunal was frightening. At our urging, on August 11, 2005, the tribunal's statute was revised by the Iraqi National Assembly to make it clear that the defendants had to be represented by their lawyers in the courtroom. We expected this to mean that Saddam would not be able to address the court until the end of the trial, when he would have an opportunity to testify on his own behalf. What we did not anticipate was that the presiding judges would follow an Iraqi judicial tradition of allowing the defendant to ask questions of the witness at the conclusion of his lawyer's cross-examinations. Perhaps more than anything else, this decision would affect the conduct of the Saddam Hussein trial and how it was perceived by the outside world.

From the point of view of fairness (if not efficient courtroom management) the IHT judges must be given credit for continuing to allow Saddam and the other defendants to participate in the proceedings even after it became evident that they would use that opportunity to sow division and disruption. In fact, the non-Arabic-speaking audiences around the world never understood the real dynamic of what was happening day after day in the courtroom. In a courtroom where there were no Westerners, the Iraqi judge would respond to disruptive defendants, often with patience, but with occasional irritation born of sheer repetition. The dialogue was always along these lines: "I am the judge, you are the defendant, we are bound by law and procedure, now sit down." Those present in the courtroom saw Saddam and the others accede to the power of the bench many times, and occasionally heard him actually apologize to the judge. Unfortunately, such scenes were not selected for broadcast by the major media outlets.

"Watching the Saddam Hussein proceedings on CNN was like watching the cross-examination of Göring at Nuremberg all over again," Henry

King told the authors. "Like Göring, Hussein had a sort of undeniable charisma. He took control of the courtroom, won the battle of the wills with the judges, and scored a lot of points with his followers." By the authors' count, Hussein used his right to ask follow-up questions to hijack the proceedings on thirty separate occasions. Like Göring and Milosevic, Saddam used every speaking opportunity to justify his attacks on the civilian population. "The president of any country of the world would have acted as I had done, when dealing with terrorists and insurgents during a period of war," Saddam repeatedly asserted. And like Milosevic, Saddam tried to turn his trial into a trial of the U.S. invasion.

## ECHOES OF NUREMBERG IN BAGHDAD

At the end of the Nuremberg trials, the world was stunned to learn that an American guard had smuggled cyanide to Hermann Göring, who cheated the hangman by taking his own life. The Milosevic trial also ended in a worldwide outcry when, a few months before the scheduled finish of the proceedings, the former Serb leader was found dead in his cell. His family claimed he had been poisoned. The tribunal claimed he died of natural causes. The autopsy was inconclusive. In any event, Milosevic's death set back the cause of justice by literally preventing history from being written since the tribunal's rules prohibit issuing a judgment in absentia.

Saddam's demise was no less contentious. As we've seen, in what was supposed to be a solemn undertaking, a leaked cell phone video that was soon broadcast countless times around the world showed the executioners mocking Saddam as they placed the noose around his neck and then jubilantly dancing around his body after it was cut down from the gallows. The prosecutor admitted that the images were unseemly and immoral, though he could find no criminal violation in their dissemination to the media.

Incredibly, the flickering images managed to lend an eerie air of dignity to the death of one of the cruelest and most calculating tyrants of his era. Saddam was a cold-blooded murderer whose narcissism dominated a nation. There is no question that the conduct of the executioners will always cloud the historic perception of the fairness and legitimacy of the Iraqi High Tribunal. But the abysmally implemented execution cannot overshadow the Iraqi-led process that riveted the region for over a year. Nuremberg is not judged today based on Göring's success at frustrating Robert Jackson's cross-examination or cheating the hangman.

"The Saddam trial had one other unmistakable parallel to Nuremberg," Henry King points out. Seated next to Saddam in the first row of the dock during the trial was Awad Hamad al-Bandar, the former chief judge of Saddam's Revolutionary Court. Awad al-Bandar was charged with ordering the execution of 148 Iraqi villagers after conducting a sham trial. According to Professor King, "Judge Awad al-Bandar is the modern-day version of [Josef] Alstoetter, the Nazi judge who was convicted sixty years ago at Nuremberg for using his court as a political weapon."

The *Alstoetter* case was immortalized in the 1961 Academy Award–winning film *Judgment at Nuremberg*, starring Spencer Tracy, Marlene Dietrich, Burt Lancaster, Judy Garland, Montgomery Clift, Richard Widmark, Maximilian Schell, and introducing a young William Shatner. As the media gathered in Baghdad the night before the Dujail trial on charges of crimes against humanity was scheduled to begin, they attended a U.S.-sponsored screening of the classic film. The film explored the questions of whether a judge can be criminally responsible for presiding over an unfair trial if it comported with the domestic law then in effect, and whether departures from normal fair trial norms can be justified in time of war. During the trial, the conduct of Judge Awad al-Bandar was one of the central issues.

In thinking about these questions, it may be helpful to consider the seminal passage from this classic film, in which the judge played by Spencer Tracy delivers the tribunal's judgment: "This trial has shown that under a national crisis, ordinary, even able and extraordinary men can delude themselves into the commission of crimes against humanity. How easily it can happen. There are those in our own country too that today speak of the protection of country, of survival. A decision must be made in the life of every nation, at the very moment when the grasp of the enemy is at its throat; then it seems that the only way to survive is to use the means of the enemy, to rest survival on what is expedient, to look the other way. Only the answer to that is—survival as what? A country isn't a rock; it's not an extension of one's self. It's what it stands for. It's what it stands for when standing for something is the most difficult."

As these stirring words suggest, the legal issue at the core of both the *Alstoetter* trial and the Dujail trial is relevant also to the United States and its allies, which today find themselves in a "war on terrorism." Where is the line to be drawn between those actions that can be justified by the necessities of such a war and those that are criminal? This may be the most important legal question of our generation.

## THE TRIAL OF THE CENTURY?

Despite the many criticisms, few would deny that Nuremberg earned the label "trial of the century." In the years since Nuremberg, the term has been employed with respect to other major war crimes trials, including the 1961–1962 Eichmann trial, the 1987 Klaus Barbie trial, the 1989 Nicolae Ceauşescu trial, and the 2002–2005 Milosevic trial. Does the Saddam Hussein trial deserve a place among these seminal cases? The authors themselves are not sure about the answer to this question, but we suggest the following six criteria as appropriate for measuring the importance of the Dujail trial.

The first criterion is the scale of the atrocities. At Nuremberg the Nazis were accused of exterminating over six million Jews and three million other minorities. In Cambodia, two million civilians were annihilated in Pol Pot's killing fields. In Rwanda, eight hundred thousand Tutsis were murdered by machete-wielding Hutus. Although Saddam Hussein was accused of genocide with respect to the mass murder of nearly a million northern Iraqi Kurds and southern Marsh Arabs, the Dujail trial involved at most a few hundred victims. And his execution at the end of the trial ensured that he would never be convicted of those greater crimes. As one of the defense counsel said during the trial, "Dujail was no Rwanda."

On the other hand, Saddam was convicted of crimes against humanity, rendering him literally an enemy of all mankind. Although the Dujail trial involved a relatively minor atrocity compared with others of which he was accused, the incident did represent a snapshot of evil, ably documenting the character of his regime. And like the defendants at Nuremberg, Saddam Hussein was convicted largely on the strength of his own documents, thus increasing the chances that the historic record contained in the lengthy trial opinion will one day be viewed as definitive. Unlike Hitler, Saddam Hussein attended his trial and made a number of statements under oath and in court that also helped to establish his guilt beyond a reasonable doubt.

The second criterion is the status of the accused. At Nuremberg, Hitler escaped trial by committing suicide, leaving his second in command, Hermann Göring, to be prosecuted as a proxy. Eichmann and Barbie were merely sycophantic underlings. Ceauşescu was a petty dictator. And Milosevic was revealed to be less of a monster than Bosnian Serb leader Radovan Karadzic and Bosnian Serb general Ratko Mladic, who are still at large. Saddam Hussein, in contrast, was the top official responsible for the actions of the Baathist regime, and he was shown during the Dujail trial to have maintained extraordinary control over the Iraqi military and security forces. Unlike Milosevic, a frumpy apparatchik who fit Hannah Arendt's description of the "banality of evil," Saddam was an imposing and terrifying figure in the courtroom.

The third criterion is the level of interest of the international community. Because a broad coalition fought against Saddam Hussein with UN approval in 1991, and because the 2003 U.S. invasion of Iraq was so controversial, Saddam was extremely well known throughout the world and the media and public interest in his trial was immense. For this reason, it is likely that more people around the globe tuned in to the televised Dujail trial than any previous trial in history, and in the United States it probably ranks second only to the O. J. Simpson case for most-watched trial. As *The Washington Post* put it, "The trial of Saddam Hussein was an utterly compelling made for TV spectacle."

The fourth criterion examines whether the trial served as a model for a reformed Iraqi justice system. As detailed in chapter 6, the Dujail trial did not turn out to be the exemplar of justice its proponents had hoped for. Nor was it the kangaroo court proceeding its opponents tried to paint it as. Its judgment may one day be viewed as the definitive documentation of the character of the Baathist regime and its notorious leader. But when one of the authors met during the trial with a delegation of Iraqi mayors who were visiting the United States, the Iraqis said that with the assassination of defense counsel, the resignation of the chief judge, all the courtroom disruptions, and the defense boycotts, they believed the legacy of the Dujail trial will be a mixed one.

The fifth criterion is the likely effect of the trial on the situation in Iraq. In the short run, the trial certainly did not do much to facilitate peace and a transition to democracy. Indeed, there were spikes in the level of violence following each of Saddam's in-court diatribes, and the month following Saddam's execution was the bloodiest since the invasion in 2003. Moreover, whatever potential the trial had for making a positive contribution to peace and reconciliation was swept aside by the tsunami of sectarian violence in Iraq that reached a zenith during the proceedings. Twelve months later, things had begun to improve, and surprisingly there were no violent protests or terrorist attacks on the one-year anniversary of Saddam's execution. If Iraq survives this period of internal strife and makes a successful transformation to a democratic and unitary state, history will no doubt attribute part of that success to the trial of Saddam Hussein before a court of law governed by international standards of due process.

A final way to assess the trial is on the basis of its value as precedent. During the training sessions with the Iraqi High Tribunal judges in 2004 and 2005, the authors spent hours discussing the precedents of Nuremberg and other international war crimes tribunals. At one point a senior Iraqi judge asked, "Professors, do you think someday in the future you will be training judges for another tribunal, and you will be discussing the precedents from the Iraqi High Tribunal?" Just two years later, in October 2006, one of the authors (Michael Scharf) spent two weeks in Phnom Penh training the judges who would preside over the Cambodia Genocide Tribunal. Because Cambodia is a civil law country like Iraq, and, like the Iraqi High Tribunal, the Cambodia Tribunal's statute and rules mix international and domestic provisions, there was a great deal of interest in the precedents and lessons learned from the Saddam Hussein trial—a trial that has already earned a place in history.

# 10

## CONCLUSION

**No words on paper** can capture the full scope of the human drama that was behind the trial of Saddam Hussein. During the decades of suffering, no one dreamed that Saddam would ever face an accounting for his crimes. Each Iraqi complainant and witness who came into the Iraqi High Tribunal in the Dujail case figuratively spoke for thousands of his or her fellow citizens. The headline at the bottom of Baghdad's leading newspaper on the day after Saddam's capture asked the rhetorical question in large print: "Can This Day Be Possible?!" Expressing the sentiment of many Iraqis, the paper quoted a man on the street named Mohammed Khala, who said, "Saddam was a germ forcefully planted in all of us. He should've killed himself. He was a coward. People were driving and shooting in joy—this is a big defeat for anyone who aided him. There is not a single person in Iraq who was not hurt by him. We all must now unite and love each other." As we write, many Iraqis risk their lives every day to rise up against the injustice of evil. Iraqis will determine the fate of their nation, just as they sifted through the evidence of Baathist crimes to determine the fate of the defendants in the Dujail trial.

In many ways, Saddam's Iraq shared all of the characteristics of Hitler's Germany: a repressive and seemingly omniscient intelligence apparatus; the overarching visage of the supreme leader; the corruption of state bureaucratic processes into instruments of oppression; the aggressive wars waged on neighboring nations; and wholesale crimes committed by the government against its own citizens in pursuit of the leader's iron will. The Dujail trial represented a barometer for the progress of civilized society in the sixty years between the opening statements in Nuremberg and those in Baghdad. As a famous American trial lawyer has written, "Perfect justice is an illusion. Perfect injustice is a reality."[1] One thing is clear—Saddam stood trial before a process unlike any ever seen in the Middle East.

As a conclusion to this insider account of the Saddam Hussein trial, this chapter explores four questions about the legacy and value of the proceedings: Was the Dujail trial a success? Was it fair? Was the courtroom chaos preventable? And what effect will the trial have on the future of Iraq and international criminal law? In addressing these issues, we are reminded of what Chief Prosecutor Robert Jackson said at the end of the Nuremberg trials: "Many mistakes have been made and many inadequacies must be confessed. But I am consoled by the fact that in proceedings of this novelty, errors and missteps may also be instructive to the future."[2] In the spirit of Jackson's sage remark, this chapter also provides advice to those who follow in our footsteps, preparing judges and prosecutors for future war crimes trials around the world, based on the lessons from Baghdad.

## WAS THE DUJAIL TRIAL A SUCCESS?

The emerging system of international criminal justice is composed of a pyramid of judicial institutions. On the upper tier are the purely international courts, such as the International Criminal Court in The Hague and the Security Council–created international criminal tribunals for the former Yugoslavia and Rwanda. On the next rung are hybrid international-domestic tribunals such as the ad hoc Court for East Timor, the Special Court for Sierra Leone, and the Extraordinary Chambers in the Courts of Cambodia. These hybrid courts were created through a treaty between the United Nations and the particular states, and their benches were made up of a combination of domestic and international appointed judges. And at the base of the pyramid are purely domestic courts and military commissions. A recent addition to this collection of penal institutions, which fall somewhere between hybrid tribunals and domestic courts, are the so-called internationalized domestic tribunals exemplified by the Iraqi High Tribunal in Baghdad.

The Iraqi High Tribunal merits this appellation because significant aspects of its statute and rules of procedure were modeled upon the UN war crimes tribunals for the former Yugoslavia, Rwanda, and Sierra Leone; its statute provides that the IHT may refer to the precedent of the UN tribunals for guidance and that its judges and prosecutors are to be assisted by international experts. Though it imports international law into the domestic code, the IHT cannot be considered an international tribunal because its authority derives wholly from domestic law, its seat is in Baghdad, and all of the court employees are Iraqis (with the notable exception of the very few non-Iraqi legal advisers who have worked within the IHT). So-called internationalized domestic tribunals are a necessary supplement to the limited resources of the newly established International Criminal Court in The Hague. The ICC is neither designed nor intended to replace domestic prosecutions, and in fact can only do so in cases where the domestic state is "unwilling or unable genuinely" to handle the cases over which it has a proper claim of jurisdiction. The IHT provides lessons that are directly applicable in nations around the world as they establish internationalized domestic tribunals under their own domestic law.

Unfortunately, the IHT was snake-bitten from its conception. Many countries, international organizations, and human rights organizations opposed the IHT from the start because it followed an invasion that they believed to be unlawful, because it provided for the death penalty, and because it was inaccurately seen as preventing deployment of a truly international court. Then, once the Dujail trial began, the proceedings were marred by the assassination of three defense counsel, the resignation of the presiding judge, the boycott of the defense team, the disruptive conduct of the defendants, and, finally, by an execution that was widely perceived as an utter fiasco. In light of all that went awry, attempting to provide an objective appraisal of the IHT is a bit like inquiring on the tragic evening of April 14, 1865, "Well, other than that, Mrs. Lincoln, how did you enjoy the show?"

But we are confident that history will end up viewing the IHT in a more favorable light, acknowledging several positive aspects of the venture. To begin with, the IHT statute and rules represent a novel (and mostly successful) attempt to blend international standards of due process with Middle Eastern legal traditions. It is particularly noteworthy that the Dujail trial was the first ever criminal proceeding in the Middle East that was televised live, gavel-to-gavel, enabling millions of people throughout the region to see the process of justice unfold, with its highs and lows, over a nine-month period. While the judges of the IHT might not have followed every provision of the tribunal's internationally inspired statute and rules as scrupulously as we hoped they would, the judges did bend over backward to grant Saddam Hussein the right to personally cross-examine his accusers and make statements to the bench—an opportunity he took advantage of on thirty different occasions during the trial. And while the media reported that the court-appointed public defenders, who represented the defendants while their retained lawyers boycotted most of the trial, were not up to the task, in fact they were ably assisted by a distinguished Canadian lawyer who had previously served as defense counsel in cases before the Yugoslavia and Rwanda tribunals.

The performance of the tribunal defense counsel as they stood to deliver powerful legal arguments on live television in spite of Saddam's aura represented the very highest expression of the legal art. The IHT was the first war crimes tribunal to incorporate an Office of Defense Counsel as an integral part of the court structure, though of course the IHT defense counsel were independent in representing their clients and in their consultations. They stepped forward in the service of the law when needed, and one defense lawyer has been described by an international adviser as "one of the bravest and most principled guys I have ever met." The four days of closing arguments delivered by the court-appointed defense counsel (in the face of Saddam's thinly veiled death threat) were particularly impressive, and ultimately led to the acquittal of one of the eight Dujail defendants and relatively light sentences for three others. In the view of the authors, the establishment of a tribunal Office of Defense Counsel is an innovation of the IHT that should become a model for other war crimes tribunals in the future.

Most importantly, though drafted in a repetitive manner that renders it a difficult read, the 298-page, single-spaced opinion of the trial chamber issued on November 22, 2006, is a thorough recitation of the law and evidence warranting criminal punishments for the events related to Dujail.

The trial chamber did a commendable job of addressing the arguments raised by the defense and meticulously describing the court's findings of fact and conclusions of law. The judgment is also strengthened with numerous and specific citations to the past decisions of international tribunals. To assist the judges in preparing their written opinion, the U.S. Embassy's Regime Crimes Liaison Office provided translations of the major war crimes judgments of our time, from Nuremberg to The Hague—the first time this body of jurisprudence has ever been made available in Arabic. And behind the scenes, the distinguished foreign judge recruited by the International Bar Association to assist the IHT judges worked tirelessly to help them understand and apply the international precedent in their judgment. He is a true hero, and because he has asked to remain anonymous, his sacrifices will never be fully acknowledged. The opinion, whose first fifty-four pages are devoted to responding to the numerous motions and arguments of the defense counsel, answers many of the objections of the tribunal's critics. And, as detailed in chapter 7, the judgment tackles one of the most difficult legal questions of our time: where is the line to be drawn in a country's fight against terrorists?

These may seem like modest accomplishments in light of all that went wrong during the Dujail trial, but in assessing the IHT one must also keep in mind that there were no other feasible alternatives for bringing Saddam Hussein to justice after his capture in 2003. While many experts would have preferred an international venue, France, Russia, and China let it be known that they would veto any effort to establish such a tribunal for Iraq since they felt the U.S. invasion had been unlawful. In any event, the United Nations had withdrawn from Iraq during the critical period when negotiations were under way to form the IHT. Simply turning Saddam Hussein over to the ordinary Iraqi courts, on the other hand, was not seen as a viable option either, since the Iraqi judiciary had been left in shambles after three decades of Baathist rule.

## WAS THE DUJAIL TRIAL FAIR?

On November 20, 2006, the highly respected human rights organization known as Human Rights Watch published a ninety-four-page report that concluded that the Dujail trial fell far short of fundamental fair trial standards. The timing of the report was unfortunate, since many of the organization's criticisms were proven to be unfounded in the pages of the court's judgment, which was issued just two days later. When in January 2007 one of the authors asked the director of Human Rights Watch, Ken Roth, why he had not waited until after the judgment was available to issue his report, Roth replied simply that the timing was calculated to ensure that the report received the greatest possible media attention. He added that his organization planned to issue a second report critiquing the opinions of the IHT trial and appeals chambers a few months later. Given the important role Human Rights Watch plays as a bulwark against injustice across the globe, this approach might seem warranted. But just as the IHT must be fair, so too must critics be fair in judging the court.

When the authors read the first Human Rights Watch report, we were reminded of the old adage "Where one sits often determines where one stands." Despite our own cynical nature and efforts to be as objective as possible, as experts who helped train the Iraqi High Tribunal's judges, the authors acknowledge that this book might reflect a subconscious inclination to view the tribunal sympathetically. In contrast, the Human Rights Watch report seemed to be shaped by a desire to discredit the institution at every turn as a way of saying, "See, we told you so. Saddam should have been tried by an international tribunal, not an Iraqi court!"

Eric Blinderman of the U.S. Regime Crimes Liaison Office has published a detailed response to the Human Rights Watch report, entitled "Judging Human Rights Watch."[3] His comprehensive fifty-five-page critique of the report convincingly establishes that many of the organization's criticisms were off base. While it may seem surprising that there could be such divergent views about the fairness of the Dujail proceedings, it is important to keep in mind that every major war crimes trial in history has had both outspoken supporters and voracious critics. As described in chapter 9, the Nuremberg Tribunal initially fared quite poorly in the court of public opinion. Fifty-five years later, the Slobodan Milosevic trial before the International Criminal Tribunal for the Former Yugoslavia was similarly subject to widespread criticism, including about the suspicious timing of the indictment (in the middle of the NATO bombing campaign), the manner of Milosevic's surrender (in violation of a judicial order by the Serb Supreme Court), the judges' demeanor (the presiding judge often yelled at the defendant), the replacement of the presiding judge who fell ill halfway through the trial with a judge who had not been present for the first two years of the proceedings, and the fact that the defendant himself died before the conclusion of the trial.

Moreover, due to the defense tactics in the Dujail trial, the challenge of ensuring both actual fairness and the perception of fairness while at the same time maintaining order in the courtroom was enormously daunting for the IHT judges. Saddam's chief lawyer, Khalil al-Dulaimi, gave an interview to *The New York Times* at the trial's midpoint in which he explained the unusual defense strategy. According to Khalil, the defense was convinced that Saddam would be found guilty no matter what and that Saddam's best chance was to use the proceedings to inflame the insurgency and to stretch the trial out as long as possible, so that in the end the United States would agree to set Saddam free in return for his help in restoring peace to Iraq.[4]

What would even the most distinguished American or European jurist do if faced with a defendant and his lawyers whose trial strategy was to be as disruptive as possible, provoke the judge at every opportunity, and continuously attempt to turn the trial into political theater? For an answer, one need only turn to the recent proceedings against accused al-Qaeda terrorist Zacarias Moussaoui, who was thrown out of court by U.S. District Judge Leonie Brinkema four times in a single day, and then temporarily banned from returning to court because of his belligerent outbursts. Newspapers reported that the consensus of legal experts was that Judge Brinkema acted appropriately; in contrast, the critics of the Iraqi High Tribunal decried that Judge Ra'ouf Rasheed Abdel Rahman violated international fair trial standards when he did the exact same thing.

What was truly amazing about the Dujail trial is that it was televised gavel-to-gavel in Iraq, and the international media broadcast daily highlights with translations. This means that observers around the world had the chance to watch justice unfold over thirty-eight trial days in Baghdad, warts and all. It is worth noting that few countries in the world have had the courage to go to such lengths to ensure transparency of their judicial proceedings, including the U.S. federal courts, which continue to this day to ban television coverage of criminal trials. True, this was among the messiest trials in history, and many mistakes were made for all to see—and for TV commentators like the authors to dissect. But as the U.S. Supreme Court has often said, "We do not live in a perfect world, and a criminal defendant is not guaranteed a perfect trial, just a fair one."[5]

In assessing whether the Iraqi High Tribunal's errors and missteps amounted to a miscarriage of justice, it is significant that the Dujail trial (much like the Nuremberg trials) turned out to be based almost entirely on the Baathist regime's own documents. The authenticity of those documents was demonstrated in open court and confirmed by the statements of Saddam Hussein in his infamous "I am responsible" testimony before the cameras on March 1, 2006. Since Saddam was convicted on the strength of these documents, even an American court would likely have dismissed Human Rights Watch's catalog of alleged judicial blunders as "harmless error," whether or not they had all been supported by the actual events during trial.

But we also have to keep in mind that this was not an American court. Although the Iraqi High Tribunal statute and rules adopt the fundamental due process safeguards enumerated in Article 14 of the International Covenant on Civil and Political Rights, they also make clear that the tribunal is to be governed by Iraqi criminal procedure, which is based on the civil law (inquisitorial) model prevalent in the Middle East. While Americans and Europeans may not be accustomed to a system that does not provide for disposition of preliminary motions until the final judgment, that allows the defendant to conduct cross-examination alongside his lawyer, or that issues a detailed charging instrument at the end of the prosecution's case—that does not mean the IHT process violated international fair trial standards.

Take, for example, the oft-repeated assertion of Human Rights Watch's international justice director, Richard Dicker, during the trial that the process was unfair because the IHT statute did not require the court to find Saddam and his codefendants guilty "beyond a reasonable doubt."[6] It is true that Article 19 of the IHT statute merely provided that "the accused is presumed innocent until proven guilty before the court" and did not stipulate a standard of proof. But the statute must be read together with the Iraqi criminal code and practice, under which a judge must be "satisfied of a defendant's guilt"—the traditional standard which civil law judicial systems (like France and Holland) employ, and a phrase that the IHT judges interpreted as the functional equivalent of the American "beyond a reasonable doubt standard." It should also be noted here that the U.S. Supreme Court has refused to define what "beyond a reasonable doubt" means and has held that American courts do not have to provide any definition of this amorphous phrase in their instructions to a jury in a criminal case.[7] In the end, the phrase "beyond a reasonable doubt" appeared over two dozen times in the Dujail trial chamber opinion.

Finally, "different" does not always mean inferior. Indeed, in one important respect, the Iraqi High Tribunal improves upon the American judicial model: the IHT statute required the court to produce a written reasoned opinion, explaining in detail the factual and legal basis of its judgment—something that is not required of an American jury verdict, which emerges from a proverbial "black box." Had the Iraqi High Tribunal instead followed the American model, there would have been no 298-page opinion for the analysts at Human Rights Watch to pick apart.

## WAS THE COURTROOM CHAOS PREVENTABLE?

It is often said that just as courts try cases, so too do cases try courts. As the first trial before the Iraqi High Tribunal, the Dujail case was the test run for this novel judicial institution. It was indeed a bumpy start. As detailed in chapter 6, during the nine-month trial, Saddam Hussein, his seven codefendants, and their dozen lawyers regularly disparaged the judges, interrupted witness testimony with outbursts, turned cross-examination into political diatribes, and staged frequent walkouts, hunger strikes, and boycotts.

While tolerating dissent is a healthy manifestation of a democratic government, a war crimes trial is not an arena in which dissension, particularly of a disruptive nature, should supplant, or even take precedence over, the task of administering justice. Unlike other forms of acceptable political expression, a disruptive defendant or defense lawyer who interferes with the "grandeur of court procedure" (as Hannah Arendt once described the judicial process)[8] threatens the proper administration of criminal justice. Disruptive conduct renders it more difficult for the defendant and any codefendants to obtain a fair trial. In addition, it hampers the court's ability to facilitate the testimony of victims and other witnesses. And it undermines the public's confidence in and respect for the legal process.

As the first case before a novel institution, the Dujail trial served as a kind of judicial laboratory in which defendants, like mad scientists, experimented with every conceivable form of disruption while the judges struggled to find appropriate remedies that would enable them to regain control of the proceedings. Perhaps the most important lesson in this regard is that allowing a former leader to act as counsel, questioning witnesses and addressing the judges throughout the trial, is a virtual license for abuse. The Iraqi National Assembly was prudent to require that defendants before the Iraqi High Tribunal be represented by Iraqi lead counsel, who came before the tribunal subject to the professional training and ethics of the Iraqi "law on lawyers" and could thus be subject to the various professional sanctions available under Iraqi law. This proved to be necessary, for example, when some members of the defense team were caught manufacturing evidence in a ham-handed attempt to impugn the motives of the chief prosecutor, Ja'afar. It was a huge mistake, however, for the presiding judges in the Dujail trial to allow the defendants to address the court at will and to question witnesses following their lawyers' cross-examinations, as this completely undermined the objective of the National Assembly's revisions to the IHT statute. Instead of permitting the defendants to have free rein, the judges should have recognized that departures from traditional Iraqi practices were warranted in an extraordinary trial of this nature, especially as the traditional practice was required by neither Iraqi nor international law.

They could instead have followed the example of U.S. courts, which have ruled that a defendant who is represented by a lawyer has no right to act as co-counsel by, for example, cross-examining witnesses or addressing the bench. American courts have said such a rule is necessary to "maintain order, prevent unnecessary consumption of time or other undue delay, to maintain the dignity and decorum of the court and to accomplish a variety of other ends essential to the due administration of justice."[9]

Even if the IHT judges felt that they had no choice but to permit defendants to act as co-counsel, they should have made clear that this was a qualified privilege. Drawing on international tribunal precedent, the privilege should be rescinded where the defendant attempts to boycott his trial;[10] the defendant's self-representation would prejudice the fair trial rights of codefendants;[11] or the defendant is being persistently disruptive or obstructionist.[12]

Since most war crimes tribunal courtrooms are partitioned by soundproof glass, a judge may effectively deal with minor disruptions by simply turning off the defendant's microphone. Adolf Eichmann was placed in a glass enclosure of exactly this sort as he stood trial in Jerusalem for engineering the destruction of millions of victims. In the case of persistent disruptions, the judge should give a specific warning before revoking the right to serve as counsel or co-counsel. And if the defendant continues to misbehave, the judges should expel him from the courtroom, after issuing an appropriate warning. The warning should also explain that in addition to exclusion, the judge may impose other sanctions on the defendant, such as relocating him to a smaller cell, decreasing the time he gets for recreation, or reducing his access to other prisoners and family.

Judge Ra'ouf and his colleagues on the bench were operating "under the lights," to use the phrase of another Iraqi judge. They tried to balance the needs of justice and judicial demeanor against what they knew the Iraqi people and the wider world expected to see during court sessions.

While the judicial process may well proceed more smoothly without the defendant in the courtroom, his absence may diminish the educative function of the trial. During Saddam Hussein's boycott of the Dujail trial, for example, print and broadcast media attention quickly dwindled, denying the public a chance to learn about some of the most important documents and testimony admitted into evidence. Thus, there are good reasons to avoid the sanction of expulsion if possible. Consequently, if disruptive conduct persists despite the initial warning, the judge should issue a firmer warning, recess to discuss the matter with the defendant and his lawyer, or briefly adjourn the proceeding to allow a cooling-off period. Further disruption should result in temporary exclusion, followed by a calibrated response proportionate to the degree and persistence of disruption. In addition, the defendant must be accorded at least a chance to return to the courtroom if he manifests a willingness to conduct himself consistently with the decorum and respect inherent in the concept of courts and judicial proceedings. Saddam returned to court and apologized to the judge on a number of occasions.

Another lesson of the Dujail trial is that a war crimes tribunal must appoint standby counsel, present from the beginning of the trial, and ever ready to step in when needed.[13] Such occasions would include when the defendant or his counsel persistently disrupt or obstruct orderly proceedings in open court, or when they stage a walkout or boycott of the proceedings. Standby counsel should be highly qualified, receive the same international training as prosecutors and judges, and be assisted by international experts. The very presence of standby public defenders can have a deterrent effect on misconduct by a self-represented defendant or by retained defense counsel because they will recognize that their disruptive actions will not successfully derail the trial, which can proceed without pause with standby counsel.

Ironically, the Iraqi High Tribunal did in fact appoint standby public defenders for the Dujail trial, but failed to provide timely notice to the media of their appointment, describe their credentials or those of their advisers, or explain their function. Consequently, several print and broadcast media outlets erroneously reported that Saddam Hussein was not represented by any counsel during those periods in which his retained counsel were boycotting the proceedings. Similarly, human rights organizations that were publicly critical of the skills and experience of the public defenders failed to recognize that they were in fact being assisted by international experts of the highest caliber recruited by the International Bar Association.[14]

With respect to disorderly defense counsel, the problem in the Dujail trial was that the judges did not clearly set the ground rules of the trial from the beginning, warning that disruptive conduct would not be tolerated and describing the sanctions that would be imposed in response to such transgression. Although the demeanor and conduct of counsel that is deemed acceptable may vary somewhat from country to country, most of the world's legal professions follow the basic principle that a lawyer must be "respectful, courteous, and aboveboard in his relations with a judge" before whom he appears.[15] Especially in a major war crimes trial, deferential courtroom behavior is necessary to ensure that the judge's decisions are not perceived to be based on emotional reactions to insult. As with so many other aspects of this process, the presiding judge for the Anfal genocide trial learned from the Dujail experience and conducted a pretrial session with the parties to ensure order from the first moments of trial.

Following the practice of the Special Court for Sierra Leone, all war crimes tribunals should adopt a code of professional conduct, which spells out the rules of courtroom decorum applicable to both the prosecution and defense counsel. Consistent with such a code, after an appropriate warning, persistent insults and disrespectful comments should be met with sanctions, including fines, jail time, suspension, and even disbarment. Since a judge has inherent power to remove a disruptive defendant from the courtroom, he also possesses the inherent power to deal with a disruptive lawyer in the same way and to temporarily or permanently replace him with standby counsel.

It is important in this regard to stress that the obligations of a defense counsel are not just to the client but also to the court and to the larger interests of justice that the court is serving. Defense counsel is not merely an agent of the client, permitted and perhaps even obliged to do for the accused everything he would do for himself if he were trying his own case. As the American Bar Association has explained, "it would be difficult to imagine anything which would more gravely demean the advocate or undermine the integrity of our system of justice than the idea that a defense lawyer should be simply a conduit for his client's desires."[16] If a client insists on his attorney asking improper questions, making irrelevant speeches, insulting the bench, or staging walkouts or boycotts, the lawyer must reject those instructions, for he cannot excuse his own professional misconduct on the ground that his client demanded it. Likewise, if defense counsel advises a client to act disruptively (or suggests methods for doing so), counsel should be fined, replaced, and even disbarred.

## WHAT ARE THE CONSEQUENCES OF THE DUJAIL TRIAL?

December 2003 was the month that the huge statues of Saddam's head were removed from the top of the Republican Palace. It was the month that Saddam was captured in his "spider hole." And it was the month that saw the establishment of the tribunal that would prosecute him. In December 2003 the first judges to grapple with the combination of Iraqi and international principles gathered to dissect the law that would in time topple a tyrant. One of those Iraqis admonished his comrades that "nationalism makes an ignorant friend and a liar historian." His clear intent was that they look at the practices of the Iraqi legal and political system with clear-eyed confidence that their society and culture is strong enough to face the truth. Amen, say these authors. The Dujail trial has profound lessons for those who are willing to study its processes and examine its precedents. Its mistakes are instructive, but it is fitting that we end this work by highlighting three of the primary consequences of the trial that will inform the future.

In the short term, as we have pointed out, the trial did little to bring peace and stability to Iraq. It failed to serve as a unifying ideal that transcended the boundaries of tribe, region, and religion. The Iraqi government was nonetheless essentially correct in the gamble that the trial and execution of Saddam would end his practical influence over the affairs of the nation. There were no mass disturbances to mark his burial or the one-year anniversary of his execution.[17] To paraphrase Mark Twain, the fears of his martyrdom were greatly exaggerated. The Iraqis knew Iraq best, and *that* is one of the lessons of the Dujail trial.

Lawrence of Arabia, author of one of the most penetrating exposés on the Arab mind ever penned in the English language, wrote, "Better the Arabs do it tolerably than you do it perfectly. It is their war, and you are to help them, not to win it for them."[18] Though his experiences came from World War I, it is clear to the authors that exercising a form of legal colonialism and imposing a process on the Iraqis would have created lasting illegitimacy in the region that would have undermined the real respect for the rule of law across the Middle East and perhaps across cultures and continents. While its operation has been pockmarked with tragedy and occasional mistakes, the IHT is one of the bulwarks that even today guard against the tide of lawlessness and unrestrained power sweeping across Iraq. Nations need to be encouraged and supported in their efforts to create a holistic and synergistic system of international criminal law that can punish those who wage war against civilized societies.

Of course, the second significant consequence of the Dujail trial is simply the power of the beaten path. The fact that Iraqis took the lead in prosecuting the officials responsible for terrorizing their nation is, in itself, rather remarkable. For the first time, scholars and jurists in the region can read the Arabic text of a full legal opinion that applies international criminal law within the context of a Middle Eastern legal system. On the eve of the trial, newspaper headlines in the region trumpeted that the Dujail trial represented "a watershed in the history of Arab justice." In hindsight, even with the immense difficulties experienced in conducting such a complex endeavor in the midst of a raging insurgency, the Dujail trial stands as a beacon pointing toward a better future. Even as the transition to a peaceful and democratic future collapsed around the court, the process of justice was not held hostage to the desire of murderers and maniacs whose lawlessness continues to wrack the nation. Paraphrasing Justice Jackson's assessment of the International Military Tribunal at Nuremberg, "no history" of the era of Iraq under Baathist rule "will be entitled to authority" if it ignores the factual and legal conclusions found in the Dujail judgment.[19] Yes, there were more significant cases to be prosecuted, and there are hundreds more potential defendants awaiting trial in Iraq today. But the work of the IHT demonstrated that the people who suffered at the hands of the regime may yet live to watch as justice is done in accordance with law and procedure.

The importance of Dujail is captured by the reality of what happened inside the courtroom and what is captured in the written legacy of the judges rather than what was transmitted for minutes each day of the trial by the broadcast media. The importance of the momentary news headline seems so trivial and ephemeral in light of the larger truth. An Arab tyrant was captured, confronted, and convicted by his countrymen. To date, the work of the court has been tainted by the perception of insidious external politics. So long as the IHT functions as a neutral, independent, and apolitical servant of the people's interests in upholding legal precepts, its work will become emblematic as a modern chapter in the age-old struggle to implement law as a constraining and constructive force in society.

Lastly, in yet another parallel to Nuremberg, the Dujail trial provided a snapshot of what tyranny looks like. Robert Jackson described Nuremberg as "the world's first postmortem examination of a totalitarian regime." The Dujail judgment documents the suppression of basic freedoms and human rights. It catalogs the cruel techniques by which what Jackson termed a "militant minority" seized power, suppressed opposition, set up concentration camps, and "destroyed all judicial remedies for the citizen and all protection against terrorism."[20] The trial and its historical record should reenergize us in our common commitment to stand alongside the deep truths of human dignity and freedom of conscience. Dujail reminds us, in the words of Franklin Delano Roosevelt, that "the mighty action we are calling for cannot be based on a disregard of all things worth fighting for."[21]

The struggle against unconstrained evil is a common bond that crosses cultural and religious boundaries to unite humankind. Though Dujail itself was but one small incident in the sweep of Saddam's criminality, who among us is not moved by the plight of the families who watched their livelihood destroyed as the orchards were razed? Or the children whose parents were murdered, and who spent their childhood behind the barbed wire of a desert detention facility because their family happened to live in Dujail in July 1982? In the words of the Iraqi judges, humanity shares a common heritage that cannot be torn apart. "Millions of women, men and children have fallen victims during the last century to unimaginable horrors which have strongly shaken the human conscience. [These] serious crimes threaten the peace, security and prosperity of the world and arouse the concern of the entire international community. [They] must not be allowed to pass without punishment and prosecuting their perpetrators in an effective way through measures taken at the national level that aim to put an end to impunity."[22] That is the legacy of Dujail.

# EPILOGUE

**In the years since** the fall of the Baathist regime, Judge Ra'id Juhi survived at least three attempts on his life, and his family has been repeatedly threatened. When an American journalist asked him why he continued to come to work, his answer was as basic as his faith in the future of Iraq: "If I stay at home, and you stay at home, and the other guy stays at home, who will build Iraq? This is a battle, mister. And we're all soldiers in this battle. So there are only two choices, either to win the battle or to die. There's no third choice."[1]

In his own way, Judge Ra'id won the battles that he could wage. He successfully led the efforts to compile the investigative files running to thousands of pages that spawned the Dujail trial and the second Anfal genocide trial. His investigative acumen and commitment to the law left a lasting imprint on the IHT, and the investigative judges whom he trained continue to work.

After completing his work as the chief investigative judge, Judge Ra'id left Iraq for a fellowship at a prestigious American university. While his wife and children have thrived in America, Judge Ra'id recently told the authors that he still feels the pull of returning to Iraq to help build a better society, perhaps in a political role.

Judge Ra'ouf, who presided over the second half of the Dujail trial, was exhausted by the intensity of that experience and the associated long-term separation from his family. The grueling effort to produce the 298-page trial judgment also took its toll. Judge Ra'ouf rested in Europe for some months and has now returned to Iraq to preside over the IHT's fourth trial. The so-called Merchants' Case involved the murder of Baghdad merchants following summary proceedings in regime special courts; its most well known defendant was Tariq Aziz, the Iraqi diplomat who served as the face of the regime. The threatened charges against him in Britain for presiding over an unfair trial never materialized.

Speaking of Britain, in 2008 Her Majesty's government nominated our colleague from the London IHT judicial training session, London School of Economics professor Christopher Greenwood, to be the new UK judge on the International Court of Justice (the World Court) in The Hague. Chris's nomination was steeped in controversy since he had prepared a memorandum for the UK government on the eve of the 2003 invasion of Iraq, making the case that military action to topple Saddam was legally justified.

As this book goes to press, the RCLO operations have drastically downsized. This has left the IHT largely on its own in coordinating the myriad administrative activities associated with running the court. The international advisers that served inside the IHT structure have either departed the country or will do so shortly.

Sandy Hodgkinson came home to serve in the U.S. Department of State, and was subsequently appointed as the Deputy Assistant Secretary of Defense for Detainee Affairs, where she is grappling with controversies concerning Guantánamo Bay. Her husband, Dave, continues to serve in the U.S. Department of State.

Upon completing their assignments in Iraq, many of the members of the RCLO returned to their original positions. Others left government service altogether. Greg Kehoe, the first Regime Crimes Liaison Officer, is currently in The Hague serving as a member of the defense team defending a Croatian general before the International Criminal Tribunal for the Former Yugoslavia, while Christopher Reid is in Lebanon working in a rule of law capacity. Eric Blinderman returned to private practice at a major law firm and is the co-owner of one of New York's trendiest new restaurants.

Nevertheless, the work of the IHT continues to move forward. Following Saddam's execution, public attention in the West shifted to other matters, but in Iraq the Anfal genocide case continued to be highly watched and debated. The judges of Trial Chamber 2 issued their verdicts on June 24, 2007, convicting five former Baathists of genocide, war crimes, and crimes against humanity, and dismissing charges against one defendant. Ali Hassan al-Majid, Saddam's cousin who was known to the world as Chemical Ali, was one of the three defendants sentenced to death, while the others received life sentences. As this book goes to press, the complex legal and political issues associated with the Anfal appeals have not been resolved and no sentences have yet been carried out.

The case against the officials responsible for the brutal suppression of the Shiite rebellion in 1991 has gone forward in fits and starts. IHT investigative judges continue to collect evidence related to other massive crimes such as the invasion of Kuwait, the destruction of the Iraqi southern marshes, which was one of the most serious environmental crimes in human history, and the persecution of other groups by Saddam's regime.

Meanwhile, the maturation of the IHT as a self-sufficient and autonomous component of the Iraqi legal system continues. As one IHT judge told the authors, "The government is on one hill and the court is sitting on another hill." Though it functions within the swirl of Iraqi domestic politics, the work of the IHT remains emblematic as a modern chapter in the age-old struggle to implement law as a constraining and constructive force in society, but only so long as it is seen to function as a neutral, independent, and apolitical servant of the people's interests in upholding legal precepts. While its operation has been pockmarked with tragedy and occasional mistakes, it is one of the bulwarks guarding against the tides of lawlessness and sectarian power sweeping across Iraq.

Time will tell whether the Dujail trial represented the first step toward a revitalized legal system or whether the influences of internal Iraqi politics and sectarian fighting will end up frustrating the IHT's noble aspirations.

# A TIME LINE OF EVENTS RELATED TO THE DUJAIL TRIAL

**1937** Saddam Hussein is born in the village of Tikrit, one hundred miles north of Baghdad.

**1968** Saddam Hussein seizes power in Iraq in a coup d'état.

**1980** Iraq invades Iran, beginning an eight-year war between the two nations.

**July 8, 1982** Saddam Hussein's convoy is attacked while visiting the town of Dujail. Iraqi authorities arrest and interrogate hundreds of townspeople and destroy the town's orchards and farms.

**June 14, 1984** The Iraqi Revolutionary Court, presided over by Judge Awad Hamad al-Bandar, sentences 148 Dujail townspeople to death in relation to the assassination attempt.

**June 16, 1984** Saddam Hussein signs the death warrant for the 148 convicted Dujail townspeople.

**March 20, 2003** U.S. and coalition forces begin invasion of Iraq.

**April 2003** United States lists fifty-five most-wanted members of the former regime in the form of a deck of playing cards. Former deputy prime minister and foreign minister Tariq Aziz is taken into custody.

**May 1, 2003** United States announces the end of major combat operations in Iraq.

**July 13, 2003** U.S.-led occupation authority known as the Coalition Provisional Authority (CPA) appoints a twenty-five-member Interim Governing Council of Iraqi leaders as a first step toward the reestablishment of sovereignty.

**December 10, 2003** With advice from the CPA, the Interim Governing Council promulgates the statute for the Iraqi Special Tribunal.

**December 13, 2003** Saddam captured in a "spider hole" in ad Dawr, ten miles south of his hometown of Tikrit.

**March 8, 2004** Interim Governing Council signs interim constitution known as the Law of Administration for the State of Iraq for the Transitional Period (TAL). Article 48(A) of the TAL provides that the statute establishing the Iraqi Special Tribunal issued on December 10, 2003, is confirmed.

**May 28, 2004** Interim Governing Council chooses Ayad Allawi as prime minister of the interim government.

**June 28, 2004** The CPA turns formal power over to Allawi's interim government. UN Security Council Resolution 1546 is adopted, recognizing that the interim government possesses full power and sovereignty of the state of Iraq. The record of debate on the resolution makes it clear that the Security Council considers the transfer of power from the CPA to the interim government as the end of occupation.

**July 1, 2004** Saddam comes before Judge Ra'id Juhi for the first time in a televised proceeding to hear the general nature of the charges against him and to be informed of his legal rights following his legal transfer to a sovereign Iraqi government; he rejects charges of war crimes and genocide.

**January 30, 2005** Iraqis elect 275-seat National Assembly. Shiite-dominated party wins 48 percent of votes; Kurdish alliance, 26 percent.

**March 29, 2005** The Iraqi National Assembly convenes.

**April 6, 2005** Lawmakers elect Kurdish leader Jalal Talabani as president, and Adel Abdul-Mahdi, a Shiite, and interim president Ghazi al-Yawer, a Sunni Arab, to serve as vice presidents. The next day, the President's Council selects Ibrahim al-Jaafari, a Shiite, as prime minister.

**April 28, 2005** The new Iraqi government is approved by the Iraqi National Assembly.

**July 17, 2005** First criminal case is filed against Saddam Hussein, stemming from the 1982 massacre of dozens of Shiite villagers.

**August 11, 2005** The Iraqi National Assembly approves the statute, rules, and list of judges for the Iraqi High Tribunal (formerly the Iraqi Special Tribunal).

**August 28, 2005** Constitutional Committee signs draft charter, after long negotiations and over objections of many Sunni Arab leaders.

**October 15, 2005** Referendum on proposed constitution is held.

**October 19, 2005** Start of the Dujail trial. Saddam Hussein defiantly questioned the validity of the court before he and his seven codefendants pleaded not guilty to charges of ordering the killing of 148 Shias from the village of Dujail. After just over three hours, the trial is adjourned until November 28 to give the defense time to prepare its case and to give the prosecution time to ensure security for its witnesses.

**October 20, 2005** Saddoun al-Janabi, lawyer for codefendant former judge Awad al-Bandar, is seized from his car and killed.

**November 8, 2005** Gunmen fire on car carrying Adil al-Zubeidi, who is killed, and Thamer Hamoud al-Khuzaie, who is wounded. Both are on the team defending Saddam's half-brother Barzan al-Tikriti and former vice president Taha Yassin Ramadan.

**November 28, 2005** The trial reconvenes for a day. Saddam calls Americans "occupiers and invaders" and complains about treatment by his U.S. captors. The court hears testimony from a former Iraqi intelligence officer named Waddah Ismai'il Khalil, who investigated the 1982 assassination attempt that triggered the alleged massacre in Dujail. In his testimony, taped before his recent death from cancer, Waddah stated that hundreds of people were detained after the ambush in Dujail, which was estimated to have been carried out by between seven and twelve assailants. "They rounded up 400 people from the town—women, children and old men. Saddam's personal bodyguards took part in killing people," he said. "I don't know why so many people were arrested. [Barzan Ibrahim al-Tikriti] was the one directly giving the orders." Waddah noted that Saddam Hussein had decorated intelligence officers who had taken part in the operation. At least four defense lawyers failed to turn up, and the trial was adjourned until December 5 so the defense team could replace the two lawyers murdered November 8.

**December 5, 2005** Chief Judge Rizgar Amin permits Defense Counsel Najib al-Nu'aymi to present arguments challenging the legitimacy of the proceedings.

**December 6, 2005** Five witnesses testify, including a woman identified as Witness A, who was sixteen at the time of the Dujail crackdown and tells of beatings and electric shocks by the former president's agents.

**December 7, 2005** Trial adjourns after a truncated session that Saddam refuses to attend, a day after yelling: "I will not come to an unjust court! Go to hell!"

**December 21, 2005** Saddam claims Americans beat and tortured him and other defendants and prays openly in court despite judge's order for trial to proceed. Two witnesses give accounts of torture at the hands of the Iraqi security services and say Dujail had been attacked by helicopter gunships following the attempt to assassinate Saddam. One, referred to as Witness G, who gave evidence anonymously from behind a curtain, told the court that Saddam Hussein's half-brother Barzan al-Tikriti had been present at the detention center. "When I was being tortured, Barzan was sitting and eating grapes," he said. Defendant Barzan al-Tikriti interjected. "My hand is clean," he said, holding it up.

**December 22, 2005** Investigative Judge Ra'id Juhi reports that he saw no evidence to verify Saddam's claims that he was beaten while in U.S. custody. Three witnesses testify at a brief closed session, speaking from behind a curtain to conceal their identities. One, referred to as Witness H, says he was eight years old during the killings in Dujail. He says his grandmother, his father, and his uncles were arrested and tortured, and he never saw his male relatives again. Defendant Barzan addresses the court to argue that the witness was too young at the time of the incident for his testimony to be reliable.

**January 15, 2006** Chief Judge Rizgar Amin submits his resignation after complaints by politicians and officials that he failed to control court proceedings.

**January 23, 2006** Court officials name Ra'ouf Abdel Rahman, another Kurd, to replace Judge Rizgar. His deputy, Sa'eed al-Hammashi, is also replaced amid accusations that he belonged to Saddam's former ruling Baath Party. Sa'eed denies claims.

**January 24, 2006** Trial's scheduled resumption abruptly postponed for five days amid confusion over new judges and absence of witnesses.

**January 29, 2006** Trial resumes with a new no-nonsense judge, Ra'ouf Abdel Rahman, presiding. Defendant Barzan al-Tikriti is ejected after refusing to keep quiet and calling the court "a daughter of adultery." Saddam Hussein is ejected from the courtroom after shouting "Down with the traitor" and "Down with America." The defense walks out after a stormy exchange. The judge appoints four new defense lawyers to act as standby counsel.

**February 1, 2006** The trial resumes in the absence of the defendants and retained counsel, who are boycotting the trial. The court calls on the court-appointed standby defense counsel to serve as lawyers for the defense. The court hears from five prosecution witnesses, including a woman who testifies that she was arrested by Saddam Hussein's security forces and tortured in prison. She says Barzan ordered her to be tortured with electric shocks.

**February 2, 2006** The trial continues in the absence of the defendants and retained counsel, who are still boycotting the trial. Two witnesses testify to acts of torture they endured

**February 13, 2006** Saddam Hussein causes uproar as he is forcibly returned to the court after having boycotted sessions with his seven codefendants. He shouts slogans against the United States and Judge Ra'ouf, who, he insists, must be removed on the grounds he is biased. Judge Ra'ouf presses on with the case. "The law states that if the defendant refuses to appear before the court, he will be forced to appear," he says. Ahmed Hussein, the former head of the President's Office, takes the stand. He confirms Saddam's signature on a document relating to the execution of the Dujailis—a significant confirmation because Saddam will later claim that all of the documents submitted at the trial were forgeries.

**February 14, 2006** Saddam Hussein announces that he and his seven codefendants have been on hunger strike for three days to protest the way the court is treating them. Saddam Hussein's half-brother Barzan Ibrahim al-Tikriti appears dressed in long underwear for the second day running to signal his rejection of the court. Two former intelligence officials appear—one hidden behind a curtain; the other, Fadil Tawfij, speaking in open court. A former culture minister and personal aide to Saddam Hussein, Hamed Yusuf Hammadi, also appears. He is shown a piece of paper recommending rewards for six officials for their part in the Dujail arrests, bearing the handwritten word "agreed." Barzan addresses the court, insisting that he had ordered the release of Dujail prisoners and had nothing to do with the massacre.

**February 28, 2006** Saddam Hussein's defense team makes its first appearance in a month after boycotting the trial on the grounds that the chief judge is biased. The team immediately calls for the chief judge and chief prosecutor to be removed and for the trial to be postponed. The chief judge refuses, and two top defense lawyers walk out. Chief prosecutor Ja'afar al-Moussawi presents a presidential decree dated June 16, 1984. He says it contains the signature of Saddam Hussein approving the death sentences of 148 Iraqi Shias from the village of Dujail, where the ex-president survived an assassination attempt in 1982. Another document, dated two days earlier and announcing the death sentences, is signed by codefendant Awad al-Bandar, Ja'afar alleges.

**March 1, 2006** The chief prosecutor presents more documents and letters that he claims implicate those on trial, including death certificates of nearly one hundred Dujaili villagers, as well as transfer orders showing that their families were sent into the desert and their properties seized. One letter reveals that four of the accused were executed by mistake, while two were released by mistake. Another shows that nearly fifty died during interrogation, rather than by hanging. In a dramatic turn, Saddam Hussein acknowledges he ordered trials that led to the execution of dozens of Shiites in the 1980s but says he acted within the law. "Where is the crime?" he asks.

**March 12, 2006** Former Baath Party official Abdallah Kasim Ruwayyid appears in court to deny testimony by witnesses accusing him of helping to round up Dujail residents and demolish their property. Codefendant Awad Hamad al-Bandar testifies on his own behalf. He acknowledges that he sentenced 148 Shias from Dujail to death but says this was done "in accordance with the law."

**March 15, 2006** The prosecution shows a letter, apparently signed by defendant Barzan al-Tikriti, asking for several intelligence officials to be commended for their work in Dujail. In an address to the court, Saddam Hussein praises the ongoing insurgency as "the resistance to the American invasion." After Saddam Hussein rejects the judge's warnings against using the trial as a political platform, the press is barred from the rest of the hearing.

**April 4, 2006** The Iraqi High Tribunal announces that Saddam will stand trial on new charges of genocide stemming from the Anfal campaigns, in which thousands of Kurds were killed in the late 1980s.

**April 5, 2006** The prosecution produces identification cards suggesting that twenty-eight people whose executions the former Iraqi leader approved had been under eighteen, the minimum legal age for the death sentence under his rule. Meanwhile, a defense lawyer is ordered from the court by the judge when she tries to display photos of Iraqis tortured in U.S.-run prisons.

**April 17, 2006** Judge Ra'ouf reads out a report by handwriting experts who say that Saddam Hussein signed the death warrants for 148 Shias in Dujail in 1984. Defense lawyers claim the experts cannot be independent because they have links to Iraq's interior ministry, and call for new experts from abroad.

**April 19, 2006** Judge Ra'ouf announces that handwriting experts have concluded that signatures on documents—including the death warrants of Dujaili villagers—did belong to Saddam Hussein.

**April 24, 2006** The prosecution plays a recording it says is of a telephone conversation between Saddam Hussein and former Iraqi vice president Taha Yassin Ramadan discussing the destruction of farmland in Dujail. It also hears a report by more handwriting experts confirming the signatures of Saddam Hussein and six of his codefendants on documents linking them to the crackdown on Shia villagers.

**May 15, 2006** At the conclusion of the prosecution's case, the judges issue a formal charging document.

**May 16, 2006** All defendants appear in court, as witnesses testify in defense of four of the lesser-known defendants. Witnesses screened by a curtain testify that the defendants are good men and low-ranking officials with no responsibility or involvement in the killings in Dujail.

**May 24, 2006** Tariq Aziz, former foreign minister, testifies on behalf of Saddam Hussein, saying the defendants cannot be guilty of the deaths of 148 men following a 1982 assassination attempt on Saddam Hussein because the state had a right to punish such an action. Saddam Hussein's director of personal security, Abed Hamid Mahmud, gives details of how the assassination attempt was made.

**May 29, 2006** Two defense witnesses testify on the fairness of the trial in which 148 Shia men from Dujail were sentenced to death over their alleged involvement in an assassination attempt against Saddam Hussein.

**May 30, 2006** A witness for the defense tells the court that 23 of the 148 Shia villagers said to have been executed over their alleged involvement in an assassination attempt against Saddam Hussein are in fact alive. One defense witness accuses the chief prosecutor of bribing him to give false testimony.

**May 31, 2006** The defense shows DVD footage to discredit a key prosecution witness.

**June 5, 2006** Saddam's defense team says 10 people out of 148 said to have been killed after the attempt on his life are still alive. The defense team also contests the authenticity of the documents presented in the case, demanding that the trial be halted to investigate its claims.

**June 12, 2006** Judge Ra'ouf announces that action was taken against the four witnesses who were recently arrested for falsely testifying that the prosecutor tried to bribe them to give false evidence.

**June 19, 2006** In closing statements, prosecutors ask the judges to sentence Saddam Hussein, Barzan al-Tikriti, and Awad al-Bandar to death. The prosecutor says that there is not enough evidence to convict one of the lesser defendants.

**June 21, 2006** Gunmen kidnap and kill Khamees al-Obeydi, the number two lawyer on Saddam's defense team. His body is found in the northern Ur area of Baghdad.

**July 10, 2006** Saddam and his defense counsel boycott the closing arguments to protest the security situation. Judge Ra'ouf tells the defense lawyers the court is prepared to appoint its own lawyers to take their place, adding that they will harm their clients if they continue their boycott and refuse to prepare arguments and deliver them in court.

**July 27, 2006** Defense concludes closing arguments and the trial comes to an end.

**November 5, 2006** The Iraqi High Tribunal trial chamber issues its verdict, convicting Saddam Hussein, Barzan al-Tikriti, and Awad al-Bandar of crimes against humanity and sentencing them to death. The tribunal also sentences Taha Yassin Ramadan to life in prison; sentences Abdallah Kasim Ruwayyid, Mizhir Abdallah Kasim Ruwayyid, and Ali Diyah Ali to a term of fifteen years; and acquits Mohammed Azawi Ali el-Marsoumi. A 298-page judgment supporting the verdict is published on November 22, 2006.

**December 26, 2006** The Iraqi High Tribunal appeals chamber affirms the three death sentences. It also remands the case against Taha Yassin Ramadan with the instruction to sentence him to death; the trial chamber does so on February 12, 2007.

**December 30, 2006** Saddam Hussein is executed.

# GLOSSARY OF KEY LEGAL TERMS

**abetted** See **aided and abetted.**

**actus reus** The material or objective element of a crime, from the Latin for "guilty act." The prosecutor must establish that the accused was responsible for the material act, or actus reus, that is involved in the crime, but also that the offender had knowledge of the relevant facts and intent to commit the act (known as mens rea).

**admissibility** Refers to whether or not the trial chamber will allow evidence to be part of the record. Statements that are not voluntary or evidence gathered in a way that raises questions about the integrity of the proceedings are inadmissible, and will not be referred to in the trial chamber's written judgment.

**adversarial system** See **common law.**

**affidavit** A written statement taken after the affiant, deponent, or witness has sworn an oath to tell the truth. Strict common law rules of evidence do not allow affidavit evidence in a criminal trial as a general rule. But at Nuremberg, affidavits were widely admitted as a replacement for live testimony, a subject of much criticism. Where the content is not particularly controversial, they can be admitted before the IHT.

**aggravating factors** Factors to be taken into account in sentencing that tend to lengthen a sentence. Examples include a superior or commanding position in a hierarchy and evidence of premeditation where this is not a specific element of the crime itself. The opposite of **mitigating factors.**

**aided and abetted** Also known as "complicity." An individual who has aided and abetted is responsible for a crime even if he or she does not actually commit the physical criminal act. The accomplice must either aid, by performing a material act that assists the principal perpetrator, or abet, by encouraging the perpetrator.

**appeals chamber** In the IHT context, a nine-judge panel with the authority to overturn decisions of the trial chamber and to order an acquittal or a retrial or revise a sentencing judgment. It is the court of last resort, because there is no "supreme court."

**armed conflict** The resort to armed force between states or protracted armed violence between governmental authorities and organized armed groups or between such groups within a state. International humanitarian law distinguishes between international and noninternational armed conflict.

**chambers** A collective reference to the judges of the tribunal. The IHT is divided into several trial chambers and one appeals chamber.

**Charter of the United Nations** The constitution of the United Nations, proclaimed on the stage of the San Francisco Opera in June 1945. Article 2(4) of the UN Charter prohibits use of force against another state unless (1) in self-defense in response to an armed attack pursuant to Article 51 of the Charter, or (2) when authorized by a Chapter 7 resolution of the Security Council.

**civil law** A commonly used expression to describe the procedural regime used in criminal trials in continental Europe and many other parts of the world, including Iraq, characterized by an inquisitorial approach rather than the adversarial framework of the common law.

**civil law system** See **Romano-Germanic system.**

**civilian population** Crimes against humanity must consist of an attack on a "civilian population." The adjective "civilian" is defined broadly and is meant to emphasize the collective nature of the crimes amounting to crimes against humanity rather than strictly the status of the victims. It covers not only civilians in a strict sense but also all persons who were no longer combatants.

**closing argument** Trial takes place in two phases, the first involving the production of evidence, the second attempts by the two sides to draw conclusions about issues of law and fact and explain the theory of their case to the judges. The prosecutor goes first, followed by the defense. The prosecutor can present a rebuttal argument to which the defense may present a rejoinder. The parties may also supplement their closing arguments with written submissions.

**command responsibility** A legal technique by which a commander or superior may be convicted of crimes committed by his or her subordinates, even if the prosecution cannot prove that the commander or superior actually knew of the crimes or in some way ordered or incited them. In effect, the commander or superior is punished for providing negligent supervision of subordinates.

**common design** This is a form of complicity wherein offenders have a common design; that is, they possess the same criminal intention to commit a specific act and formulate a plan to carry it out, although each coperpetrator may play a different role within it.

**common law** The procedural system that first developed in England and then spread to its colonies, almost all of which kept the system, with some modifications, after decolonization. The common law treats prosecutor and defense as adversaries who in effect duel before relatively passive judges. Each side takes strategic decisions aimed at winning its case rather than approaching the trial as a forum where the truth of the allegations is to be determined in an objective sense.

**compensation** The IHT itself cannot order compensation to victims, but its judgments may facilitate claims for compensation by victims under Iraqi national legislation.

**competence** This term is sometimes used as a synonym for "jurisdiction." It refers to the power or authority of the tribunal to judge cases, rather than to its expertise.

**complicity** Participation in a crime for which the main physical act is committed by another. Accomplices generally participate by "aiding and abetting" the commission of specific acts. But an accomplice may also be held liable for acts of other participants that are reasonably foreseeable when there is an overall plan or common design to carry out a criminal act.

**concurrent jurisdiction** War crimes, genocide, and crimes against humanity can be prosecuted both by the IHT and by the Iraqi national courts, but in case of conflict, the IHT takes precedence under the principle of primacy.

**concurrent sentences** If two or more convictions are registered by the trial chamber, it may impose distinct sentences for each crime yet order that they be served concurrently, especially if they relate to the same general fact situation or criminal transaction. In practice, then, the convicted person serves the longer of the two sentences. Alternatively, the trial chamber may specify that the sentences be served consecutively. There is no limit in the statute as to the length of sentences.

**conspiracy** An agreement between two or more persons to commit a crime.

**contempt** Misconduct before the tribunal may be punished as "contempt." Contempt includes such acts as "contumaciously" refusing or failing to answer a question, violating orders of the tribunal, and tampering with witnesses.

**counsel** A defendant in proceedings before the IHT has a right to counsel of choice, provided that lead counsel is a member of the Iraqi bar.

**crimes against humanity** The concept of crimes against humanity was first recognized at the Nuremberg trial. It filled a major gap in humanitarian law, which hitherto had regarded what a state did to its own population as being its own concern, in contrast with what a state did to populations of occupied territories or soldiers of another belligerent, who were already protected. Crimes against humanity consist of an underlying "ordinary crime," like murder, that is committed as part of a widespread or systematic attack on a civilian population.

**cumulative convictions** Although the prosecutor is free to charge an accused with several different offenses with respect to the same act, if there is a conviction, the tribunal will only enter a finding of guilt with respect to one if there is sufficient overlap.

**customary international law** A source of international law derived not from written treaties but rather from unwritten rules developed over the ages. Customary law is established by proof of constant practice by states, indicating the existence of a legal rule, coupled with some indication (other than the practice itself) that they consider themselves to be bound by such a rule.

**decision** See **order.**

**defense** The accused or the accused's counsel.

**deportation** A crime against humanity involving the forced displacement of a civilian population by expulsion or other coercive acts from the area in which it is lawfully present.

**deposition** Testimony by a witness taken out of court, sometimes by videoconference, but for use during the trial as if the witness were actually present. The trial chamber can authorize a deposition in cases where a witness cannot physically attend or for other reasons deemed acceptable.

**disclosure** Prior to trial, the prosecutor is required to disclose or make available to the defense copies of witness statements of those who will be called to testify, copies of sworn statements, books, documents, photographs, and tangible objects that are material to the defense.

**disqualification** Removal of a judge assigned to a case because the judge has a personal interest or has or has had any association that might affect his or her impartiality.

**dossier** The referral file assembled by the investigative judge. It contains both inculpatory and any available exculpatory material and must be provided to the defense forty-five days before the first day of trial. Materials in the dossier may be considered as evidence by the judges.

**double jeopardy** See **non bis in idem.**

**due process** Ancient term of the common law referring to the right to a fair trial.

**duress** A defense invoked by the accused during trial whereby the commission of the criminal act is admitted, but it is claimed that the perpetrator had no moral choice because he or she was threatened with death or some other dire consequence.

**elements of crimes** The detailed criteria that must all be established by the evidence to warrant conviction of a defendant for a particular crime. The Nuremberg Tribunal did not use elements of crimes, but all modern tribunals do.

**enslavement** A crime against humanity involving the exercise of any or all of the powers attaching to the right of ownership over a person, such as by purchasing, selling, lending, or bartering such a person or persons, including the exercise of such power in the course of trafficking in persons, in particular, women and children.

**equality of arms** Concept developed in human rights law whereby a fair trial requires that both sides, prosecution and defense, have a certain equivalence in terms of resources and opportunity to present their case.

**ethnic group** One of the groups protected by the prohibition of genocide. It is similar in many respects to a national or racial group.

**extermination** A crime against humanity by which a particular civilian population is targeted for death, by either killing or being otherwise subjected to conditions of life calculated to bring about the destruction of a numerically significant part of the population.

**extradition** Process by which an accused is sent from one state to another in order to stand trial.

**Geneva Conventions** Four international treaties adopted in 1949 to deal with the protection of victims of armed conflict: wounded soldiers and sailors, prisoners of war, and civilians. In principle applicable only to international armed conflict, each of the four conventions includes one provision, known as Common Article 3, addressing the protection of victims of noninternational armed conflict.

**genocide** The intentional destruction of a national, ethnic, racial, or religious group, in whole or in part. The definition of genocide in the IHT statute is taken essentially word for word from the 1948 Convention for the Prevention and Punishment of the Crime of Genocide. It has been described by judges as the "crime of crimes" and is, arguably, the most severe of the categories of crimes within the jurisdiction of the tribunal. Genocide is in many ways an extreme form of the crime against humanity of persecution, to which it is closely related.

**grave breaches** Particularly heinous violations of the 1949 Geneva Conventions and of Additional Protocol 1. They are punishable under the IHT statute. Grave breaches can only be committed in international armed conflict. All states have an obligation to investigate grave breaches and see that their perpetrators are brought to justice, wherever the crimes have been committed.

**habeas corpus** A remedy by which a person who is detained challenges the legality of the detention. Defendants before the IHT are not permitted to seek habeas relief before the national courts of Iraq.

**Hague Convention** International treaty adopted in 1907 that concerns the laws or customs of war. It largely codifies important customary legal rules dealing with means and methods of war, the protection of prisoners, and the rights of civilians in an occupied territory. Though it was not designed as a criminal law treaty, its prohibitions were taken as the basis of individual criminal responsibility by the Nuremberg Tribunal. Violations of the Hague Convention are included in the IHT statute.

**head of state or government** Many countries grant their own heads of state or government a form of immunity from criminal prosecution, at the very least while they are still in office. However, no similar immunity was recognized at Nuremberg in the case of international prosecution. Moreover, governments can revoke a former head of state's immunity, as Chile has done with its former president Augusto Pinochet.

**human rights law** Body of international law developed since World War II in such instruments as the Universal Declaration of Human Rights, the Convention for the Prevention and Punishment of the Crime of Genocide, and the international human rights covenants. The IHT may be guided by the precedents from regional human rights bodies like the European Court of Human Rights, particularly with respect to fair trial issues.

**humanitarian law** Sometimes called international humanitarian law, or IHL, this is the body of law that regulates armed conflict that is both international and noninternational. The core of humanitarian law comprises the four Geneva Conventions of 1949, the two Additional Protocols of 1977, and the Hague Convention of 1907. Violations of humanitarian law are war crimes within the jurisdiction of the IHT.

**imprisonment** A crime against humanity consisting of severe deprivation of liberty, usually involving inhumane conditions.

**in camera proceedings** Proceedings that are not public.

**incitement** Incitement to commit genocide can be prosecuted by the IHT even if nobody actually commits the crime. Defendants and defense counsel can be ordered not to make statements that would incite imminent violence.

**indictment** The initial indictment, known as an "order for referral," is prepared by the investigative judge and sets out the charges against the accused. It must be in sufficient detail to indicate the points that are at issue, so as not to take the accused by surprise at trial.

**inhumane acts** A crime against humanity involving infliction of great suffering, or serious injury to body or to mental or physical health, by means of any act similar in nature to those set out in the list of crimes against humanity, such as murder, sexual violence, torture, and beatings.

**inquisitorial system** See **Romano-Germanic system.**

**intent** It is a requirement for any criminal conviction that the prohibited act be committed with intent and knowledge, often referred to by the Latin expression *mens rea,* or "guilty mind."

**interlocutory motion** An issue contested during the proceedings, usually on procedural or evidentiary issues, and on which one of the parties seeks an immediate ruling.

**international armed conflict** Resort to armed force by two or more states. Certain violations of international humanitarian law that are within the jurisdiction of the IHT can only be prosecuted if it can be shown that there was an international armed conflict.

**International Court of Justice** Located in The Hague, the International Court of Justice hears cases between sovereign states.

**International Criminal Court** See **Rome Statute.**

**internationalized domestic tribunal** The IHT is sometimes referred to as an internationalized domestic tribunal since its statute and rules are derived from those of the international tribunals, it is independent of the domestic legal system, and it is assisted by international experts, but at the same time its judges and prosecutor are Iraqi and it sits in Baghdad.

**Iraqi High Tribunal** The Iraqi High Tribunal, or IHT, was established in 2003 and approved by the democratically elected Iraqi National Assembly in 2005 to prosecute Saddam Hussein and other top figures of the former Iraqi government for crimes against humanity, war crimes, genocide, aggression, corruption of the judiciary, and wastage of natural resources in Iraq.

**joinder** Persons accused of the same or different crimes committed in the course of the same transaction may be jointly charged and tried. In the first IHT trial, Saddam Hussein was jointly tried with seven other defendants for crimes against the inhabitants of the town of Dujail in 1982.

**joint criminal enterprise** A venture by two or more persons to effect a criminal result, in which each member is held responsible for the specific acts perpetrated by the other members of the enterprise, but only to the extent these acts were likely to lead to such an act. Where a defendant is charged with a crime committed by another participant that goes beyond the agreed object of the joint criminal enterprise, the prosecutor must establish that the crime was a natural and foreseeable consequence of the enterprise, and that the accused was aware of this when he or she agreed to participate in the enterprise.

**joint trial** A trial of two or more accused.

**judgment** Ruling by the judges of the trial chamber or by a majority of them at the conclusion of the trial on the question of guilt or innocence. The final determination of an appeal by the appeals chamber is also called a judgment.

**judicial notice** As a general rule, if the judges are to take facts into account in their deliberations, such facts must be proven in open court. But some facts are so notorious and well-accepted that judges may take "judicial notice" of them.

**jurisdiction** The limits that circumscribe the power of the tribunal. See also **subject matter jurisdiction, personal jurisdiction, temporal jurisdiction**, and **territorial jurisdiction.**

**killing** See **murder.**

**laws of war** Historic rules governing means and methods of warfare, and the treatment of the wounded, prisoners, and civilians. Many of them date back to the age of chivalry, and they are regularly referred to in classical Greek histories as well as in the plays of Shakespeare. The first great modern codification is the Hague Convention of 1907. They were referred to as part of the expression "laws or customs of war" in Article 6(b) of the charter of the Nuremberg Tribunal.

**lawyer-client privilege** Communications between lawyer and client are privileged, and cannot be disclosed at trial without the consent of the client, unless the client has voluntarily disclosed the content of the communication to a third party, and that third party then gives evidence of that disclosure.

**mens rea** The mental or subjective element of a crime, from the Latin for "guilty mind." A guilty act (actus reus) is only punishable as a crime if the offender had knowledge of the relevant facts or circumstances and actually intended to commit the act. But this should not be confused with motive, which is the reason why the act was committed. For most crimes, the tribunal does not require proof of motive, although it may find such evidence to be helpful in clarifying any doubts about whether or not the accused actually committed the crime. But in the case of the crime against humanity of persecution, the prosecutor must establish that the accused did this on "political, racial and religious grounds" or, in other words, for a discriminatory motive.

**military necessity** A justification for the commission of war crimes, in certain circumstances. For example, wanton destruction or devastation of cities, towns, or villages is a violation of the laws or customs of war, but only to the extent it is not justified by military necessity.

**mitigating factors** So that the punishment actually fits the crime, an accused may invoke a range of personal circumstances, including age, infirmity, and mental illness, in order to reduce the sentence that might otherwise be imposed.

**motion** An application to the tribunal that normally takes place prior to or during the trial, asking the judges to make a ruling on a specific issue. Motions may deal with the admissibility of evidence or with a variety of procedural questions. A motion is not generally subject to appeal to the appeals chamber.

**murder** The statute refers to both "murder" and "killing." This is for historical reasons, because the crimes defined in the statute are derived from various texts that use slightly different terminology. But the Yugoslavia and Rwanda tribunals have concluded that the grave breach and genocidal act of "killing," and the crime against humanity of "murder," amount to the same thing: intentional homicide.

**national court** A court that is part of the ordinary Iraqi justice system. The IHT is independent of the national courts of Iraq, including the Supreme Constitutional Court.

**national group** A category of group protected by the prohibition of genocide. Kurds may either be a national group or an ethnic group.

**non bis in idem** Latin expression for what is known in the common law as "double jeopardy." An accused cannot be tried by a national court if he or she has already been tried by the tribunal. This also works in the other direction, but subject to important exceptions, such as sham trials held to shield someone from international prosecution.

**nongovernmental organizations (NGOs)** The IHT received assistance and training by several NGOs including the International Bar Association, based in London; the International Legal Assistance Consortium, based in Stockholm; the International Association of Penal Law, based in Paris and Siracusa, Italy; and the Public International Law and Policy Group, based in Washington, D.C., and Cleveland. Other NGOs, such as Human Rights Watch, participated as trial observers during the IHT proceedings.

**noninternational armed conflict** In popular parlance, a civil war. But international humanitarian law takes care to distinguish between noninternational armed conflict and situations of internal disturbances and tensions, such as riots, isolated and sporadic acts of violence, or other acts of a similar nature. There may also be a requirement that there be evidence of protracted armed violence between governmental authorities and organized armed groups or between such groups within a state. Serious violations of the laws or customs of war committed during noninternational armed conflict include violations of Common Article 3 of the Geneva Conventions, as well as some serious violations of Additional Protocol 2. They are punishable under the IHT statute. A noninternational armed conflict may become "internationalized" if another state intervenes in that conflict through its troops or, alternatively, if some of the participants in the internal armed conflict act on behalf of that other state.

**notice of appeal** Written declaration, following judgment, indicating a party's intent to appeal.

**nullum crimen sine lege** Latin for "no crime without law." This is the prohibition of retroactive crimes.

**office of the prosecutor** The organ within the IHT that is responsible for preparing prosecutions and presenting them to the tribunal at trial.

**official position** Official position is not a defense. In the past, tyrants alleged that they were merely acting on behalf of a state, and that they could not be held responsible individually for criminal offenses. The Pinochet judgment of the English House of Lords rejects this view, and it is set out clearly in the statute of the IHT, which says official position "shall not relieve such person of criminal responsibility nor mitigate punishment."

**opening statements** Before presentation of evidence by the prosecutor, each party may make an opening statement. The defense may, however, elect to make its statement after the conclusion of the prosecutor's presentation of evidence and before the presentation of evidence for the defense.

**order** A ruling by a judge or a trial chamber that relates to the preparation of the trial, transfer of suspects, protection of witnesses and other trial participants, televising the proceedings, and similar matters.

**pardon** An executive act that cancels a conviction and leads to the release of the convict.

**persecution** A crime against humanity consisting of the deprivation of fundamental rights; acts that are not inherently criminal but that may nonetheless become criminal and persecutorial if committed on political, racial, or religious grounds.

**personal jurisdiction** The IHT only has personal jurisdiction over persons of Iraqi nationality.

**precedent** A previous decision of a court that resolves a legal issue. The IHT statute provides that the tribunal will be guided by the precedent of the International Criminal Tribunal for the Former Yugoslavia and the International Criminal Tribunal for Rwanda. Judgments of post–World War II war crimes tribunals, international judicial bodies like the International Court of Justice and the European Court of Human Rights, and even rulings of national courts may also be invoked by the judges of the IHT as they interpret the statute.

**preliminary motion** An application to the tribunal by one of the parties made prior to the trial itself in order to resolve issues that affect the future proceedings, such as the joinder of defendants or details about the indictment.

**presiding judge** Each of the trial chambers elects a presiding judge who directs the proceedings.

**prisoner of war** A prisoner of war is a captured enemy combatant who wears a distinctive sign, carries arms openly, and does not violate the laws or customs of war. Prisoner-of-war status is presumed upon capture but may be contested before a court. Prisoner-of-war status is regulated by the Third Geneva Convention of 1949.

**prosecutor** See **office of the prosecutor.**

**racial group** Archaic term used to describe what we now know as "ethnic group." One of the four groups protected by the prohibition of genocide.

**record on appeal** The appeal is not a new trial, and as a general rule it does not consider evidence that was not initially presented to the trial chamber during the trial. The appeals chamber bases its decision exclusively on the "record on appeal," consisting of transcripts of the testimony at the trial, documents and other material evidence entered in evidence, and the various written proceedings of the court file.

**recusal** See **disqualification.**

**referral file** See **dossier.**

**religious group** A group protected by the prohibition of genocide. Intentional destruction of a religious group is a form of genocide. The category was included in the prohibition to ensure that disputes as to whether Jews or Muslims, for example, were not an ethnic but rather a religious group would not provide a loophole for defendants.

**Romano-Germanic system** A system of criminal procedure widely used in continental Europe and other parts of the world, including Iraq, sometimes also called "civil law system" or "inquisitorial system." Unlike the common law system, where this is done by prosecution and defense lawyers, it is a judge (known as the investigating or instructing magistrate) who prepares the case for trial.

**Rome Statute** The treaty that creates the International Criminal Court. Adopted by a diplomatic conference in July 1998, it came into force in mid-2002. Much like the IHT, the ICC can prosecute genocide, crimes against humanity, and war crimes. It has jurisdiction over crimes committed on the territory of countries that have ratified the Rome Statute, or by their nationals. Iraq has not ratified the Rome Statute. But the United Kingdom has, and complaints have been filed before the ICC about war crimes allegedly committed by UK personnel in Iraq during the 2003 invasion. Because the United Kingdom has prosecuted such cases domestically, the complementarity principle prevents the ICC from pursuing the matter further.

**rules of procedure and evidence** Detailed rules guiding the operation of the tribunal. They were approved, along with the IHT statute, by the Iraqi National Assembly on August 11, 2005. The rules are to be supplemented by the Iraqi Criminal Code, but in cases of conflict, the IHT rules prevail.

**sentence** If the tribunal decides to convict, it can impose an appropriate sentence, ranging from a term of years to life imprisonment or capital punishment. Any evidence or arguments that the defense wishes to submit in order to mitigate sentence must be produced during the trial itself, before the trial chamber has ruled on the issue of guilt.

**statute** The legal basis for the operations of the IHT. It was first promulgated by the Coalition Provisional Authority on December 10, 2003, and later repromulgated with revisions by the Iraqi National Assembly on August 11, 2005.

**subject matter jurisdiction** The crimes that the IHT is empowered to try, namely, grave breaches of the Geneva Conventions, violations of the laws or customs of war, genocide, crimes against humanity, aggression against an Arab country, corruption of the judiciary, and wastage of natural resources. In legal Latin, this is "ratione materiae jurisdiction."

**subordinate** See **command responsibility.**

**subpoena** An order issued by a judge or a trial chamber directing a person to testify in person or to produce a document.

**superior orders** A classic defense in war crimes trials, in which the obedient soldier admits committing a war crime but says, "I was only following orders." Even in post–World War II trials, superior orders was rejected as a defense in cases where the order was manifestly unlawful. To avoid any debate on this point, the IHT statute simply prohibits the defense. But the tribunal can take the issue into account in mitigation of punishment.

**temporal jurisdiction** The tribunal can only punish crimes committed within its temporal jurisdiction, that is, from 1968 to 2003. In legal Latin, this is "ratione temporis jurisdiction."

**territorial jurisdiction** The IHT can punish crimes committed by Iraqi citizens within the territory of Iraq or within neighboring states, such as Iran or Kuwait. In this way, its jurisdiction is more expansive than that of the Yugoslavia and Rwanda tribunals.

**torture** Torture can be prosecuted as a grave breach of the Geneva Conventions, a serious violation of the laws or customs of war, or a crime against humanity. It consists of the intentional infliction of severe pain or suffering, whether physical or mental, upon a person in the custody or under the control of the accused. Torture must be conducted for a prohibited purpose, such as obtaining information or a confession, punishing, intimidating, humiliating, or coercing the victim or a third person, or discriminating, on any ground, against the victim or a third person.

**trial chamber** Five judges of the tribunal, led by a presiding judge, who actually hear the case and rule on guilt and innocence. The trial chamber also has some responsibilities over pretrial matters.

**tu quoque** Latin for "you too." It is an argument used in war crimes trials in which the defense argues that "since you have committed the same crime, you cannot legitimately prosecute me." The tu quoque argument was rejected as an illegitimate defense by both the Nuremberg Tribunal and the Yugoslavia Tribunal.

**war crimes** This general expression refers to grave breaches of the Geneva Conventions and other serious violations of the laws and customs of war. In 1995, the Yugoslavia Tribunal's appeals chamber ruled that war crimes could be committed in noninternational armed conflict as well as in international armed conflict, a principle that was later codified in the Rome Statute.

**willful blindness** Where it is established that a defendant suspected that a fact existed, or was aware that its existence was highly probable but refrained from finding out whether it did exist so as to be able to deny knowledge, this is deemed to be equivalent to real knowledge for the purpose of establishing the mental element, or mens rea, of the crime.

# NOTES

## PROLOGUE: HIGH CRIMES, HIGH DRAMA

1. The story of the Charles I trial is captured in a wonderful book written by Geoffrey Robertson, an internationally renowned human rights lawyer who helped prepare the Iraqi jurists during the London training sessions in late 2004, *The Tyrannicide Brief: The Story of the Man Who Sent Charles I to the Scaffold* (New York: Pantheon Books, 2005). The transcript of the Charles I trial is on the Hanover College Department of History Web site, at http://history.hanover.edu/courses/excerpts/212trial.html.

## 1. LIBERATION

1. This name was chosen to symbolize the Iraqi incarnation of the speed and ultimate success of the breakout from the Normandy beachhead in 1944. Operation Cobra paved the way for the defeat of Germany, the institution of democratic government, and the achievement of lasting peace in Europe for the first time in more than two centuries.

2. For a riveting account of the armored reconnaissance mission that proved to be the rapid thrust into the heart of the regime, see David Zuccino, *Thunder Run: The Armored Strike to Capture Baghdad* (New York: Atlantic Monthly Press, 2004).

3. The International Center for Transitional Justice and the Human Rights Center of the University of California at Berkeley, *Iraqi Voices: Attitudes Toward Transitional Justice and Social Reconstruction* (International Center for Transitional Justice, May 2004), at http://www.ictj.org/images/content/1/0/108.pdf (accessed January 20, 2008). This source captures the results of interviews taken from a broad cross-section of the Iraqi population by a team of researchers in July and August 2003.

4. Michael R. Gordon and General Bernard E. Trainor, *Cobra II: The Inside Story of the Invasion and Occupation of Iraq* (New York: Vintage Books, 2006), 579.

5. Judge Gilbert Merritt, who was on President Clinton's short list for the U.S. Supreme Court and currently serves on the U.S. Court of Appeals for the Sixth Circuit, wrote an exclusive series of eight articles describing his experiences in Iraq as one of thirteen judges selected by the Justice Department sent to discuss the establishment of a revitalized Iraqi judicial system with lawyers inside Iraq. He was ordered to cease publication of his insights by the Coalition Provisional Authority. This is Judge Merritt's last public comment regarding what he termed a gag order: "It is, to say the least, ironic that, as a federal judge, I was asked to come here to try to help erect and establish constitutional values for the Iraqis, including the rights of freedom of speech and other civil liberties. Americans are entitled to speak their minds, especially on matters involving government, politics, law, foreign policy, and other public concerns. We value robust debate because our founding fathers believed that open debate was good in itself and would lead to better public policy, more scientific and technological progress and better artistic expression. That is what Iraqis admire about us and wish to have for themselves. They are thankful that we have liberated them from the tyrant so that they may now have prosperity through freedom of contract and freedom of speech. Yet, irony of ironies, our own citizens here must now clear our own speech with CPA so that our American values and policies, according to the directive, 'are launched in a coherent and coordinated manner' pleasing to the Directorate of Strategic Communication of the Coalition Provisional Authority. Having 'launched' our bombs and won the war quickly, I do not think that this kind of control of free speech is the kind of free speech policy most Americans want us to 'launch' in Iraq." Gilbert S. Merritt, "'Gag' Order Contradicts U.S. Values Iraqis Like," *Nashville Tennessean*, June 28, 2003, A2.

6. "Iraqi Coalition Casualty Count," iCasualties.org, at http://icasualties.org/oif/BY_DOD.aspx.

7. Headquarters Department of the Army, "Field Manual 3-24, Marine Corps Warfighting Manual 3-33.5 Counterinsurgency," Appendix B, December 2006, at http://www.fas.org/irp/doddir/army/fm3-24.pdf.

8. "Tip-off Led to Seizure," Aljazeera.net, at http://english.aljazeera.net/english/archive/archive?archiveid-42181.

9. Robin Moore, *Hunting Down Saddam: The Inside Story of the Hunt and Capture* (New York: St. Martin's Press, 2004), 248.

10. Ibid.

11. Named after a popular movie that portrayed domestic resistance to an invasion of American soil by enemy paratroopers.

12. The meekness of his capture led some sympathetic Iraqis to fabricate a story that, in fact, he was captured after a firefight in which two Americans were killed. According to this fictitious account, at http://www.watchingamerica.com/almadina000001.html, Saddam had been captured up to three weeks earlier and held by Kurdish insurgents. The Kurds allegedly held Saddam in the hopes of claiming the $25 million reward for his capture. A fictitious former American soldier, Nadim Abou Rabeh, who was allegedly one of the twenty closest to the capture, was reported to have said that Saddam was detained on Friday, December 12, 2003, and not on Saturday, December 13, as has been reported by the American military in Iraq. "Eight of us of eastern origin and who speak Arabic, were assigned to raid and inspection operations with support from helicopter gunships and tanks. The operation took place over three days in houses close to Tikrit, about 15 km [9.3 miles] away. Saddam was arrested in a rural home, and not in a hole, and only after offering fierce resistance. One soldier of Sudanese origin was killed." Nadim claimed that Saddam was detained after a large number of forces imposed control over the area. The military film-

making group worked throughout Friday night and into Saturday preparing to make the movie and arranging the scene, including the hole in the ground. "Saddam's guards offered little resistance, but Saddam himself shot more than 20 bullets from his gun, from a room on the second floor of the house, and it was I and a colleague of Moroccan origin that entered the house and spoke to him in Arabic," Nadim said. "We told him to surrender and offer us no resistance, and he answered us: 'If you were Americans I would have fired at you.' He then aimed his gun at us, and when he saw an American officer he became agitated, clung to a concrete post near the second-floor balcony and flung himself off the porch to the ground, where he was caught and had his hands tied."

The U.S. Department of State factually rebutted these wild claims as "a total fabrication." See http://usinfo.state.gov/media/Archive/2005/Mar/15-731732.html.

13. John D. Banusiewicz, "Rumsfeld Says Saddam Compliant, but Not Cooperative," American Forces Press Service, December 15, 2003, at http://www.defenselink.mil/news/newsarticle.aspx?id-27628.

14. "President Bush Addresses the Nation on the Capture of Saddam Hussein," December 14, 2003, at http://www.whitehouse.gov/news/releases/2003/12/20031214-3.html. The official White House message reads in full as follows:

> Good afternoon. Yesterday, December the 13th, at around 8:30 p.m. Baghdad time, U.S. military forces captured Saddam Hussein alive. He was found near a farmhouse outside the city of Tikrit, in a swift raid conducted without casualties. And now the former dictator of Iraq will face the justice he denied to millions.
>
> The capture of this man was crucial to the rise of a free Iraq. It marks the end of the road for him, and for all who bullied and killed in his name. For the Baathist holdouts largely responsible for the current violence, there will be no return to the corrupt power and privilege they once held. For the vast majority of Iraqi citizens who wish to live as free men and women, this event brings further assurance that the torture chambers and the secret police are gone forever.
>
> And this afternoon, I have a message for the Iraqi people: You will not have to fear the rule of Saddam Hussein ever again. All Iraqis who take the side of freedom have taken the winning side. The goals of our coalition are the same as your goals—sovereignty for your country, dignity for your great culture, and for every Iraqi citizen, the opportunity for a better life.
>
> In the history of Iraq, a dark and painful era is over. A hopeful day has arrived. All Iraqis can now come together and reject violence and build a new Iraq.
>
> The success of yesterday's mission is a tribute to our men and women now serving in Iraq. The operation was based on the superb work of intelligence analysts who found the dictator's footprints in a vast country. The operation was carried out with skill and precision by a brave fighting force. Our servicemen and women and our coalition allies have faced many dangers in the hunt for members of the fallen regime, and in their effort to bring hope and freedom to the Iraqi people. Their work continues, and so do the risks. Today, on behalf of the nation, I thank the members of our Armed Forces and I congratulate them.
>
> I also have a message for all Americans: The capture of Saddam Hussein does not mean the end of violence in Iraq. We still face terrorists who would

rather go on killing the innocent than accept the rise of liberty in the heart of the Middle East. Such men are a direct threat to the American people, and they will be defeated.

We've come to this moment through patience and resolve and focused action. And that is our strategy moving forward. The war on terror is a different kind of war, waged capture by capture, cell by cell, and victory by victory. Our security is assured by our perseverance and by our sure belief in the success of liberty. And the United States of America will not relent until this war is won.

May God bless the people of Iraq, and may God bless America. Thank you.

15. Ambassador Bremer, "Text of Ambassador Bremer's Opening Remarks at the CPA Conference Center" (comments, CPA Conference Center, Baghdad, Iraq, December 14, 2003). A full transcript of Ambassador Bremer's opening comments is available at http://www.iraqcoalition.org/transcripts/20031214_Dec14_Saddam_Capture.htm.

## 2. THE GENESIS OF JUSTICE

1. Samir Shakir Mahmood Sumaida'ie, Iraqi ambassador to the United States, speech, Frederick K. Cox International Law Center, Case Western Reserve School of Law, Cleveland, Ohio, October 6, 2006.

2. "Genocide in Iraq: The Anfal Campaign Against the Kurds," Human Rights Watch report, July 1993, at http://www.hrw.org/reports/1993/iraqanfal.

3. The events of the 1991 uprising would later serve as the basis for the third trial of the Iraqi High Tribunal, which is ongoing at the time of this writing. The Dujail trial, which is the subject of this book, came first, having begun on October 19, 2005. The Anfal genocide case began in August 2006.

4. Part 1 of the unofficial English translation of the trial chamber opinion (hereafter, Dujail Trial Judgment), at http://law.case.edu/saddamtrial/dujail/opinion.asp. See also "Judgment of *Al-Dujail* Law," *Case Western Reserve Journal of International Law* 39, nos. 1–2, App. A (2006–2007): 7.

## 3. HAMMURABI WAS AN IRAQI: THE CREATION OF THE IRAQI TRIBUNAL

1. *New York Times* advertising section, July 1, 1980, quoted in Sandra Mackey, *The Reckoning* (New York: Norton, 2002), 238–239.

2. Quoted in Andrew Cockburn and Patrick Cockburn, *Out of the Ashes: The Resurrection of Saddam Hussein* (New York: HarperCollins, 1999), 76.

3. A cuneiform tablet written in the Sumerian language contains the code of Lipit-Ishtar and marks the earliest known codification of law, dating back to his reign from 1868 to 1857 B.C. See Sara Robbins, ed., *Law: A Treasury of Art and Literature* (New York: Harkavy Publishing Service, 1990), 19. Some provisions of Hammurabi's code included the following:

> If a man accuse a man, and charge him with murder, but cannot convict him, the accuser shall be put to death.
>
> If a man owe a debt and Adad [the storm god] inundate the field or the flood carry the produce away, or through lack of water, grain have not grown in the field, in that year he shall not make any return of grain to the creditor, he shall alter his contract-tablet and he need not pay any interest for that year.
>
> If the wife of a man be taken in lying with another man, they shall bind them and throw them into the water. If the husband of the woman spare the life of his wife, the king shall spare the life of his servant.

4. Leonard W. King, *A History of Sumer and Akkad* (London: Chatto and Windus, 1923), 184.

5. Interview with Judge Zuhair Jumma Bash al-Maliki, December 9, 2007.

6. Samir Shakir Mahmood Sumaida'ie, Iraqi ambassador to the United States, speech, Frederick K. Cox International Law Center, Case Western Reserve School of Law, Cleveland, Ohio, October 6, 2006.

7. Universal Declaration of Human Rights (December 10, 1948), UNGA Res 217A (III), UN Doc A/810 (1948), at http://www.un.org/Overview/rights.html.

8. *Encarta*, "Stele of Hammurabi," at http://encarta.msn.com/media_461514617/Stele_of_Hammurabi.html (accessed January 23, 2008).

9. Grotian Moment: The International War Crimes Blog, "Iraqi Penal Code 1969," at http://law.case.edu/grotian-moment-blog/documents/Iraqi_Penal_Code_1969.pdf.

10. Interview with Judge Zuhair Jumma Bash al-Maliki, December 9, 2007. Judge Zuhair is well known in Iraq for his efforts against corruption in official circles. He is working on behalf of the rule of law at the time of this writing to assist the Iraqi people as part of the Provincial Reconstruction Team in Baghdad.

11. Final Report on the Transitional Justice Project in Iraq (2002), 11–12.

12. Nehal Bhuta, *Iraqi Voices: Attitudes Toward Transitional Justice and Social Reconstruction* (New York: International Center for Transitional Justice, May 2004), 31.

13. The Gallup data is recited at http://globalsecurity.org/wmd/library/news/iraq/2003/12/51_111203.htm. The political dynamic for the formation of the Balkans Tribunal is recounted in chapter 3 of Kingsley Chiedu Moghalu, *Global Justice: The Politics of War Crimes Trials* (Westport, Conn.: Praeger Security International, 2006), 50–75. Ironically, this book features a picture of Saddam standing and forcefully making a point to the presiding judge in the Dujail trial as its cover art.

14. Susan Sachs, "The Prosecution of a Dictator: A Decade's Worth of Digging Is Already Done," *New York Times*, December 16, 2003.

15. When the Iraqis shut down the power grid in Baghdad in the face of the invading coalition army, it could not be restarted even though coalition forces had deliberately elected not to target its physical facilities during the invasion. Given the anarchy and lawlessness that accompanied the small military footprint across Iraq, the dilapidated power grid could not be restored quickly, especially since the copper and aluminum from the power lines were looted and sold by Iraqi civilians. According to Thomas Wheelock, a senior U.S. official from the Agency for International Development, "they just started at one end of the transmission line and worked their way up, taking down the towers, taking away the valuable metals, smelting it down, selling it into Iran and Kuwait. The price of metal

in the Middle East dropped dramatically during this period of time." Quoted in Michael R. Gordon and General Bernard E. Trainor, *Cobra II: The Inside Story of the Invasion and Occupation of Iraq* (New York: Vintage Books, 2006), 536.

16. Kenneth Katzman, *Iraq: Post-Saddam Governance and Security* (Washington, D.C.: Congressional Research Service, 2007), 14.

17. David Rieff, "Blueprint for a Mess," *New York Times Magazine*, November 2, 2003, 28.

18. The project cost $5 million and had fifteen working groups on major issues. Information on the project, including summaries of the findings of its seventeen working groups, can be found at "Duty to the Future: Free Iraqis Plan for a New Iraq," U.S. Department of State, http://usinfo.state.gov/products/pubs/archive/dutyiraq/.

19. George Packer, *The Assassins' Gate: America in Iraq* (New York: Farrar, Straus and Giroux, 2005), 125.

20. Testimony of Mr. Sermid al-Sarraf, Iraqi Jurists Association, June 25, 2003, U.S. Senate Committee on the Judiciary, at http://judiciary.senate.gov/testimony.cfm?id-826&wit_id-2346.

21. John Hamre, testifying for the Center for Strategic and International Studies on October 8, 2003, before the U.S. House of Representatives Committee on Armed Services, "Reconstruction and Rehabilitation in Iraq," available at http://www.csis.org/media/csis/congress/ts031008hamre.pdf. The context of Mr. Hamre's comments is particularly disturbing; here is the pertinent text excerpted.

> I strongly encourage the Defense Department to continue its efforts to provide as complete and comprehensive an assessment as possible of the costs that we are incurring and are forecast to incur during the coming year. Up until just a day ago, we had too narrow an institutional base to support the reconstruction efforts in Iraq. I think it was an excellent idea for Ambassador Bremer to establish a liaison office here in Washington, headed up by Mr. Ruben Jeffries. But until the President named his National Security Advisor, Condoleezza Rice to lead a broader interagency effort, it was a problem that Mr. Bremer had to rely on a small staff in Washington to support him. In general, the efforts to enlist a wider base of support in the federal government for the reconstruction effort is a step in the right direction, and I'm more hopeful that we are getting on the right path. This raises the question of whether or not the federal responsibilities for rebuilding Iraq should have been assigned exclusively to the Defense Department. I understand and appreciate Secretary Rumsfeld's view that the Defense Department would overwhelmingly field the assets required for reconstruction, and therefore he should have complete authority to undertake the task. In theory I agree with this. But in practice it has not worked. The patterns of cooperation inside the Government broke down during the past year. DoD found itself having to manage tasks for which it has no background or competence, and it has not been effective in inviting the support of others in the government who have that background and competence. So the President's direction to Condoleezza Rice to take over the coordinating function for reconstruction should improve collaboration with other, better skilled parts of our government. The challenge of rebuilding Iraq is enormous. We have been eroding too much of our effectiveness caused by bureaucratic struggles here in Washington.

22. DIILS has presented programs to over twenty-nine thousand senior military and civilian government officials in 102 countries worldwide since its inception in late 1992. Typically, the program is accomplished through multiple phases that allow for tailoring curriculum to the host country. The U.S. presenters are members of the military services and civilian subject matter specialists. Seminars are designed for an audience of forty to sixty military and civilian executive personnel from the host country. DIILS works closely with the embassy team and the host country to develop appropriate seminars that are practical, timely, and effective. Seminars address legal-related topics, but the majority of audiences are nonlawyers who need a better understanding of how to operate within the parameters of international law and regulations. Participants include military and civilian personnel of appropriate rank and assignment for the seminar topic. There are unlimited possibilities once a relationship has been established with the host nation and specific needs identified. Potential topics include legal aspects of combating terrorism, legal and ethical concerns in public agencies, peace operations, military justice, operational law, trial advocacy, domestic operations, and legal issues in developing a professional military.

23. Before his retirement from active duty with the U.S. Army Judge Advocate General's Corps, one of the authors, Lieutenant Colonel Michael Newton, was the senior member of that team responsible for organizing the training, teaching, and meeting with the working groups of Iraqis.

24. Interview with David B. Hodgkinson, December 15, 2006, by Michael Newton.

25. Steven R. Ratner and Jason S. Abrams, *Accountability for Human Rights Atrocities in International Law: Beyond the Nuremberg Legacy*, 2d ed. (New York: Oxford University Press, 2001), 228–253.

26. Jane Stromseth, David Wippman, and Rosa Brooks, *Can Might Make Rights? Building the Rule of Law After Military Interventions* (Cambridge, UK: Cambridge University Press, 2006), 249–309.

27. Baghdad Penal Code (1919), para. 41.

28. The first documented suggestion of a war crimes trial for Saddam Hussein came in an editorial published on September 12, 1990. The authors stated that "any such trial must be scrupulously fair and all defendants must be given the opportunity to be present, give evidence, be represented by counsel, challenge evidence and the like; the refusal of a defendant to appear, however, should not preclude a trial." John Norton Moore and Robert F. Turner, "Apply the Rules of Law," *International Herald Tribune*, September 12, 1990.

29. Ironically, this was the same title used throughout World War II by the Allied efforts, spearheaded by the Americans, to collect detailed data that would later be used to support the International Military Tribunal at Nuremberg and other postwar military commission prosecutions.

30. General Accounting Office, *State Department Issues Affecting Funding of the Iraqi National Congress Support Foundation*, GAO Report GAO-04-559, April 2004.

31. A typical example is House Concurrent Resolution 137 (http://bulk.resource.org/gpo.gov/bills/105/hc137ih.txt.pdf), passed in the first session of the 105th Congress. Enacted on November 13, 1997, it read as follows:

> Whereas the regime of Saddam Hussein has perpetrated a litany of human rights abuses against the citizens of Iraq and other peoples of the region, including summary and arbitrary executions, torture, cruel and inhumane treatment, arbitrary arrest and imprisonment, disappearances and the repression of freedom of speech, thought, expression, assembly and association;

Whereas Saddam Hussein and his associates have systematically attempted to destroy the Kurdish population in Iraq through the use of chemical weapons against civilian Kurds, the Anfal campaigns of 1987–1988 that resulted in the disappearance of more than 182,000 persons and the destruction of more than 4,000 villages, the placement of more than ten million landmines in Iraqi Kurdistan, and the continued ethnic cleansing of the city of Kirkuk;

Whereas the Iraqi Government, under Saddam Hussein's leadership, has repressed the Sunni tribes in western Iraq, destroyed Assyro-Chaldean churches and villages, deported and executed Turkomen, massacred Shiites, and destroyed the ancient Marsh Arab civilization through a massive act of ecocide;

Whereas the status of more than six hundred Kuwaitis who were taken prisoner during the Gulf War remain unknown and the whereabouts of these persons are unaccounted for by the Iraqi Government, Kuwait continues to be plagued by unexploded landmines six years after the end of the Gulf War, and the destruction of Kuwait by departing Iraqi troops has yet to be redressed by the Iraqi Government;

Whereas the Republic of Iraq is a signatory to the Universal Declaration on Human Rights, the International Covenant on Civil and Political Rights, the Convention on the Prevention and Punishment of the Crime of Genocide and other human rights instruments, and the Geneva Convention on the Treatment of Prisoners of War of August 12, 1949, and is obligated to comply with these international agreements;

Whereas Saddam Hussein and his regime have created an environment of terror and fear within Iraq and throughout the region through a concerted policy of violations of international customary and conventional law; and

Whereas the Congress is deeply disturbed by the continuing gross violations of human rights by the Iraqi Government under the direction and control of Saddam Hussein: Now, therefore, be it

*Resolved by the House of Representatives (the Senate concurring)*, That it is the sense of the House of Representatives that—

(1) the Congress—

(A) deplores the Iraqi Government's pattern of gross violation of human rights which has resulted in a pervasive system of repression, sustained by the widespread use of terror and intimidation;

(B) condemns the Iraqi Government's repeated use of force and weapons of mass destruction against its own citizens, as well as neighboring states;

(C) denounces the refusal of the Iraqi Government to comply with international human rights instruments to which it is a party and cooperate with international monitoring bodies and compliance mechanisms, including accounting of missing Kuwaiti prisoners; and

(2) the President and the Secretary of State should—

(A) endorse the formation of an international criminal tribunal for the purpose of prosecuting Saddam Hussein and all other Iraqi officials who are responsible for crimes against humanity, including unlawful use of force, crimes against the peace, crimes committed in contravention of the Geneva Convention on POW's and the crime of genocide; and

(B) work actively and urgently within the international community for the adoption of a United Nations Security Council resolution establishing an International Criminal Court for Iraq.

Passed the House of Representatives November 13, 1997.

32. Regulations annexed to Hague Convention IV Respecting the Laws and Customs of War on Land, 1907 [1907 Hague Regulations] entered into force January 26, 1910, reprinted in A. Roberts and R. Guelff, eds., *Documentation on the Laws of War,* 3d ed., (New York: Oxford University Press, 2000), 73; Geneva Convention Relative to the Protection of Civilians in Time of War [Fourth Geneva Convention], articles 47–78, opened for signature August 12, 1949, 75 UNTS 287, 6 UST 3516.

The legal test for occupation law to apply is met when the following circumstances prevail on the ground: first, that the existing governmental structures have been rendered incapable of exercising their normal authority; and second, that the occupying power is in a position to carry out the normal functions of government over the affected area. See UK Ministry of Defence, *The Manual of the Law of Armed Conflict* (New York: Oxford University Press, 2004), 275, para. 11.3; see also Department of the Army, Field Manual 27-10, *The Law of Land Warfare,* para. 351 [FM 27-10] (Washington, D.C., 1956). The whole of chapter 6 of the U.S. Army Field Manual related to the law of armed conflict is devoted to explicating the text of the law related to occupation as well as the U.S. policy related to occupation.

33. The Permanent Representatives of the UK and the U.S. to the UN, addressed to the President of the Security Council, May 8, 2003, UN Doc S/2003/538, available at http://www.globalpolicy.org/security/issues/iraq/document/2003/0608usukletter.htm.

34. Security Council Resolution 1483, May 22, 2003, para. 5, at http://www.un.org/Docs/sc/unsc_resolutions03.html.

35. General Eisenhower's proclamation said: "Supreme legislative, judicial, and executive authority and powers within the occupied territory are vested in me as Supreme Commander of the Allied Forces and as Military Governor, and the Military Government is established to exercise these powers." Reprinted in *Military Government Gazette, Germany, United States Zone,* Office of Military Government for Germany (U.S.), Issue A, June 1, 1946, 1.

36. Coalition Provisional Authority Regulation 1, available at http://www.cpa-iraq.org/regulations/20030516_CPAREG_1_The_Coalition_Provisional_Authority_.pdf.

37. 1907 Hague Regulations, article 42.

38. Ibid. The conceptual limitations of foreign occupation also warranted a temporal limitation built into the 1949 Geneva Conventions that the general application of the law of occupation "shall cease one year after the general close of military operations." Fourth Geneva Convention, article 6. Based on pure pragmatism, article 6 of the Fourth Geneva Convention does permit the application of a broader range of specific treaty provisions "for the duration of the occupation, to the extent that such Power exercises the functions of government in such territory." The 1977 Protocols eliminated the patchwork approach to treaty protections with the simple declarative that "the application of the Conventions and of this Protocol shall cease, in the territory of the Parties to the conflict, on the general close of military operations and, in the case of occupied territories, on the termination of occupation." Protocol 1, article 3(b).

39. Sandra Mackey, *The Reckoning* (New York: Norton, 2002), 287.

40. *Coalition Provision Authority, Achieving the Vision to Restore Full Sovereignty to the Iraqi People (Strategic Concept)*, October 1, 2003, 5, available at http://www.globalsecurity.org/military/library/congress/2003_hr/03-10-08strategicplan.pdf.

41. Coalition Provisional Authority administrator L. Paul Bremer appointed the Iraqi Governing Council on July 13, 2003. The UN Security Council described the IGC as "broadly representative" and praised its formation as "an important step towards the formation by the people of Iraq of an internationally recognized, representative government" in Resolution 1500. The following list and description of the appointees appears at http://www.cpa-iraq.org/government/governing_council.html.

**Dr Ebrahim Jafari Al Eshaiker:** Main Spokesman of the Islamic Da'wah Party. Born in Karbala, educated in Mosul University as a medical doctor.

**Dr Ahmad Chalabi:** Head of the Iraqi National Congress (INC), mathematics professor and a businessman. Founder of the INC [which received $88 million from the U.S. government to support anti-regime activities from the time of its formation until the invasion].

**Ahmad Shya'a al-Barak:** General Coordinator for the Human Rights Association of Babel; Graduate of the Law Faculty, Babel University. Graduate of the College of Management and Economy, Baghdad University. One of the tribal leaders of Al Bu Sultan tribe in Babel.

**Dr Ayad Allawi:** Secretary General of the Iraqi National Accord. PhD in medicine. Started to oppose the dictatorial regime in the early 1970s and was in the forefront of efforts to organise opposition both within Iraq and abroad.

**Dr Jalal Talabani:** Jalal Talabani is Secretary General of the Patriotic Union of Kurdistan and a leading figure of the Iraqi democratic movement during the last 50 years.

**Hamid Majeed Mousa:** Secretary of the Iraqi Communist Party since 1993. Born in Babil province. An economist and petroleum researcher. Left Iraq in 1978 and returned in 1983 to continue his political activities against the dictatorial regime

**Judge Dara Nor al Din:** A Judge who as a member of the Court of Appeals, held one of Saddam's edicts (confiscating land without proper compensation) unconstitutional. Was sentenced to 2 years in jail. Served 8 months at Abu Ghraib before being released in the general amnesty last October.

**Dr Raja Habib Khuzai:** Head of maternity hospital in Diwanyia. Studied and lived in the United Kingdom from the late 1960s until 1977 when she returned to Iraq.

**Samir Shakir Mahmood Sumaidy:** From the Al-Sumaidy clan with documented lineage from the Prophet Mohammed through Mousa Al-Khadhum. Ancestral lands located near Haditha in the Al-Anbar region. Writer, designer and entrepreneur. A prominent figure in the opposition to the Saddam regime.

**Salahaddin Muhammad Bahaddin:** Elected as Secretary General of the Kurdistan Islamic Union in the first conference of the party in 1994, was reelected in the second and third conferences and still holds the post. Born in Halabja. Has written several books in Kurdish and Arabic.

**Songul Chapouk:** From Kirkuk and from the Iraqi Turkoman Community. A trained Engineer and teacher. She heads the Iraqi Women's Organisation (based in Kirkuk) which aims to bring together all the female communities of Iraq.

**Abdul Aziz al-Hakim:** Abdul Aziz al-Hakim is a religious and political leader and the current leader of the Supreme Council for Islamic Revolution in Iraq. He is the brother of Muhammad Baqr al-Hakim. They both returned to Iraq after 20 years of exile and are both the sons of the late Ayatollah Sayyid Mohsin al-Hakim.

**Abdul Karim Al Muhammadawi:** Head of Iraqi Party of God in Al Amara. Member and Rotating Chairman of Interim Supervisory Council in Maysan Province. Dubbed "Prince of the Marshes" for leading the resistance movement against Saddam in the Southern Marshes for 17 years, for which he spent 6 years in prison.

**Dr Adnan Pachachi:** President of the Iraqi Independent Grouping. Former Foreign Minister and Permanent Representative to the United Nations.

**Ghazi Ajil Alyawar:** Born in Mosul. A civil engineer. Recently Vice President of Hicap Technology Co. Ltd., Riyadh.

**Dr. Mohsen Abdul Hameed:** Secretary General of the Iraqi Islamic Party (IIP). Born in the city of Kirkuk. Author of more than 30 books in the field of interpretation of the Holy Quran. Detained in 1996 on the charge of reorganising the IIP. Professor in the College of Education in Baghdad University.

**Dr Seyyid Muhammed Bahr ul-Uloom:** Highly-respected Shi'a clergyman. Returned from London where he headed the Ahl al-Bayt charitable center. Elected as the Shi'a member of a leadership triumverate by the Iraqi opposition after the Gulf Conflict.

**Mahmoud Othman:** Independent politician and long-term leader of the Kurdish National Struggle.

**Masood Barzani:** President of the Kurdistan Democratic Party (KDP). He rose to this position from peshmerga. He was elected President in 1979 and reelected in 1999.

**Mowaffak al-Rubaie:** Born in al-Shatra. Member of British Royal Doctors' College. Consultant in internal medicine and neurology. Author of the Declaration of the Shia of Iraq. Activist in human rights. Student of the martyr Imam Baaker al-Sadr, who was murdered by Saddam.

**Naseir al-Chadirchi:** Leader of the National Democratic Party. Resident of Baghdad. Lawyer, businessman and farm owner.

**Judge Wael Abdulatif:** Born in Basra and practiced civil and criminal law before being disbarred and imprisoned by Saddam. Had been head judge at Nasiriya and now deputy head judge in Basra. Elected Governor of Basra on 4 July 2003 by the interim local council with the support of all the leading political and religious parties.

**Yonnadam Kanna, Assyrian Democratic Movement (ADM):** Secretary General of the Assyrian Democratic Movement. Former Minister of Public Works and Housing and Former Minister of Industry and Energy in Iraqi Kurdistan. Engineer since 1975. Activist against the dictatorial regime since 1979.

**Salama al-Khufaji:** Shiite, Appointed to the Council following the assassination of Dr. Hakila Al-Hashimi on September 20th, 2003. Diplomat. Led Iraqi delegation to New York donors' conference. PhD in Modern Literature and Bachelors in Law. Working with UN programmes in Iraq since 1991 in the Ministry of Foreign Affairs.

42. Security Council Resolution 1483, UN Doc S/RES/1483 (2003), at http://www.un.org/Docs/sc/unsc_resolutions03.html. An explanation and analysis are available on the American Society of International Law Web site, at http://www.asil.org/insights/insigh107.htm.

43. Charles Garroway, "The Statute of the Iraqi Special Tribunal: A Commentary," in Susan C. Breau and Agnieszka Jachec-Neale, eds., *Testing the Boundaries of International Humanitarian Law* (London: British Institute of International and Comparative Law, 2006), 155.

44. *Governing Iraq. IGC Middle East Report No. 17* (Baghdad, Washington, D.C., Brussels: International Crisis Group, Aug. 25, 2003), at http://www.crisisgroup.org/home/index.cfm?id=1672=1.

45. Coalition Provisional Authority Order No. 2, "Dissolution of Entities," at http://www.iraqcoalition.org/regulations/20030823_CPAORD_2_Dissolution_of_Entities_with_Annex_A.pdf.

46. *Prosecutor v. Nahimana et al.*, International Criminal Tribunal for Rwanda, Case No. ICTR-99-52-T, December 3, 2003, para. 109, quoting the Security Council resolution passed under Chapter 7 authorizing the tribunal's formation, SC Res 955, S/RES/944 (1994), November 8, 1994.

47. Gilbert S. Merritt, "Judge Jailed by Saddam Hopes for Return of Rule by Law," *The Tennessean*, May 26, 2003, 4A.

48. Ibid.

49. Peter Landesman, "Who V. Saddam," *New York Times Magazine*, July 11, 2004, 34, 37.

50. Ibid.

51. Interview with Charles Garroway, December 28, 2007.

52. UN Charter, article 39 (giving the Security Council the power to "determine the existence of any threat to peace, breach of the peace, or act of aggression" and to "make recommendations, or decide what measures shall be taken in accordance with Articles 41 and 42, to maintain or restore international peace and security").

53. Letter from Mr. Poos, president in Office of the Council of Ministers of the European Communities, to the secretary-general of the United Nations, April 16, 1991, in *The Path to the Hague: Selected Documents on the Origins of the ICTY* (New York: United Nations, 1996), 17.

54. Security Council Resolution 827, May 25, 1993, at http://www.un.org/Docs/sc/unsc_resolutions03.html.

55. UN Charter, article 25.

56. See Coalition Provisional Authority Order No. 48, "Delegation of Authority Regarding an Iraqi Special Tribunal," at http://www.cpa-iraq.org/regulations/20031210_CPAORD_48_IST_and_Appendix_A.pdf.

57. In international legal circles, this principle is respected as the principle of nullem poena sine lege (literally, "no punishment without law").

58. International Covenant on Civil and Political Rights, 1966, article 15, entered into force March 23, 1976.

59. Iraqi Special Tribunal (IST) statute, article 17(a).

60. Ibid., article 17(b).

61. Ibid., article 21(b).

62. Ibid., article 20.

63. Ibid., article 19. This provision of the IST statute preventing any adverse inference from the silence of the accused is noteworthy because it is the first time that such a protection was specifically found in Iraqi law.

64. For a summary of state practice and its implementation in treaty norms and military manuals around the world, see Jean-Marie Henkaerts and Louise Doswald-Beck, eds., *Customary International Humanitarian Law*, vol. 1 (Cambridge, UK: Cambridge University Press, 2005), 352–375; hereafter, ICRC Study.

65. Fourth Geneva Convention, article 3.

66. Adam Roberts and Richard Guelff, eds., *Documents on the Laws of War*, 3d ed. (Oxford, UK: Oxford University Press, 2000), 358.

67. ICRC study, vol. 1, 355.

68. Iraqi Special Tribunal statute, article 16.

69. Ibid., article 17 (first).

70. Ibid. (second).

71. I. Müller, *Hitler's Justice: The Courts of the Third Reich* (Cambridge, Mass.: Harvard University Press, 1991), 153–173.

72. Rajiv Chandrasekaran, "Tribunal Planners Hope to Start Case by Spring," *Washington Post*, December 16, 2003, 1.

73. Iraqi Special Tribunal statute, article 1(a).

74. Chandrasekaran, "Tribunal Planners Hope to Start Case by Spring," 1.

75. Landesman, "Who V. Saddam," 39.

## 4. PROVING INCREDIBLE EVENTS

1. Robert H. Jackson, "Report to the President," June 7, 1945. Upon his return from Europe, having laid the groundwork for negotiation of the charter to establish the International Military Tribunal of Nuremberg, Justice Jackson made a report to the president that was issued with a statement of White House approval on June 7, 1945. It was issued as official U.S. policy to all the nations that came to negotiate the London Charter. In context, this historic and oft-repeated sentiment read as follows:

> The groundwork of our case must be factually authentic and constitute a well-documented history of what we are convinced was a grand, concerted pattern to incite and commit the aggressions and barbarities which have shocked the world. We must not forget that when the Nazi plans were boldly proclaimed they were so extravagant that the world refused to take them seriously. Unless we write the record of this movement with clarity and precision, we cannot blame the future if in days of peace it finds incredible the accusatory generalities uttered during the war. We must establish incredible events by credible evidence.

Quoted in "Remarks of the Chief Justice: Dedication of the Robert H. Jackson Center," May 16, 2003, at http://www.supremecourtus.gov/publicinfo/speeches/sp_05-16-03.html.

2. David J. Scheffer, "Address on the 50th Anniversary of the Universal Declaration of Human Rights," Ramapo College, Mahwah, N.J., September 16, 1998.

3. David J. Scheffer, "The Case for Justice in Iraq," Monday, September 18, 2000, at http://www.fas.org/news/iraq/2000/09/iraq-000918.htm.

4. Ibid.

5. Human Rights Watch, *Basra: Crime and Insecurity Under British Occupation*, vol. 15, no. 6(E), June 2003, 8, at http://www.hrw.org/reports/2003/iraq0603/.

6. Human Rights Watch, *Iraq: State of the Evidence*, vol. 16, no. 9(E), November 2004, at http://www.hrw.org/reports/2004/iraq1104/.

7. Ibid., 17, note 37.

8. Ibid., 19.

9. Michael P. Scharf, "Is It International Enough? The Iraqi Special Tribunal in Light of the Goals of International Justice," *Journal of International Criminal Justice* 2 (June 2004): 130–338.

10. President Theodore Roosevelt, "The Man in the Arena: Citizenship in a Republic," Address at the Sorbonne, Paris, April 23, 1910, at http://theodoreroosevelt.org/research/speeches.htm.

11. For details about the assassination of Riyadh, see Schuster, Henry, "An Iraqi Victim," Wednesday, February 23, 2005, at http://edition.cnn.com/2005/WORLD/meast/02/23/schuster.column/index.html.

## 5. TRIAL AND ERROR

1. The phrase is commonly found in Iraqi courtrooms and comes from the fourth surah (chapter) of the Koran, titled "Al-Nisaa" ("the women"). In its entirety, surah 4, verse 58, says, "Surely Allah commands you to make over trusts to their owners and that when you judge between people you judge with justice; surely Allah admonishes you with what is excellent; surely Allah is Seeing, Hearing."

2. Obituary: Taha Yassin Ramadan, BBC News, March 20, 2007, at http://news.bbc.co.uk/2/hi/not_in_website/syndication/monitoring/media_reports/2333287.stm.

3. Jess Bravin, "Putting Former Dictator on Trial Is Next Test Facing U.S. and Iraq," *Wall Street Journal*, December 15, 2003, A1.

4. Louis Arbour, *In the Matter of Sentencing Taha Yassin Ramadan: Application for Leave to Intervene as Amicus Curiae and Application as Amicus Curiae of the United Nations High Commissioner for Human Rights*, February 8, 2007.

5. International Commission of Jurists, *Iraq and the Rule of Law* (New York: Human Rights Watch, 1994), 109–113.

6. Part 1, Dujail Trial Judgment, 14.

7. Death Certificate of Qasem Mohammed Jasim. Trial Exhibit IST.A4000.001.007 (March 23, 1989).

8. Memorandum from Counsel of the Revolutionary Command Intelligence Service, 9. Trial Exhibit IST.A4019.007.078 (February 9, 1987).

9. Trial Exhibit IST.A4019.009.003-002.

10. Quoted in *Economist*, July 16, 2004, 16.

11. The official transcript records a different version of the Koranic verse: "In the name of God, the Compassionate, the Merciful. Those who were said by the crowd that people had collected donations for them, increased their faith and said 'Sufficient unto us is God, He is our best representative.'"

12. Kanan Makiya is one of the extraordinary Iraqis whose courage and conviction represents the hope of his people. He was born in Baghdad but was able to leave for study in Cambridge and at MIT. He published *Republic of Fear* under a pseudonym, and followed that up with another award-winning work entitled *Cruelty and Silence*. He is the founder of the Iraq Memory Foundation.

13. Kanan Makiya, "An Iraqi Discovers Arendt," *World Policy Journal* 23, no. 4 (2006): 83.

14. "Affiya ya shaab al-Iraqi."

15. Peter Landesman, "Who V. Saddam," *New York Times Magazine*, July 11, 2004, 39.

16. Ibid.

17. Press conference with the chief investigative judge, Ra'id Juhi, Combined Press Information Center, Baghdad, Iraq, Thursday, October 13, 2005.

18. Interview with David Crane, conducted by Michael Newton on January 11, 2008.

19. Law on Criminal Proceedings with Amendments, No. 23 of 1971, Decree No. 230 Issued by the Revolutionary Command Council, February 14, 1971, para. 154, reprinted in United States Institute of Peace, *Iraqi Laws Referenced in the Statute of the Iraqi Special Tribunal* (2004) (hereafter, Iraqi Law No. 23 on Criminal Proceedings; copy on file with author), at http://law.case.edu/saddamtrial/documents/Iraqi_Criminal_Procedure_Code.pdf.

20. Iraqi High Criminal Court statute, article 20.

21. Article 19 reads as follows:

> First: All persons shall be equal before the Court.
>
> Second: The accused shall be presumed innocent until proven guilty before the Court in accordance with this law.
>
> Third: Every accused shall be entitled to a public hearing, in pursuance with the provisions of this law and the Rules issued according to it.
>
> Fourth: In directing any charge against the accused pursuant to the present Law, the accused shall be entitled to a just fair trial in accordance with the following minimum guarantees:
>
> A. To be informed promptly and in detail of the nature, cause and content of the charge against him;
>
> B. To have adequate time and facilities for the preparation of his defense and to communicate freely with counsel of his own choosing and to meet with him privately. The accused is entitled to have non-Iraqi legal representation, so long as the principal lawyer of such accused is Iraqi;
>
> C. To be tried without undue delay;
>
> D. To be tried in his presence, and to use a lawyer of his own choosing, and to be informed of his right to assistance of his own choosing; to be informed, if he does not have legal assistance, of this right; and to have legal assistance and to have the right to request such aid to appoint a lawyer without paying the fees, case if he does not have sufficient means to pay for it; if he does not have the financial ability to do so.
>
> E. The accused shall have the right to request the defense witnesses, the witnesses for the prosecution, and to discuss with them any evidence that support his defense in accordance with the law.

F. The defendant shall not be forced to confess and shall have the right to remain silent and not provide any testimony and that silence shall not be interpreted as evidence of conviction or innocence.

22. Niko Price, "Iraqi Genocide Tribunal Forming: Among Those Who May Be Tried: Hussein and Allies," Associated Press, December 6, 2003.

23. Joseph E. Persico, *Infamy on Trial* (New York: Praeger Press, 1994), 83.

24. The actual phrase used in court, in Arabic, was "Bidun tajreeh."

25. Iraqi High Criminal Court statute, article 1.

26. Ibid., article 33.

27. See http://www.iraqcoalition.org/regulations/20030516_CPAORD_1_De-Ba_athification_of_Iraqi_Society_.pdf.

28. Many American officials are defensive in conversation about the actual de-Baathification order, pointing out that it applied only to the first four levels of Baath Party members, while the more draconian steps taken by Iraqi politicians had a much more extensive, and some argue damaging, effect on post-Saddam society.

29. See http://www.iraqcoalition.org/regulations/20030516_CPAORD_1_De-Ba_athification_of_Iraqi_Society_.pdf.

30. Protocol Additional to the Geneva Conventions of 12 August 1949, and Relating to the Protection of Victims of International Armed Conflicts 1977 (Protocol 1), article 75(4).

31. Iraqi High Criminal Court statute, article 4.

32. Ibid.

33. ICTJ observers' notes, October 19, 2005.

34. Law of Judicial Organization, No. 160 of 1979, Res. No. 1724, issued by the Revolutionary Command Council, October 12, 1979, article 7. Published by the Ministry of Justice, *Official Gazette of the Republic of Iraq*, 23, no. 27 at 2 (July 2, 1980), reprinted in United States Institute of Peace, *Iraqi Laws Referenced in the Statute of the Iraqi Special Tribunal* (2004) (copy on file with author).

## 6. DISORDER IN THE COURTROOM

1. *United States v. Seale*, 461 F.2d 345 (7 Cir. 1972); *United States v. Dellinger*, 472 F.2d 340 (7 Cir. 1972).

2. Ibid.

3. For references by the tribunal to Milosevic misusing hearings and cross-examinations as a platform for making political speeches, see *Prosecutor v. Milosevic*, Initial Appearance, Case No. IT-02-54-T, July 3, 2001; *Prosecutor v. Milosevic*, Status Conference, Case No. IT-02-54-T, October 30, 2001; *Prosecutor v. Milosevic*, Hearing, Case No. IT-02-54-T, November 10, 2004 (T. 33293); *Prosecutor v. Milosevic*, Pre-Defense Conference, Case No. IT-02-54-T (T.32115-32116); see also Jerrold M. Post, "Tyranny on Trial Personality and Courtroom Conduct of Defendants Slobodan Milosevic and Saddam Hussein," *Cornell International Law Journal* 38 (2005): 823.

4. Michael P. Scharf and Christopher M. Rassi, "Do Former Leaders Have an International Right to Self-Representation in War Crimes Trials?" *Ohio State J. Dispute Resolution* 20 (2005): 3–42, 6–7.

5. Jerrold M. Post, "Saddam Hussein: A Political Psychological Profile," in Michael P. Scharf and Gregory S. McNeal, eds., *Saddam on Trial: Understanding and*

*Debating the Iraqi High Tribunal* (Durham, N.C.: Carolina Academic Press, 2006), 23, 53.

6. Statement of Jonathan Turley, George Washington Law School, on CNN, *Anderson Cooper 360 Degrees*, December 5, 2005, at http://edition.cnn.com/TRANSCRIPTS/0512/0512/05/acd.02.html.

7. See transcript, at http://transcripts.cnn.com/transcripts/0406/29/pzn.00.html.

8. Brian Bennett, "Saddam's Revenge," *Time*, October 9, 2006, 30–31.

9. There is also some international tribunal precedent for the approach of the IHT. After assigning counsel over the objection of the accused, the Yugoslavia Tribunal permitted Krajisnic "as an exception to the usual regime, to supplement counsel's cross-examination with his own questions." *Prosecutor v. Krajisnic*, Reasons for Oral Decision Denying Mr. Krajisnik's Request to Proceed Unrepresented by Counsel, Case No. IT-00-39-T, August 18, 2005, para. 3.

10. Robert Jackson, "Lawyers Today: The Legal Profession in a World of Paradox," *American Bar Association Journal* 26 (January 1947).

11. Interview with Chris Reid, former director of the Regime Crimes Liaison Office, conducted by Michael Scharf on October 6, 2006.

12. See *In Re Soliman*, 134 F. Supp. 2d 1238 (N.D. Ala. 2001); *Grand Jury Subpoena John Doe v. United States*, 150 F.3d 170 (2d Cir. 1998); *Martinez v. Turner*, 977 F.2d 421 (8th Cir. 1992); *White v. Narick*, 292 S.E. 2d 54 (W.VA. 1982); *Von Holden v. Chapman*, 450 N.Y.S. 2d 623 (N.Y. App. Div. 1982).

13. Robert Worth, "Prosecutors in Hussein Case Tie Him to Order to Kill 148," *New York Times*, March 1, 2006.

14. Exhibit 1, IST.A4019.008.074-077.

15. Exhibit 2, IST.A1369.001-004.

16. Exhibit 3, IST.A4021.001.059-062.

17. Exhibit 4, IST.A1655.040.001-002.

18. Exhibit 5, IST.A4021.001.053-057.

19. Exhibit 7, IST.A4019.008-034.

20. Exhibit 8, IST.A0480.002.010-011.

21. Exhibit 9, IST.A0480.002.008-009.

22. Exhibit 10, IST.A0480.002.002-003.

23. Exhibit 13, IST.A4019.009.003-004.

24. Exhibit D, IST.A0490.005.041-044.

25. See Gustav Becker, Wilhelm Weber, et al., UN War Crimes Commission, *Law Reports of Trials of War Criminals* (London: HMSO, 1947–1949), 7:67.

26. Eric H. Blinderman, "Judging Human Rights Watch: An Appraisal of Human Rights Watch's Analysis of the Ad-Dujayl Trial," *Case Western Reserve Journal of International Law* 39 (2006): 129–130.

27. See Transcript of Record, Al-Dujail Trial (June 12, 2006) (No. 2), 27–28, cited in Blinderman, "Judging Human Rights Watch," 140–141.

28. Ibid, 141–142.

29. Post, "Saddam Hussein," 23, 31, 182.

## 7. JUDGMENT DAY

1. See John F. Burns and Kirk Semple, "The Struggle for Iraq: Hussein Is Sentenced to Death by Hanging," *New York Times*, November 6, 2006, A1.

2. Dujail Trial Judgment, at http://law.case.edu/saddamtrial/dujail/opinion.asp.
3. Part 1, Dujail Trial Judgment, 24.
4. Ibid.
5. Ibid.
6. Ibid., 31.
7. Ibid.
8. Security Council Resolution 1511, 2003, para. 1, at http://www.un.org/Docs/sc/unsc_resolutions03.html.
9. Ibid., para. 4.
10. The Yugoslavia Tribunal and the Iraqi High Criminal Court are thus intellectual twins as they rest on the authority of the Security Council's Chapter 7 power. Former U.S. attorney general Ramsey Clark has attacked the legal authority for forming the ad hoc tribunals in a number of public comments and letters that raise almost identical arguments to those raised in the Dujail trial strategy: "The former President of Yugoslavia is on trial for defending Yugoslavia in a court the Security Council had no power to create. . . . The ICTY and other ad hoc criminal tribunals created by the Security Council are illegal because the Charter of the United Nations does not empower the Security Council to create any criminal court. The language of the Charter is clear. Had such power been placed in the Charter in 1945 there would be no UN. None of the five powers made permanent members of the Security Council in the Charter would have agreed to submit to a UN criminal report." See "The Milosevic Trial Is a Travesty," *Medialens*, comment posted on February 18, 2004, at http://www.medialens.org/forum/viewtopic.php?p=1168&sid=951fac4d77699450a10f09dadbfc2d0a.
11. Part 1, Dujail Trial Judgment, 31.
12. Michael A. Newton, "Comparative Complementarity: Domestic Jurisdiction Consistent with the Rome Statute of the International Criminal Court," *Mil. Law Review* 167 (Spring 2001): 20.
13. M. Greenspan, *The Modern Law of Land Warfare* (Berkeley: University of California Press, 1959), 223–227.
14. For example, the oath of the Nazi party was: "I owe inviolable fidelity to Adolf Hitler; I vow absolute obedience to him and to the leaders he designates for me." Drexel D. A. Sprecher, *Inside the Nuremberg Trial: A Prosecutor's Comprehensive Account* (Lanham, Md.: University Press of America, 1999), 1037–1038. Accordingly, power resided in Hitler, from whom subordinates derived absolute authority in hierarchical order. This absolute and unconditional obedience to the superior in all areas of public and private life led, in Justice Jackson's famous words, to "a National Socialist despotism equaled only by the dynasties of the ancient East." Opening Statement to the International Military Tribunal at Nuremberg, *Trial of the Major War Criminals Before the International Military Tribunal*, vol. 2, November 21, 1945; also cited at http://www.yale.edu/lawweb/avalon/imt/proc/11-21-45.htm.
15. *Prosecutor v. Krnojelac* (Appeals Chamber), September 17, 2003, para. 31; Blagojevic and Jokic (Trial Chamber), January 17, 2005, para. 698; *Prosecutor v. Simic* (Trial Chamber), October 17, 2003, para. 156.
16. Ibid.
17. Human Rights Watch, "The Poisoned Chalice: A Human Rights Watch Briefing Paper on the Decision of the Iraqi High Tribunal in the Dujail Case," no. 1, June 2007, 13, at http://hrw.org/backgrounder/ij/iraq0607/index.htm.

18. Robert Goldman, "Trivializing Torture: The Office of Legal Counsel's 2002 Opinion Letter and International Law Against Torture," *Human Rights Brief* 12, no. 1 (2004).

19. See *Kolk and Kislyiy v. Estonia*, ECHR Judgment, Application No. 24018/04, January 26, 2006. According to the European Court of Human Rights, crimes against humanity were proscribed and defined sufficiently by 1949 to permit the conviction of Estonian nationals in 1994 based on a domestic statute enacted in 1992 that created jurisdiction over crimes against humanity.

20. Part 1, Dujail Trial Judgment, 35–44.

21. Guenael Mettraux, "Crimes Against Humanity in the Jurisprudence of the International Criminal Tribunals for the Former Yugoslavia and for Rwanda," *Harvard International Law Journal* 43, no. 237 (Winter 2002).

22. Part 1, Dujail Trial Judgment, 41.

23. Part 2, Dujail Trial Judgment (2006), 4.

24. *Prosecutor v. Kupreskic, et al.*, IT-95-16-T, Trial Judgment, January 14, 2000, para. 563, cautioning, however, that there "is a concern that this category lacks precision and is too general to provide a safe yardstick for the work of the Tribunal and hence, that it is contrary to the principle of the 'specificity' of criminal law. It is thus imperative to establish what is included within this category."

25. Iraqi High Criminal Court statute, article 12(1)(f).

26. "The Justice Case," 3 T.W.C. 1 (1948), 6 L.R.T.W.C. 1 (1948), 14 Ann. Dig. 278 (1948), at http://www.law.umkc.edu/faculty/projects/ftrials/nuremberg/Alstoetter.htm.

27. International Commission of Jurists, *Iraq and the Rule of Law*, 109–113.

28. The signed death warrants were available at trial and entered into evidence; see http://law.case.edu/saddamtrial/exhibits/.

29. Part 1, Dujail Trial Judgment, 14.

30. Ibid.

31. Part 2, Dujail Trial Judgment, 13. Some of the facts leading to this conclusion were that "after carrying out the death penalty in 1985, at least between 4 and 14 individuals who were sentenced to death were still alive." Part 2, Dujail Trial Judgment, note 137, 20. Also, "In any case, the tribunal spent enormous efforts in this regard and secured all the papers of case No. 944/C/1984, comprised of 361 pages, and gave all the lawyers of the defence, including the lawyer of the defendant Awad al-Bandar, copies of all of those papers, as demonstrated by receipt attached to the case papers dated June 19, 2006. The tribunal notes that all of these 361 pages did not contain any of the procedures of the alleged trial, including the absence of any of the victims (defendants') testimonies before the (disbanded) Revolutionary Court in this case," part 2, Dujail Trial Judgment, 22.

32. Ibid.

33. "The Justice Case."

34. "Nuremberg Trials 60th Anniversary: Justice Case," *Dimensions: A Journal of Holocaust Studies* 19 (Fall 2006), at http://adl.org/education/dimensions_19/section3/justice.asp.

35. Ibid.

36. See, e.g., Human Rights Watch, "The Poisoned Chalice"; "UN Rights Chief Files Brief to Prevent Death Sentence on Iraq's Ex-Vice President," *UN News Centre*, February 8, 2007, at http://www.un.org/apps/news/story.asp?NewsID=21502&Cr=iraq&Crl=.

37. See "Prosecuting Saddam's Trial Judge in the UK," *Jurist Legal News and Research*, April 27, 2007, at http://jurist.law.pitt.edu/hotline/2007/04/prosecuting-saddams-trial-judge-in-uk.php.

## 8. APPEAL AND EXECUTION

1. Mark S. Ellis, "The Saddam Trial: Challenges to Meeting International Standards of Fairness with Regard to the Defense," *Case Western Reserve Journal of International Law* 39, nos. 1–2 (2006): 192.

2. See Sabrina Tavernise, "For Sunnis, Dictator's Degrading End Signals Ominous Dawn for the New Iraq," *New York Times*, January 1, 2007, A7; Hassan M. Fattah, "For Arab Critics, Hussein's Execution Symbolizes the Victory of Vengeance over Justice," *New York Times*, December 31, 2006, 13. Ironically, this Muslim holiday commemorates the willingness of Abraham to sacrifice his son. For Christians, Abraham was willing to sacrifice Isaac to Jehovah, but for Muslims, the holiday observes his readiness to sacrifice Ishmael to Allah.

3. Law on Criminal Proceedings with Amendments, No. 23 of 1971, Decree No. 230 Issued by the Revolutionary Command Council, Febrary 14, 1971, para. 290, reprinted in United States Institute of Peace, *Iraqi Laws Referenced in the Statute of the Iraqi Special Tribunal* (2004) (copy on file with author), at law.case.edu/saddamtrial/documents/Iraqi_Criminal_Procedure_Code.pdf (hereafter, Iraqi Law No. 23 on Criminal Proceedings), para. 290.

4. "There is no God but God, and Muhammad is his Prophet."

5. Iraqi Law No. 23 on Criminal Proceedings, para. 212.

6. Part 1, Dujail Trial Judgment, 24.

7. Ibid.

8. John Simpson, "Iraqi PM on Saddam and the Future," *BBC News*, http://news.bbc.co.uk/2/hi/middle_east/6126532.stm.

9. Kirk Semple, "Iraqi Predicts the Hanging of Saddam by the Year's End," *New York Times*, November 9, 2006.

10. Ibid.

11. Rajiv Chandrasekaran, "Tribunal Planners Hope to Start Case by Spring," *Washington Post*, December 16, 2003, 1.

12. Ibid.

13. "Saddam Should Be Executed '20 Times a Day,' Iraqi President Says," *International Herald Tribune*, September 7, 2005, at http://www.iht.com/articles/2005/09/07/africa/web.0907iraq.php.

14. Reuters, "Saddam Should Hang '20 Times a Day': President," *Sydney Morning Herald*, September 7, 2005, at http://www.smh.com.au/news/world/saddam-should-hang-20-times-a<->day-president/2005/09/07/1125772574459.html.

15. Iraqi Penal Code of 1969, Chapter 5, sec. 1, para. 85, at http://www.law.case.edu/saddamtrial/documents/Iraqi_Penal_Code_1969.pdf. "The primary penalties are: 1) death penalty, 2) life imprisonment, 3) imprisonment for a term of years, 4) penal servitude, 5) detention, 6) a fine, 7) confinement in a school for young offenders, 8) confinement in a reform school." Ibid. The subsequent sections specify a range of procedural obligations and limitations on the actual imposition of capital sentences.

16. For a summary of state practice and its implementation in treaty norms and military manuals around the world, see ICRC Study.

17. UN General Assembly note verbale, February 2, 2008, UN Doc A/62/658 (2008), states: "The Permanent Missions wish to place on record that they are in persistent objection to any attempt to impose a moratorium on the use of the death penalty or its abolition in contravention to existing stipulations under international law. . . . [Capital punishment] must therefore be viewed from a much broader perspective and weighed against the rights of the victims and the right of the community to live in peace and security."

18. Coalition Provisional Authority Order No. 7, Doc No CPA/ORD/7, Sec. 3(1) (June 9, 2003), at http://www.cpa-iraq.org/regulations/index.html#Orders.

19. Iraqi High Criminal Court statute, article 24 (first).

20. Colum Lynch, "U.N. Refuses to Assist Iraqis with War Crimes Trials," *Washington Post*, October 22, 2004, A18.

21. Security Council Resolution 1483, para. 4, UN Doc S/RES/1483, May 22, 2003, at http://www.un.org/Docs/sc/unsc_resolutions03.html.

22. Marlise Simons, "With Trials Looming, Iraqi Judges Agree They Need Help," *Inernational Herald Tribune*, October 23, 2004, 4.

23. Human Rights Watch, "The Poisoned Chalice: A Human Rights Watch Briefing Paper on the Decision of the Iraqi High Tribunal in the Dujail Case," no. 1, June 2007, 13.

24. Cassation Panel, Iraqi High Tribunal, al-Dujail Final Opinion Unofficial Translation, 9, at http://law.case.edu/saddamtrial/content.asp?id-88.

25. Ibid.

26. Ibid., 18.

27. Ibid., 9–10.

28. International Covenant on Civil and Political Rights, 1966, article 15.

29. Cassation Panel, 11.

30. Ibid.

31. Article 15 of the International Covenant on Civil and Political Rights reads:

> No one shall be held guilty of any criminal offence on account of any act or omission which did not constitute a criminal offence, under national or international law, at the time when it was committed. Nor shall a heavier penalty be imposed than the one that was applicable at the time when the criminal offence was committed. If, subsequent to the commission of the offence, provision is made by law for the imposition of the lighter penalty, the offender shall benefit thereby.

32. See law.case.edu/grotian-moment-blog/documents/Iraqi_Penal_Code_1969.pdf.

33. Commission on Human Rights, 5 Session (1949), 6 Session (1950), 8 Session (1952) [E/CN.4/SR.112, p. 8 (F)].

34. Momir Nikolic, Case No. IT-02-60/1-S, Judicial Supplement No. 46, para. 163, Sentencing Judgment, December 2, 2003.

35. Christopher Greenwood, *Essays on War in International Law* (London: Cameron May, 2006), 357; *Manual of Military Law*, part 3, *The Law of War on Land* (London: UK War Office, 1958), para. 510; see also Gerhard von Glahn, *The Occupation of Enemy Territory: A Commentary of the Law and Practice of Belligerent Occupation* (Minneapolis: University of Minnesota Press, 1957), 27–37; U.S. Army Field Manual, 27–10, para. 358:

> Being an incident of war, military occupation confers upon the invading force the means of exercising control for the period of occupation. It does

not transfer the sovereignty to the occupant, but simply the authority or power to exercise some of the rights of sovereignty. The exercise of these rights results from the established power of the occupant and from the necessity of maintaining law and order.

36. "Geneva Convention Relative to the Protection of Civilian Persons in Time of War," in Jean S. Pictet, ed., *The Geneva Conventions of 12 August 1949*, vol. 4, *Commentary* (Geneva: International Committee of the Red Cross, 1958), 274 ("the occupation of territory in wartime is essentially a temporary, de facto situation, which deprives the occupied Power of neither its statehood nor its sovereignty; it merely interferes with its power to exercise its rights"); Frederic L. Kirgis, "Security Council Resolution 1483 on the Rebuilding of Iraq," *ASIL Insights* (May 2003), at http://www.asil.org/insights/insigh107.htm ("Internationally, though, the fact that a country is occupied and is under the effective, but temporary, control of the occupying powers does not affect its continuing status as a sovereign state. Iraq remains a state as a matter of international law, with rights and obligations toward other sovereign states").

37. Part 1, Dujail Trial Judgment, 3.

38. Paul Bowers, "Iraq: Law of Occupation," Research Paper 03/51, House of Commons Library 19 (June 2, 2003).

39. Cassation Panel, 13.

40. Toby Harnden, "Man with a Mission to Put Saddam in the Dock: Pierre-Richard Prosper, the US Ambassador for War Crimes, Tells Toby Harnden in Washington Why He Would Love to Look the Fallen Dictator in the Eye," *Daily Telegraph*, April 21, 2003, 12.

41. House of Parliament Councils Debate, cc32-3 at 29 (April 28, 2003), at http://www.parliament.uk/commons/lib/research/rp2003/rp03-051.pdf.

42. See Associated Press, "Saddam Letter Says Iraq's 'Liberation' at Hand; New Slaying Linked to Trial," October 16, 2006, at http://www.usatoday.com/news/world/iraq/2006-10-16-saddam-letter_x.htm.

43. John F. Burns and Marc Santora, "U.S. Questioned Iraq on the Rush to Hang Hussein," *New York Times*, January 1, 2007, A1.

44. Marc Santora, "On the Gallows, Curses for U.S. and Traitors," *New York Times*, December 31, 2006, A1.

## 9. ECHOES OF NUREMBERG: THE DUJAIL TRIAL IN HISTORIC PERSPECTIVE

1. Michael P. Scharf, *Balkan Justice: The Story Behind the First International War Crimes Trial Since Nuremberg* (Durham, N.C.: Carolina Academic Press, 1997), 3–17.

2. Peter Maguire, *Law and War: An American Story* (New York: Columbia University Press, 2000), 241, 246.

3. Andre Purvis, "Star Power in Serbia: Slobodan Milosevic's Performance at His War Crimes Trial Has Won Him Increased Popularity at Home," *Time*, September 30, 2002, 46; Gary J. Bass, "Milosevic in The Hague," *Foreign Affairs*, May–June 2003, 82.

4. Telford Taylor, *The Anatomy of the Nuremberg Trials: A Personal Memoir* (New York: Alfred A. Knopf, 1992), 335–336.

## 10. CONCLUSION

1. Alan Dershowitz, "Imperfect, but Fair Enough," *Wall Street Journal*, November 7, 2006, 12.

2. Robert H. Jackson, "Report to the President by Mr. Justice Jackson," October 7, 1946, quoted in *American Journal of International Law* 49 (1955): 44, 49, reprinted in *Report of Robert H. Jackson, United States Representative to the International Conference on Military Trials, London, 1945*, Department of State Publication 3080 (Washington, D.C.: GPO, 1949), 432, 438.

3. Blinderman, "Judging Human Rights Watch."

4. See Edward Wong, "Hussein Thinks He Will Get Death Penalty but Sees Escape Hatch, His Lawyer Says," *New York Times*, June 25, 2006, 6.

5. *Bruton v. United States*, 391 U.S. 123 (1968).

6. Mohamad Bazzi, "Saddam on Trial," *Newsday*, October 18, 2005, A24; Roula Khalat, Neil MacDonald, and Steve Yeyus, "A Dictator in the Dock: Iraq Justice Is Also on Trial as Saddam Faces Judgment," *Financial Times*, October 19, 2005, 17.

7. See *Victor v. Nebraska*, 511 U.S. 1 (1994).

8. Hannah Arendt, "Civil Disobedience," in Eugene Rostow, ed., *Is Law Dead?* (New York: Simon & Schuster, 1971), 212.

9. *United States v. Foster*, 9 F.R.D. 367, 372 (S.D.N.Y. 1949).

10. *Prosecutor v. Barayagwiza*, Decision on Defense Counsel Motion to Withdraw, Case No. ICTR-07-19-T, November 2, 2000; see also *Diaz v. United States*, 223 U.S. 442, 458 (1912) (holding that a trial could continue when the defendant refused to appear in the courtroom; to hold otherwise would enable the defendant to "paralyze the proceedings of courts and juries and turn them into a solemn farce").

11. *Prosecutor v. Norman et al.*, Decision on the Application of Samuel Hinga Norman for Self-Representation under Article 17(4)(d) of the Statute of the Special Court, Case No. SCSL-4-14-T, para. 14.

12. *Prosecutor v. Seslj*, Decision on Appeal Against the Trial Chamber's Decision on Assignment of Counsel, IT-03-67-AR73.3, October 20, 2006, para. 21.

13. The concept of standby counsel was first developed in U.S. practice and refers to an attorney who is appointed to assist a self-represented defendant. D. Klein, "Annotation Right, Under Federal Constitution, of Accused to Represent Himself or Herself in Criminal Proceeding—Supreme Court Cases," *Lawyers' Edition* 145, no. 2 (2004): 1177.

14. See Blinderman, "Judging Human Rights Watch."

15. See, e.g., ABA Code of Professional Responsibility, EC 7-36.

16. ABA Project on Standards for Criminal Justice, Standards Relating to the Prosecution Function and the Defense Function (1971), 53.

17. Akeel Hussein and Colin Freeman, "Few Gather to Remember Saddam as Other Ba'athists Await Same End; Year After Tyrant Was Hanged, His Tomb Has Failed to Become a Shrine," *Sunday Telegraph* (UK), December 30, 2007.

18. Malcolm Brown, ed., *T. E. Lawrence in War and Peace: An Anthology of the Military Writings of Lawrence of Arabia* (London: Greenhill Books, 2005), 55. Lawrence's observation rings through the years with an almost haunting prescience when seen in light of the work of the IHT in the Dujail trial, as he added to the quoted text, "Actually, also under the very off conditions of Arabia, your practical work will not be as good as, perhaps, you think it is."

19. Jackson, "Report to the President," October 7, 1946.

20. Ibid., 438–439.

21. Franklin Delano Roosevelt, "The Four Freedoms," U.S. House of Representatives, January 6, 1941, reprinted in Gregory R. Shapiro, ed., *Great American Speeches* (New York: Gramercy Books 1993), 161.

22. Cassation Panel, 18.

## EPILOGUE

1. George Packer, *The Assassins' Gate: America in Iraq* (New York: Farrar, Straus and Giroux, 2005), 332.

# INDEX

# ABOUT THE AUTHORS

## MICHAEL A. NEWTON

Mike Newton is a West Point graduate and Professor of the Practice of Law at Vanderbilt University Law School. He advised Iraqi jurists as they drafted the statute for the Iraqi tribunal and was a member of the small team of international experts who taught them international criminal law. He has made four trips to Baghdad to provide expertise on a wide range of legal issues and served as an international legal adviser to the Iraqi High Tribunal in 2006 and 2007.

During the Clinton and George W. Bush administrations, he served in the Office of War Crimes Issues, U.S. Department of State. He advised the U.S. Ambassador-at-Large for War Crimes Issues, helped establish the Special Court for Sierra Leone, and participated on the U.S. delegation negotiating the elements of crimes for the International Criminal Court. He has taught around the world and was elected to the International Institute of Humanitarian Law. He has published more than forty articles and book chapters. His op-eds have appeared in *The New York Times*, the *International Herald Tribune*, *The Denver Post*, and *The Washington Times*. He has appeared on CNN, BBC, *Good Morning America*, *Fox and Friends*, *Court TV*, NPR, and other media outlets. He currently advises a working group of the Task Force on Genocide Prevention established by the U.S. Holocaust Memorial Museum and the U.S. Institute of Peace. He has also coordinated legal advice for the Public International Law and Policy Group on behalf of the governments of Afghanistan, Kosovo, and Sri Lanka.

During his distinguished military career, he deployed to assist Kurdish civilians in northern Iraq, developed and led the human rights and rules of engagement education for all multinational forces and international police in support operations in Haiti, and organized U.S. support to the Milosevic indictment during operations in Kosovo. He taught at the Judge Advocate General's School and the Department of Law, United States Military Academy. At Vanderbilt, he developed the innovative International Law Practice Lab. His students participate in a demanding yet richly rewarding course that exposes them to cutting-edge questions in international law and emphasizes pragmatic lawyering skills. He has supervised Vanderbilt law students providing support to a wide range of governmental, judicial, and nongovernmental clients. He also teaches international criminal law and coordinates student participation in the academic consortium, providing substantive advice to lawyers in Iraq, the Sierra Leone Special Court, and other tribunals.

## MICHAEL P. SCHARF

MICHAEL SCHARF is Professor of Law and director of the Frederick K. Cox International Law Center at Case Western Reserve University School of Law. In 2004 and 2005, Scharf served as a member of the international team of experts that provided training to the judges of the Iraqi High Tribunal, and in 2006 he led the first training session for the investigative judges and prosecutors of the newly established UN Cambodia Genocide Tribunal. In February 2005, Scharf and the Public International Law and Policy Group, a nongovernmental organization he cofounded, were nominated for the Nobel Peace Prize by six governments and the prosecutor of an international criminal tribunal for their work in the prosecution of major war criminals such as Slobodan Milosevic, Charles Taylor, and Saddam Hussein.

During the George H. W. Bush and Clinton administrations, Scharf served in the U.S. Department of State, Office of the Legal Advisor, where he held the positions of attorney-adviser for law enforcement and intelligence, attorney-adviser for UN affairs, and delegate to the UN Human Rights Commission. A graduate of Duke University School of Law (Order of the Coif and High Honors) and judicial clerk to Judge Gerald Bard Tjoflat on the Eleventh Circuit Federal Court of Appeals, Scharf is the author of over sixty scholarly articles and ten books, including two that have won National Book of the Year awards. Scharf has also testified before the U.S. Senate Foreign Relations Committee and the House Armed Services Committee; he has published op-eds in *The Washington Post*, the *Los Angeles Times*, *The Boston Globe*, *The Christian Science Monitor*, and the *International Herald Tribune*; and he has appeared on *ABC World News Tonight*, *CBS Evening News*, *Today*, *Nightline*, *The O'Reilly Factor*, *The NewsHour with Jim Lehrer*, *The Charlie Rose Show*, the BBC, CNN, C-SPAN's *Book TV*, and NPR.

Recipient of the Case School of Law Alumni Association's 2005 Distinguished Teacher Award and *Ohio Magazine*'s 2007 Excellence in Education Award, Scharf teaches international law, international criminal law, the law of international organizations, and the War Crimes Research Lab. In 2002, Scharf established the War Crimes Research Office at Case Western Reserve University School of Law, which provides research assistance to the prosecutors of the International Criminal Tribunal for Rwanda, the Special Court for Sierra Leone, the International Criminal Court, the Cambodia Genocide Tribunal, and the Iraqi High Tribunal on issues pending before those international tribunals.